Raising the Dead

NEW AMERICANISTS A Series Edited by Donald E. Pease

RAISING THE DEAD

Readings of Death and (Black) Subjectivity

SHARON PATRICIA HOLLAND

Duke University Press Durham and London

2000

© 2000 Duke University Press   All rights reserved

Printed in the United States of America on acid-free paper ∞

Designed by C. H. Westmoreland   Typeset in Palatino with Antique Olive display

by Wilsted & Taylor Publishing Services

Library of Congress Cataloging-in-Publication Data appear on the last

printed page of this book.

TO ALL THOSE I HAVE KNOWN IN THE PLACE OF THE LIVING

Robert Edward "Flip" Holland

Theola Priscilla Green Martin

John L. Smith

Jesse Evans

Michael Scott

Vera Lewis

Alfonso Ortiz

My Beloved "Sula" Dog

Lora Romero

Contents

Acknowledgments

This book grew out of one of those trips to the library, when just by happenstance I pulled a copy of Leslie Fiedler's *Love and Death in the American Novel* from the shelves and found the beginnings of what would become *Raising the Dead*. But happenstance is a small gift for the unaware, and I was not so lucky. The rough seed of this book germinated in the winter of 1988, when my father died from a self-inflicted wound during my first year of graduate school. It was an event that changed the trajectory of my intellectual endeavors; I was no longer on the outside looking in—I was surrounded by death, subjected to its silence and awed by the insights it provided. I reread Morrison's *Beloved* and saw the potential for a reading of death and the dead in that work and many others. The dead staged a performance for my private viewing, and I began to search for an open door, for critical intervention in the "space of death" in which I suddenly traveled.

Of all those in Ann Arbor who chose to travel with me, I'd like to thank Cathy Cohen, Michelle Johnson, Meghan Lewis, and Wasentha Young, who were there in the beginning along with my advisers and mentors, Michael Awkward, Ruth Behar, Julie Ellison, and Rafia Zafar. I'd also like to thank the CIC Fellowship Office at the University of Michigan; without their support of my early work this book would not have been possible. A Ford Foundation Dissertation Grant in the summer of 1991 allowed me to travel to Belcourt, North Dakota; Kyle, South Dakota; Laguna Pueblo, New Mexico; and Albuquerque, New Mexico, to connect with scholars and writers there. During that journey I met Mari Scout's Enemy, Alfonso Ortiz, and Jolean Peltier, all of whom helped me to understand a myriad of issues at stake for Indians on and off the reservation. A special thanks to Marjorie Levinson, Richard Harris, Olivia, and Cecily—your love (and food) during my last year in Ann Arbor literally kept me on my feet. Thanks also to

Robin and Diedre Kelley for the kind of mentoring and example that stretched my ideas about the profession and my own place in it.

A postdoctoral fellowship at Wesleyan University put me in touch with a wonderful group of scholars at the Center for African American Studies. I'd like to thank Henry Abelove, Erness Brody, Ann duCille, and Ashraf Rushdy for making that year one of the best. The Baldwin essay in this book germinated during one of my many "after hours" conversations at the center with Ann duCille. Because of Erness Brody's capable and inspiring example, I will always think of Wesleyan as my first intellectual home.

Much of the revision of the manuscript could not have been completed without the advice and support of my colleagues at Stanford. I will always remember Lora Romero for her wit, beauty, and brutally honest comments on the early drafts. A big thank you to Sandra Drake, Harry Elam, Estelle Freedman, Horace Porter, and David Riggs, who provided extensive feedback on the book's first draft. A small grant from the Feminist Studies Program contributed to the collection of archival material for chapter 5, and I'd like to thank Cathy Jensen at Feminist Studies for her help along the way. Joss Marsh directed Emily Perez to my office, and she is responsible for compiling much of the review research for the *Beloved* and *Almanac* chapters. Without the friendship and love of Akhil Gupta, Margaret Kelly, Purnima Mankekar, Cherríe Moraga, Paula Moya, Ramon Saldívar, Eleanor Soto, Mitzie Van Sant, Robert Warrior, Yvonne Yarbro-Bejarano, and Tim Young I would have taken up another profession altogether. I'd also like to thank all the students in Yost House and the staff of Governor's Corner (Lisa Webb and Sharon Wong); I worked on refining book ideas during my three years as a resident fellow at Yost, and their energy and grace helped move me along.

I would also like to thank my anonymous readers at Duke University Press as well as Ken Wissoker, Katie Courtland, and Jean Brady. I am grateful to Cynthia Morrill and Jonathan Green of the California Museum of Photography for allowing me to reproduce Arnie Zane's "The Figure of Death," which appears on the cover. And last, but not least, I extend much appreciation to my indexer, Carol Roberts.

And finally, a big shout out to my extended family—you're all I have. For Mrs. Kathleen J. McCabe, who still believes that I can do anything and whose writerly example always gives me pause. To Lila

Karp, who is *always* there, and whose imagination permeates these pages as much as my own; to Renos Mandis for being so "right on" about everything. To H. Yoshi Campbell and Thomas Paine Beyer, who put up with all the crazy years and still love me. To Sharon Grant Henry, Atiya, and Makana—my home away from home since my days as an undergraduate at Princeton. To Emory Elliott who encouraged many of us at Princeton (1982–1987) to stay when we would have much rather fled. To Sly Villarreal for being my rock all these years; to Stacey Hart who understands me; to my mijita, Marcia Ochoa, and her girl, Sara. To Jennifer De Vere Brody for helping me over the last hurdle and especially for being with me. And finally, to my mother—where it all began. Thank you.

Introduction:

Raising the Dead

Anything dead coming back to life hurts.
—Amy Denver, in *Beloved*

In the late fall of 1987 Toni Morrison published *Beloved*. It is a story *not* about slavery, Morrison asserts, but about an infanticide that refuses to remain in the past and imbues the present with a haunting so profound that memory is jolted from its moorings in forgetfulness. Much of the critical response to the novel involved the representation of Beloved, her rising from the dead and the plausibility of such a resurrection.[1] Reviewers and critics were enthralled by Morrison's "ghost story" but also were sometimes skeptical of her reversal of a trenchant Western paradigm: that those who die do not come back, that the line between "us" and "them" is finite and, therefore, never porous.[2] As Marilyn Atlas's review of the novel's critics found, "*Beloved* simply makes some reviewers extremely uncomfortable, forcing confrontations not usually required by literature. These critics do not want to reflect upon these particular human issues and they are unable to see how exploring these new details from new perspectives permanently expands the tradition of American literature, and allows valuable characters into the world, ones they can see no value in examining."[3] Moreover, critics claimed that Morrison's *Beloved* was an amazing departure for American literature.[4] What seemed like a departure for most, however, was actually a phenomenon deeply rooted in the novel of the Americas. Following an American tradition stemming from Alejo Carpentier's and Arturo Uslar Pietri's intellectual work in the late 1940s expounding on what has now erroneously been coined "magical realism," Morrison uses the "fantastic" to comment on the experience of "being" marginal to the historical record of a culture that refuses to recognize difference as its own creation.[5]

Why did Morrison's Beloved seem so different from Hawthorne's or Poe's ghosts? Although *Beloved* appeared to follow a familiar trajectory in American literature, it also offered something more jolting to the American psyche—a BLACK FEMALE "ghost" with agency to possess and to destroy both house and sense of home. Although *Beloved* is a work of fiction, its ghostly presence merged with America's worst nightmares of both past and self. To imagine Beloved, readers and even critics had to work with what was available to them—this imaginary palate was already imbued with its own little shop of horrors—people had to work around what Fanon has called "negrophobia." Morrison's *Beloved* confronted readers with a persistent sense of simultaneity until all fact, all knowledge about slavery, about history begins to exist as in-between, and therefore fragile, as "all the inhabitants . . . at 124 Bluestone Road are suspended between the past and the present, the living and the dead."[6] More disturbing than the presence of a BLACK FEMALE ghost was the idea that the novel's structure so closely mirrored that of the American imaginary and its subconscious machinations to disremember a shared past.

On 7 October 1988, within less than a year of *Beloved*'s publication, Morrison delivered the 1988 Tanner Lecture on Human Values at the University of Michigan. Her lecture, "Unspeakable Things Unspoken: The Afro-American Presence in American Literature," called for a return to the meaning of the "Africanist" presence in American life and letters. Attempting to intervene in the ongoing "canon debates" that raged during the mid-1980s,[7] Morrison proclaimed that "Afro-American culture exists and though it is clear (and becoming clearer) how it has *responded* to Western culture, the instances where and means by which it has *shaped* Western culture are poorly recognized and understood."[8] Morrison, then well on her way to a Nobel Prize with the publication of *Beloved*, sought to use both African American "literature and the awareness of its culture" to "resuscitate the study of literature in the United States." Early in the essay Morrison employs the word *miscegenation* to describe contemporary fears about the canon's revision, indicating that "canon defense is national defense. Canon debate, whatever the terrain, nature and range . . . is the clash of cultures" (8). Ultimately, Morrison signals the need for a "reinterpretation of the American canon, the founding nineteenth-century works,"[9] where "the impact of Afro-American presence on modernity becomes clear and is no longer a well-kept secret" (11).

Returning to Michael Rogin's 1983 study, *Subversive Genealogy: The Politics and Art of Herman Melville*, which argues that ideas like American freedom were just as important to Melville as the nation's struggle with and abolition of slavery, Morrison called on academics to recast the net—to extend Rogin's critical matrix even further. It was time for us to rethink the existing canon's grand metaphors—like self-reliance, home, and destiny—to include the presence of and what some would call the "problem" presented by African Americans moving toward becoming subjects *in* rather than subjects *of* an America in the making. What Morrison revised was the notion that black culture was as invisible to the dominant culture as were most of the nation's black subjects. More than any canonical debate, Morrison's ideas in the fall of 1988 changed the direction and energy of scholarship in *both* African American studies and American literary studies. This shift and subsequent connection between two "literatures" is still being contested and renunciated in departments across the country, where debates about African American studies occur as if such a moment of confluence—where the study of African American literature and culture *becomes* the rubric for the study of American literature—never took place.[10] For those in my cohort at graduate school, Morrison's directive read like a Bible, and we set about the task of making good on our promise to change the profession, to recast the connection between African American literature and culture and canonical literatures as imbricated rather than segregated.

Somewhere between *Beloved* and "Unspeakable Things Unspoken" the seeds of "Raising the Dead" germinated. In 1988 I began to take Morrison's notion of "resuscitation" literally, and returning to "Unspeakable," I read: "We can agree, I think, that invisible things are not necessarily 'not-there'; that a void may be empty, but is not a vacuum. In addition, certain absences are so stressed, so ornate, so planned, they call attention to themselves; arrest us with intentionality and purpose, like neighborhoods that are defined by the population held away from them" (11). The connection between *Beloved* and "Unspeakable Things Unspoken" lay in a seemingly inarticulate but populated place. Raising the dead became a figurative enterprise, as well as an intellectual and therefore concrete endeavor. The task was both to hear the dead speak in fiction and to discover in culture and its intellectual property opportunities for not only uncovering silences but also transforming inarticulate places into conversational territories. I was convinced that Morrison's use of the word *miscegenation* obliterated the segregation of peoples and bodies inherent in the belief that between the living and the dead exists a finite line. Perhaps the more interesting place of inquiry was on the other side of that finite line; perhaps once in this populated place the line would no longer represent a demarcation but a suturing, a connection in the flesh. Ultimately, Morrison called for critics to transgress boundaries, to undertake a type of travel that necessitated another kind of understanding: that retrieving both literatures and imaginary subjects from a space that is simultaneously "spiteful," "loud," and "quiet" is necessary and dangerous work.

In *Shamanism, Colonialism, and the Wild Man*, anthropologist Michael Taussig argues that "the space of death is important in the creation of meaning and consciousness, nowhere more so than in societies where torture is endemic and where the culture of terror flourishes. We may think of the space of death as a threshold that allows for illumination as well as extinction."[11] Although some would argue that the United States is now a "kinder, gentler nation," we cannot escape the raw fact that our boundary is filled with the blood from five hundred years of slavery, removal, and conquest and that our border is a constant space of death and terror. We have chosen to relegate these experiences to the calmer reaches of our national subconscious, and most Americans would tell a far different story about the founding of our fair republic and contemporary life among its peoples. We have left the horror to our imaginations. Discovering who resides in the nation's imaginary "space of death" and why we strive to keep such subjects there is the central inquiry of this book.

The writers, artists, and critics discussed here have discovered that the line is not so finite. They are raising the dead, allowing them to speak, and providing them with the agency of physical bodies in order to tell the story of a death-in-life. Perhaps the most revolutionary intervention into conversations at the margins of race, gender, and sexuality is to let the dead—those already denied a sustainable subjectivity—speak from the place that is familiar to them. Moreover, speaking from the site of familiarity, from the place reserved for the dead, disturbs the static categories of black/white, oppressor/oppressed, creating a plethora of tensions *within* and *without* existing cultures. Embracing the subjectivity of death allows marginalized peoples to speak about the unspoken—to name the places *within* and *without* their cultural milieu where, like Beloved, they have slipped between the cracks of language.

Like many cultural studies projects—with no comprehensive study of the dead in the literature discussed here available—this one searches in sometimes unusual territories for its fuel. The book embraces both popular and academic texts in the search for keys to understanding what is at stake when the critic ventures into conversations at the boundaries between worlds, what Taussig has described as the "space of death."

Even with the somewhat liberal, if not outrageous, borrowing from different (re)sources, the book grounds itself at several junctures. It relies heavily on recent developments in the fields of African American, Native American, feminist, and queer studies, and it seeks to intersect these discourses whenever possible. When theorists think of margins, they often conjure competing forces, a dominance without and a subordination within. Radical and cultural feminists have posited that the margin is not an area of danger or suspicion but of power. Seizing that power, however, always necessitates transferring dominance from the center to the outside. I am concerned with moving away from a model of the margin as an adequate vehicle for a critique of how "oppressed peoples" experience hegemonic power. In other words, I am occupied with two things here: first, placing this marginal space on the inside, not as an entity from without but as an entity from within—a nation within, if you will—and, second, formulating an understanding and theory of marginalized existence that more adequately describes the devastating experience of being "outside" this culture. It is quite often the nation within that disrupts our ordinary sense of who we are, that has the power to dismantle blackness and nativeness, hereness and thereness. With conversations at the boundary between the dead and the living in constant interplay, the book proceeds to map the imaginative environment where authors and sometimes critics attend to the vicissitudinous "space of death." This book does not promise a reading of death that always focuses on "the dead"; instead, it offers discontinuous readings of death—as a cultural and national phenomenon or discourse, as a figurative silencing or process of erasure, and as an embodied entity or subject capable of transgression. At the outset I should also note one thing that this book does *not* do: it does not indulge in a comprehensive look at gendered bodies. It is my understanding from the literature that death, its consort—the dead—and our irrational fear of its bleeding edges create a genderless space. Our worst nightmare is truly shared space, which might be our only successful attempt at "healthy" integration.

The book comprises two parts. The first, "Imaginative Places, White Spaces: If Only the Dead Could Speak," centers on an oppositional approach to the study of the literature. This first section wrestles with dichotomies—blackness/whiteness, life/death, and past/present—in an effort to demonstrate the mistake of relying on finite categories in any critical or creative venture. The three chapters of part 1 therefore contain more traditional textual explications, where the tendency is to look outward rather than inward for the tension between communities.

Chapter 1, "Death and the Nation's Subjects," has two sections and seeks to interrogate the place of black subjectivity in the popular imagination, ultimately contending that black subjects are not just marginal to the culture. Their presence in society is, like the subject of death, almost unspeakable, so black subjects share the space the dead inhabit. Arguing that residual subject relations from slavery are still active in the American imaginary, I begin with an examination of the Hughes brothers' film *Menace II Society,* using it as a model of the interface of the nation, the dead, and blackness. Because of its emphasis on nation formation, Benedict Anderson's *Imagined Communities* serves as a theoretical palimpsest for this opening discussion. I then trace briefly attitudes toward death (and the dying) in a medical context, with attention to works by Michel Foucault and Philippe Ariès.

The second chapter, "Bakulu Discourse: Bodies Made 'Flesh' in Toni Morrison's *Beloved,*" turns to the work of Hortense Spillers to create a template for discussing Morrison's novel, placing Morrison in conversation with other black female critics about the relative status of black women, about their invisibility and their haunting of the American imagination. I treat my observation of Beloved as both spirit and orisha (deity) as an entryway into a discussion about the always already "dead" position of African Americans in the United States. Believing that blackness is truly a category one cannot transcend *and* noticing that black women under the law of slavery never arrived at the status of "mother" (according to Spillers), and therefore never achieved the category of "woman," I then ask, how might a return from the dead, from silence, be viewed as a tragic empowerment for black women?

Chapter 3, "Telling the Story of Genocide in Leslie Marmon Silko's *Almanac of the Dead*," takes this query even further. I perform a reading of Silko's text based on *both* the shortcomings and the value of theories of the grotesque. Although many critics have called Silko's novel a postmodern text, it lacks the cynicism directed at the category of the "dead" that most postmodern texts exhibit. In Silko's complex and often unnerving portrait of the Americas, the dead *drive* the narrative and can both facilitate and hinder the best efforts of the living. Silko is ever aware not only of the presence of the dead but also of their *location*. She is concerned with the forces of death that bring about genocide and those that transform disaster into possibility. For Silko death is a double-edged sword.

The ending of this chapter provides a segue into the second part of the manuscript, "Dead Bodies, Queer Subjects," which focuses on the invisibility of black gay and lesbian subjects in relationship to *internal* communities rather than in opposition to *external* hegemonies like whiteness. Whether the "home" community is the "family" of African American literature or the progressive left, the same kind of silencing experienced in external communities can occur for queer subjects seeking to connect with and simultaneously challenge familiar spaces.

Chapter 4, "(Pro)Creating Imaginative Spaces and Other Queer Acts: Randall Kenan's *A Visitation of Spirits* and Its Revival of James Baldwin's Absent Black Gay Man in *Giovanni's Room*," situates two novels by black gay men in the context of critical endeavors to name *black* gay presence within African American literary discourse. What distinguishes this chapter from the preceding ones is its almost exclusive focus on one particular field's construction of an image, a home, and a canon. I envision Kenan's novel as a gentle rewriting of Baldwin's work. Whereas Baldwin's characters are white and "exiled" in Europe, Kenan's protagonist is a black gay youth—a relation in a southern Baptist family. Kenan brings the exiled Baldwin home on several levels, placing queerness and blackness in direct confrontation with one another. I read the hallucinations of Kenan's Horace and the paranoia of Baldwin's David as manifestations of discomfort with gay presence in the African American imagination. Moreover, the attention to ghosts / ghosting in each text points toward the particular subject position of black gay men in the pantheon of African American literature. Relegated to the space of the dead, they occupy our imaginative terrain on a persistently marginal level, and they are a danger to themselves and to others.

Chapter 5, "'From This Moment Forth, We Are Black Lesbians': Querying Feminism and Killing the Self in Consolidated's *Business of Punishment*," critiques the lyrics of a thrash/hip hop band to access the translation of feminist principles in the realm of the popular. Claiming both a feminist and radical identity, Consolidated (an all-white, male band) embodies the complicated politics of maneuvering between identities. Listening to Consolidated's music requires the attending critic to adjust the distances between speaking/nonspeaking and black/white subjectivities. Group members consistently take on the identities of the people they sing about, becoming women in the sex industry, people who are HIV positive, and, finally, black lesbians. My central query is whether their "becoming" black lesbians represents a killing of a white self or an exercise of white authority through an ability to reinscribe black lesbian subjects in the familiar space of the "unspeakable." Consolidated puts whiteness in the spotlight by forcing us to ask: Can whiteness be transcended? And if so, *what* are the politics of, or at least, *how* can we theorize about, this particular killing of the self? In their attempt to respond to the HIV/AIDS crisis, the far right, and neofascism, they explore the feminist concept "the personal is political" and attempt to divest themselves of their own white supremacy. This chapter investigates not only the subtle way that Consolidated kills the self as they flirt with the space of silence and death but also the cultural context that allows for such transgression.

In the final chapter, I attempt to place several critics in conversation with one another, demonstrating that critical maneuvers are often figuratively placed at the boundary between the living and the dead. The discussion here is informed by feminist theories of the margin, coupled with theories of liminality and pollution from the discourse of anthropology. The process of naming and unnaming a literary trajectory is almost always an act of silencing someone or something, and critical interventions come dangerously close to the liminal space of death—and the silence that accompanies it. I also move into popular new age and spiritual forms of discourse to demonstrate that there might be useful material in the new subjectivities that the dead bring to life.[12] This last chapter represents the myriad places in critical, historical, and anthropological texts where discussions of death and the dead have taken place. It is hoped that these parting words move the project's future in several directions.

Many of the novelists discussed here have talked about being literally haunted by the characters who inhabit the worlds they bring to the printed page. *Raising the Dead* attempts to fill the space left by critical inattention to manifestations of the dead. I hope that cultural critics will find new fodder for explorations into imaginative landscapes— seen and unseen. When I began this work in 1989, I had no idea that Joseph Roach was engaged in similar explorations. It was only on completion of the manuscript that a colleague suggested I read his book, *Cities of the Dead*. I would like to acknowledge Roach as a fellow traveler in the endeavor to harass the border between the living and the dead. Roach identifies the "new way of handling (and thinking about) the dead" as a vestige of modernity.[13] This work perceives the difference between the living and the dead as the beginning binary, as the model for creating other dichotomous systems such as black and white or straight and queer. *Raising the Dead* is a new lens for citing alternative ways of seeing and, perhaps, believing.

PART ONE

Imaginative Places, White Spaces:

If Only the Dead Could Speak

From the moment Vicky introduced these newcomers, the consulting room seemed so alive and there were so many impressions, that, gazing at the woman beside her, who at the moment was simultaneously Marcia Lynn and Vanessa Gail Dorsett, the doctor, who had thought herself inured to the surprises that a multiple personality had to offer, could not refrain from being excited by this simultaneous sharing of the body. Nor could the doctor keep from speculating on how so many diverse characters could simultaneously flourish in the small, slight frame of Sybil Dorsett. The thought was fanciful because occupancy was not a matter of inhabiting space but of sharing being.

—Flora Rheta Schreiber, *Sybil*

1

Death and the Nation's Subjects

What the eye is to the lover—that particular, ordinary eye he or she is born with—language—whatever language history has made his or her mother-tongue—is to the patriot. Through that language, encountered at mother's knee and parted with only at the grave, pasts are restored, fellowships are imagined, and futures dreamed.
—Benedict Anderson, *Imagined Communities*

Orlando Patterson's landmark observations in *Slavery and Social Death* provide a cornerstone for the discussion of marginality, blackness, and death throughout this chapter. Examining the practice of slavery from premodern to modern societies, Patterson argues that enslaved peoples experienced varying degrees of "social death." The crux of his project rests on a series of bold introductory statements; the most compelling is certainly the following:

> Not only was the slave denied all claims on, and obligations to, his [*sic*] parents and living blood relations but, by extension, all such claims and obligations on his more remote ancestors and on his descendants. *He was truly a genealogical isolate.* Formally isolated in his social relations with those who lived, he was also culturally isolated from the social heritage of his ancestors. He had a past, to be sure. But a past is not a heritage. . . . [Slaves] were not allowed freely to integrate the experience of their ancestors into their lives, to inform their understanding of social reality with the inherited meanings of their natural forebears, or to anchor the living present in any conscious community of memory.[1]

For Patterson, enslaved subjects are genealogical isolates because they are denied access to the social heritage of their ancestors. Although it is outside the scope of this project to ascertain the commitment of enslaved peoples to their own religions or kinfolk, it is possible to interpret the "social death" in slavery as continually plagued by tacit and sometimes overt manifestations of ancestral strength and / or recognition that punctured the rigid boundary between freed and enslaved subjectivity.[2] What seems to contradict the impossibility of reviving a past, achieving a heritage, is the relationship of enslaved peoples to their legion of unnamed and unrecognized ancestors—the same ancestors who are designated as the "Sixty Million and more" lost to the middle passage in Toni Morrison's dedication of *Beloved* and the unnamed "Sixty million Native Americans [who] died between 1500–1600" in the frontispiece to Leslie Marmon Silko's *Almanac of the Dead*. In sum, it is the dead, present as ancestors, who make the complete social death of the slave, and therefore the categories of freed and enslaved, unstable at best.

Focusing as he does on enslaved subjectivity, Patterson is less likely to extend his theory of genealogical isolation to the community of masters. If we take his observations out of their global context and focus on slavery as practiced in the United States, then a series of conditions present themselves. Parallel to this phenomenon of social death for enslaved peoples is the common experience of white subjects enabling a legal discourse that extends its umbrella to them as well.[3] Under this umbrella white subjects who produced children from unions with enslaved peoples, but were unable *and* unwilling to claim such progeny in their own genealogical narratives, nevertheless experienced a similar lack of heritage. The condition of manumission further exacerbated the problem of how white subjects should relate to black counterparts, some of whom were their children.

Formal emancipation called for an abrupt about-face for a system too entrenched to change as mandated by law. Manumission dictated that the peculiar social status of enslaved people be transferred to and shared by another space altogether. Not willing to comprehend fully the freed state of formally enslaved subjects, masters and their kin reserved a special place in their *imaginations* for this new being. Although seeing the black subject as a "slave" was now prohibited by law, there was no impediment to viewing this subject in the same place s/he had always already occupied. In this way the enslaved-now-freed person, either "black" or close enough to this category, began to occupy the popular imagination.[4] Ultimately, a system such as slavery might be abruptly halted, but its dream lives in the peoples' imagination and becomes fodder for both romantic fictions and horrific realities. bell hooks comments on this customized relationship: "Reduced to the machinery of bodily physical labor, black people learned to appear before whites as though they were zombies, cultivating the habit of casting the gaze downward so as not to appear uppity. To look directly was an assertion of subjectivity, equality. Safety resided in the pretense of invisibility."[5]

The unaccomplished imaginative shift from enslaved to freed subjectivity *and* the marked gap between genealogical isolation and the ancestral past form the meeting place where the bulk of my ruminations on death and black subjectivity reside.[6] It is possible to make at least two broad contentions here: a) that the (white) culture's dependence on the nonhuman status of its black subjects was never measured by the ability of whites to produce a "social heritage"; instead it rested on the status of the black as a nonentity; and b) that the transmutation from enslaved to freed subject never quite occurred at the level of the imagination. This imaginative element carries itself into the contemporary terrain and formulates this chapter's first query: If black subjects are held in such isolation—first by a system of slavery and second by its imaginative replacement—then is not their relationship to the dead, those lodged in terms like *ancestor* or *heritage*, more intimate than historians and critics have heretofore articulated? At this intersection the investigative terrain appears filled with wide open spaces.[7]

In existential terms, knowledge of our own death determines not only the shape of our lives but also the culture we live in.[8] Even though knowledge of death fuels all cultural activity, social and cultural customs prohibit us from conversing about death, dying, or the dead in the course of living. This chapter demonstrates that such a discussion is long overdue and absolutely necessary to an understanding of how *some* subjects, in particular black subjects, function in the culture. Furthermore, what if we were to entertain another hypothesis about the relationship between the living and the dead: What if some subjects *never* achieve, in the eyes of others, the status of the "living"? What if these subjects merely haunt the periphery of the encountering person's vision, remaining, like the past and the ancestors who inhabit it, at one with the dead—seldom recognized and, because of the circum-Atlantic traffic in human cargo or because of removal, often unnamed?

On the other hand, if we were in the position of the subject denied the status of the living, how would we illustrate this social predicament? Communities of color often describe their collective experience in the United States as dystopic rather than utopic. The paradise is often within, and "hell" is a condition arising from encounters with whites. When "living" is something to be *achieved* and not *experienced*, and figurative and literal death are very much a part of the social landscape, how do people of color gain a sense of empowerment? Toni Morrison once remarked that the second word immigrants to this country learn on their arrival is *nigger*; the first word is *okay*.[9] The irony of this simultaneous embracing of an Africanism ("okay") and disparaging of an African American subject is a metaphor for the bittersweet experience of being "black" in the United States. As Anderson reminds us, through language "fellowships are imagined, and futures dreamed." Morrison is not speaking about the relationship of one group to another but commenting on the unique place that blackness has as paradigm in the quest for achieving the status of "American." It is a paradigm so powerful that even some of this nation's first peoples buckled under its discursive weight, taking into their ranks thousands of Africans as slaves, and emulating their (white) counterparts.[10] Blackness is the yardstick by which most peoples in this nation measure their worth—by something they are *not*.[11] I propose that we give blackness its due—not as a universalizing narrative for all marginalized people but as something much more tangible, provocative, and meaningful. I would like to view blackness as a measure of how *all peoples* in the United States construct an intimate idea of self in relationship to the nation—by having, in that little corner of their imagination a black seed against which all action—and therefore, in the existential sense, all being—is differentiated.

Attempting to devise a category in which liminal subjects can reside and from which they can speak, critics and authors have created terms like *marginality* and *invisibility* to aid those outside of master narratives and places of power in articulating a politics of experience.[12] At times this space is empowering, but it also can be mercurial and dangerous. Moreover, as intellectual constructs, theories of the margin hold much promise, but as paradigms for what it is like to be marked as black in this nation, they fall short of the mark. The experience of being in the margin is much like that of skating on thin ice. Josette Feral offers a theoretical tale for just such an experience: "To put discourse into question is to reject the existing order. . . . It means choosing marginality (with emphasis on the margins) in order to designate one's difference, a difference no longer conceived of as an inverted image or as a double, but as alterity, multiplicity, heterogeneity. It means laying claim to an absolute difference, posited not within the norm but against and *outside* the norms."[13] I believe that Feral has a point about the alterity of the margin, but I do not think that the marginal space referred to by writers in this book is consistently constructed against or outside the norm. I can see the importance of Feral's offering in terms of traditional power relationships: to speak from the center traditionally means to speak from a position of authority, to speak with the voice of the father, and to utter words from his language. Conversely, to talk (back) from the margin usually implies a formerly denigrated status and a sense of belonging to a tradition conceived by breaking silence. Although this outside status might be empowering on paper, literal existence "outside" makes day-to-day living just short of impossible.

Toni Morrison contextualizes the experience of being "outdoors" by offering the following critique in *The Bluest Eye*:

> Outdoors was the end of something, an irrevocable, physical act, defining and complementing our metaphysical condition. Being a minority in both caste and class, we moved about anyway on the hem of life, struggling to consolidate our weaknesses and hang on. . . . Our peripheral existence, however, was something we had learned to deal with—probably because it was abstract. But the concreteness of being outdoors was another matter—like the difference between the concept of death and being, in fact, dead. Dead doesn't change and outdoors is here to stay.[14]

Morrison's writing about "outdoors" corresponds well with the tenor of this project. In her paradigm, outside becomes "outdoors," and peripheral existence or marginal space describes a living death— a full embrace of the concept of death. Here "outoors" is synonymous with being dead. To resist outsider status, to come back from the dead, is a monumental existential feat in Morrison's world. There is no full embrace of the margin here, only the chance to struggle against both a killing abstraction and a life-in-death; neither choice is an appealing option. More than anything, Morrison's paradigm demonstrates the possibility of being among the dead in the course of living. Abstract theoretical paradigms do not do much to change or challenge the politics of life for people of color, specifically poor black people. Morrison's illustration of a metaphysical condition indicates that theorists have been looking in the wrong sites for their empowering oppositional narratives.

For those beyond the periphery, beyond even a language of the margin, for those literally "outdoors" and therefore dead to others, there needs to be a theory profound enough to explain such a devastating existence. We must investigate the viability of theoretical examinations of the margin in the context of the articulated experiences of those who seem to dwell in what Morrison calls an abstract existence. The impending task is then to define, in as much as possible, the vehicle used by authors writing about traditionally marginal(ized) experiences to speak and to legitimate the power of that discourse. One of the broader tasks of this book as a whole is to bring varying discursive communities into dialogue with one another—a critical jog suggested and performed by Elizabeth Meese in her *(Ex)Tensions: Re-Figuring Feminist Criticism*. A larger discussion of her work appears in chapter 6. In commencing such a project, it might be prudent to move from the macro to the micro—from larger structures like nations, which help to construct speaking subjects, to smaller arrangements like those between communities and among communities. For the moment I'd like to focus on a discussion of the dead and national character as a means of strengthening these observations.

"It Takes a Nation of Millions to Hold Us Back"[15]

The dead acknowledge no borders. As an example of such outrageous disrespect for boundaries, both discursive and national, I turn to two disparate genres—black film and anthropological theory—to launch a critique about the relationship among the dead, black subjects, and the nation. An old saying contends that you can tell the strength of a nation by the way it treats its poor; today, one can also ascertain this relative strength by examining the way a nation treats its dead. At the global level the dead appear before the public eye as a sign of another

Covers from *Time* magazine: May 16, 1994 (*left*) and August 1, 1994 (*right*).
During the summer that civil war continued in Rwanda, *Time* produced a
series of stories on the conflict. Most notably, these covers represent how
the magazine envisioned the crisis: as both apocalyptic and representative
of a nation torn by "ethnic" conflict. Photographs of thousands of slain
Rwandans were used to demonstrate that the nation's people had surely,
to paraphrase the missionary here, gone to the devil.

country's *lack*—of democracy, of civilization, of resources, of compas-
sion. Witness, for example, the coverage of ethnic conflict in Rwanda
on the cover of *Time* or *Newsweek*—barometers of this nation's ideas
about death at home and abroad—and we might say that the dead, in
signifying both *loss* and *lack* for other countries, represent that entity's
national character (see illustrations). The dead embody, and therefore
become so much of, what the living are unable to realize. In times of
peace the national tone is strident, and we are proud of our dead; in
times of war this pride transforms the dead into objects of our most intense and unflattering scrutiny.

In 1993 twenty-one-year-old twins Allen and Albert Hughes released
a devastatingly brutal look at life in America, *Menace II Society*. *Menace*
traces, in "gangster film" vividness, the lives of black youth in Watts

almost thirty years after the 1965 riots. Caine (Tyrin Turner) and his friends all deal in the market economy available to them—manufacturing and selling crack cocaine and breaking into and delivering cars for disreputable insurance companies. In the opening sequence of the film the camera follows the cental narrator, Caine, and his gangsta friend O-Dog (Lorenz Tate). On their way to a party O-Dog and Caine stop by a corner store owned by a Korean couple. As they make their way to the beer case, O-Dog repeatedly tells the female shop owner to "stop creepin'"—in other words, to stop following him; the background music intensifies the air of surveillance as the Cutthroats, produced in part by Guru, chant the rap "Stop lookin' at me." With a forty-oz. beer in hand and about to exit with Caine's change, O-Dog hears the Korean man behind the counter say, "I feel sorry for your mother." The shop owner does not know that he has broken an unwritten rule in the black community: you don't talk about someone's mother if you don't know the person. Those in the audience who recognize these cues know what will unfold. O-Dog reels around and asks him, "What did you say about my mama?" In the resulting altercation O-Dog shoots the man and then forces the woman to the back of the store for the video surveillance tape. In the process of retrieving the tape, O-Dog shoots the Korean woman. As he and Caine exit the store, the film fades to black, and Caine begins the story's narration: "Went in the store to get a beer, came out an accessory to armed robbery and murder. It was funny like that in the 'hood sometimes. You never knew what was going to happen or when. After that, I knew it was going to be a long summer."

Gun violence and fear become the framing thematic as the film's second opening rolls television footage and broadcast announcements of the 1965 Watts riots. As these images fade, we move to "Watts, late 1970s" and listen to Marvin Gaye's "Got to Give It Up" as Caine's parents give a party for their friends. Caine's father (Samuel Jackson) is a "dope dealer," and his mother (Khandi Alexander) is a heroin addict; we later learn that both of his parents are deceased and that he lives with his grandparents. The scene also portrays Caine's induction into "gangsta life" as we see him handle a gun for the first time and witness a murder perpetrated by his father, who shoots a family friend over a debt and a card game.

Throughout the film Caine and his gangsta friends are given limited options for survival in South Central Los Angeles—either move to another city or participate in the local drug economy and eventually end up in prison or in a body bag. As the film progresses, Caine is given another option. His incarcerated mentor's girlfriend, Ronnie (Jada Pinkett), decides to move to Atlanta and, after developing a love interest in Caine, asks him to leave with her and her young son, Anthony (Jullian Roy Doster). As they pack the car, the film moves in slow motion and cuts to a car full of young black youths out to take revenge on Caine for beating one of the riders. Ironically, this beating was the result of Caine's abandonment of the young man's cousin, Llena (Erin Leshawn Wiley), who announces that she is pregnant by Caine. On the verge of escape, Caine dies in a hail of bullets.

At the close of the film, images of Caine flash and fade to black to the rhythm of a declining heartbeat.[16] His last words are apocalyptic:

> After stomping Marllena's cousin like that I knew I was goin' to have to deal with that fool someday. I never thought he'd come back like this: Blasting. Like I said, it was funny like that in the 'hood sometimes. You never knew what was going to happen, or when. I had done too much to turn back, and I'd done too much to go on. I guess in the end, it all catches up with you. My grandpa asked me one time if I cared whether I live or die. Yeah, I do. Now it's too late.

We find in the end that Caine has not, in fact, survived. Because he narrates the film's action, we somehow believe that his voice, his authority, insures his survival. The central perspective of the film is told in the form of a reflective piece; and reflection implies change, assures the viewer of a before and an after. All of the violent images that we consume during the film are magically erased because the "hero" lives in language. When he dies at the end of the film, we feel cheated, almost lied to—the directors have displayed the ultimate "bad faith."[17] There are several ways to interpret this moment of bad faith; perhaps the directors want us to understand that in the contemporary terrain there are very few *living* narratives of black people: we literally speak from the dead. As acts of violence create cultural space in the film they parallel the force that constructs urban poor areas across this nation; and as we watch we participate in such a making and unmaking of urban territories. *Menace II Society* provides a running commentary on our "national character," placing the dead/the always already dying in the position of storyteller. Because the film's title implies the character of black subjectivity in relationship to the society at large, some insights on the function of the dead in the service of such national imaginings might be useful here. I turn to Benedict Anderson's discussion of the dead and the nation to help frame this discussion of *Menace*.

In the 1991 revision of *Imagined Communities*, Anderson again reminds us that nations are imagined political entities. What is most interesting for my examination of *Menace* and its implicit critique of American nationalisms is the way Anderson particularizes the fuel or momentum of a nation's burgeoning imaginative space. Constructing a simile around the tomb of the Unknown Soldier for the beginnings of his discussion,[18] Anderson admits that "void as these tombs are of identifiable mortal remains or immortal souls, they are nonetheless saturated with ghostly *national* imaginings."[19] Death here is merely an event, decontextualized from the body of any "known" subject and therefore embraced by everyone. Anderson then observes that the Unknown Soldier's "ghostly" presence is very much linked to ideas of death and immortality, and such a connection bears a "strong affinity with religious imaginings" (10). He then offers that the birth of the nation comes about simultaneously with the slippage of religion as a foregrounding ideology. It appears that the nation thrives on anonymity in death, and religion gives back to the individual a sense of immortality "by transforming fatality into continuity" (11). In fact, Anderson later acknowledges this possibility by stating that "confidence of community in anonymity . . . is the hallmark of modern nations" (36). It is not the *actual* dead but an *idea* of them that holds the nation together.

Although he begins with an analysis of the positionality of death in the schema of imaginative communities and their move toward a nationalist posture, he seems to abandon the centrality of death as lived experience for the abstract ease of "death" resolved through the metaphor of "fatality" in language. Anderson writes that "while it is essential to keep in mind an idea of fatality, in the sense of a *general* condition of irremediable linguistic diversity, it would be a mistake to equate this fatality with that common element in nationalist ideologies which stresses the primordial fatality of *particular* languages and their association with *particular* territorial units. The essential thing is the *interplay* between fatality, technology and capitalism" (43). I would like to posit Anderson's reckoning of "death" and its relationship to the tangible (i.e., language) as representative of modern critical maneuvers around the subject of death itself. It is as if the fear of death is so pervasive that traveling through its territory puts the critic in danger of being consumed by the unknown—a literal linguistic tower of Babel. It is particularly interesting that this fear of consumption is much like the anxiety Anderson so carefully articulates in his analysis of the rise of national identity/ies among societies on the verge of diversity and its recognition.

However, Anderson still relies, as noted earlier, on the fatality in language rather than on actual fatality as represented by a literal body. In his earlier discussion the body's absence, not presence, figures the nation and its awakening. The study of death in relationship to nationalist discourse proves all the more fascinating when we recall that scores of nationalist literatures rely on a very central image—that of the "nation" being embodied. And this national body is overwhelmingly imagined and inscribed as *female*. This would seem to stand in direct contradistinction to the kind of disembodied anonymity sought after to sustain the nation-state. Although it is not the purpose of this project to elucidate the relationship between death and the national body, it is important to conceive of death and discourse as linked to and comprising ideas about nationhood and nationality, about belonging and disenfranchisement. In fact, if hyperbole were my forte, I might want to suggest that the dead and their relations are perhaps the most lawless, unruly, and potentially revolutionary inhabitants of any imagined territory, national or otherwise. Moreover, I would add that the disenfranchised and oppressed often join the dead in this quixotic space, becoming, in common parlance, menace(s) to society.

Several parallels can be made between Anderson's assessment of the dead and the nation and the particular use of "death" in the Hughes's first film. In the imagined life of a United States citizen, black subjects constantly haunt and therefore threaten the stability of the working nation. This black subject retains a certain amount of anonymity by being "spirit" or "ghost"—by being disembodied but simultaneously recognizable as black and residing in poor urban spaces. The Hughes brothers reverse this familiarity of relationship between black subject and the U.S. citizen's imagining its presence by serving us our worst nightmare—the ultimate menace to society—*and* by keeping him "alive," thus allowing him to speak from the dead. Whereas Anderson reifies the dead, or death, as spectacle, the Hughes brothers reconfigure the space of death, pulling the audience into what appears to be spectacle or entertainment but ultimately becomes real and horrific when we learn that Caine does not survive, that his life is circumscribed by an imaginative text already scripted for him. In *Menace* we are not protected from the knowledge of Caine's death even after the fact of language, of narrative. Caine speaks precisely *because* he is dead; death provides him with an uncanny power as he "talks back" from a heretofore finite place. Once we reach the film's conclusion and realize that Caine is in fact dead, we can no longer consume the film in the way we desire. In the genre of gangster films, *Menace* closely mirrors the narrative style of Martin Scorsese's *Goodfellas*, which begins innocently in East New York in 1955, with the film's primary narrator and central character pronouncing, "As far back as I could remember, I always wanted to be a gangster." Whereas Scorsese's protagonist intends to *become* a "gangster," the Hughes brother's Caine has always already *been* one. And surely this is why Caine must not live, as Scorsese's Henry Hill (Ray Liotta) does.

In both popular culture and neonationalist rhetoric the black community is depicted as a nation within a nation. Anderson's discussion of emerging nations within existing national terrains runs parallel to my observations about black communities. In the context of this reluctant cohabitation within borders is a remark Anderson quotes from the early Javanese-Indonesian nationalist Suwardi Surjaningrat. In angry response to the proposal for a celebration of the centennial of liberation of the Netherlands from French imperialism, Suwardi published the following words on 13 July 1913:

> At the moment we are very happy because a hundred years ago we liberated ourselves from foreign domination; and all of this is occurring in front of the eyes of those who are still under our domination. Does it not occur to us that these poor slaves are also longing for such a moment as this, when they like us will be able to celebrate their independence? Or do we perhaps feel that because of our soul-destroying pol-

icy we regard all human souls as dead? If that is so, then we are deluding ourselves, because no matter how primitive a community is, it is against any type of oppression. If I were a Dutchman, I would not organize an independence celebration in a country where the independence of the people has been stolen. (117)

I wonder who this "primitive" community really is—the colonial subjects or the dead? In either case the position of the dead in figurative relationship to the nation poses an interesting territory of inquiry.[20] Here the living seek nation status, and the dead serve as the signifiers of that loss, of that impossibility. But what is even more macabre is the colonial powers' ability to render the subjugated population as "dead," as invisible, by imposing a fictitious narrative of independence on a people for whom self-determination is a futuristic concept. Ultimately, the "primitive" nature of the community *retrieves* the dead from the place of the forgotten (the disremembered) and the homeless, bringing them back into the discourse of the nation. The dead and the black subject all serve a double sentence in the national economy and imagination.

After O-Dog kills the store owners and retrieves the videotape, he uses it to entertain himself and his gangsta friends. Anderson's moment of retrieval is rehearsed as the videotape of the robbery becomes a movie within the movie and the deaths of the Korean store owners are recycled for amusement. Throughout the film we are constantly reminded of how our own voyeurism transforms violence into fodder for our leisure time. We witness how the dead are retrieved, not to be remembered but to become evidence of O-Dog's gangsta machismo— the dead couple are resurrected for their participation in a neonationalist script. The video is a scene within a scene, as well as fodder for a nation within *the* nation. But this collective show of voyeurism is only secondary to the original transgression of the film's opening action— the constant submission of black subjects to scrutiny and surveillance. The unnamed Korean store owners' watchfulness of O-Dog inscribes him in a constant space of simultaneous social erasure and presence. Their imaginations get the best of them as the narrative they impose on the two through constant vigilance fulfills itself completely. The Korean shop owners pay for the "crime" of watching, and the action of the film seems to support the sentence carried out on the two, as their looking becomes the transgressive act—becomes privileged as a more fantastic crime than O-Dog's act of murder. We witness the boys' figurative slip from under the death-like gaze of the shopkeepers as a triumph, and for the remainder of the film the videotape is both proof and celebration of their escape.

These representations of black subjectivity and (national) surveillance find their parallel in the introductory words to Anderson's eighth chapter, "Patriotism and Racism." Here Anderson admits: "It is doubtful whether either social change or transformed consciousnesses, in themselves, do much to explain the *attachment* that peoples feel for the inventions of their imaginations—or, to revive a question raised at the beginning of this text—why people are ready to die for these inventions" (141). And, literally, the Korean couple dies from what they imagine as real—from the belief that all black subjects are criminals. The film's opening action not only illustrates tensions between blacks and Koreans in urban America but also demonstrates the grotesque ease with which America's fear of blackness enacts itself in the realm of the popular. In short, our imaginative life can dictate our actions, even bring about our deaths.

The answer to Anderson's query about the people's readiness to die for their imaginative "inventions" lies in an interpretive blunder. Anderson creates an idea of imaginative space in the nation as if it were shared by everyone. To some degree national imaginings are universal, but the imaginative space itself is quite diverse. Perhaps *some* people are ready to die because the space imagined—the place of death—is not a dead space but a living space; perhaps, even with the advent of imperialism and nationalisms, a bit of the power of indigenous thought—the importance of the dead in life—has seeped into an otherwise finite and closed space. People do not die, therefore, for a national invention, but they die so that they might be able to attach themselves to an idea of life before the alien invaders.[21]

In this chapter on patriotism and racism Anderson undertakes his most extensive return to the subject of death/fatality in relation to nation formation. In one of the boldest strokes of the book he notes that "languages thus appear rooted beyond anything else in contemporary societies. At the same time, nothing connects us affectively to the dead more than language" (145). In fact, he later implies that through song, nationalist and patriotic language likens itself to a communal prayer.

If the nation relies on its ability to articulate itself in "patriotic language," then why does its survival rest on its ability to keep the dead unknown and inarticulate as Anderson observes? Who are the dead that the nation seeks so fervently to (dis)connect with?

In *Menace* nothing connects us more to the fate of—the death of— black subjectivity in the United States than the *fact* of Caine's narrative. The sense of the black subject as open to constant scrutiny, as open to national discourse, is emphasized by Caine's description of O-Dog as "America's nightmare: young, black and didn't give a fuck." In the tradition of the "gangster" movie there is always a member of the gang who does not mind the killing. Here, however, the "nightmare" extends not just toward the victim of crime but to all America. O-Dog is perpetually guilty—of past crimes and of any potential crime he might commit in the near future, as with his literary precursor, Bigger Thomas. O-Dog is also confined by historic events that begin the action of the movie—the 1965 riots in Watts and the L.A. rebellion some twenty-seven years later.

As Henry Louis Gates observes in his review of the film for the *New Yorker*, "The film gets at the way the ghetto has become the social equivalent of what scientists refer to as the 'black hole'; *it's a place where the American id collapses on itself.*"[22] Gates does not qualify this American id as "white," implying in his own evaluation an understanding of the class difference among black subjects so that black resistance through hip hop culture is also marked as the anger of an underclass of black subjects left behind by their upwardly mobile counterparts. If the *ghetto* is America's unconscious, and most Americans, when they think of the term, can't help but see or say "black," then black subjects are indeed absorbed into the landscape of anonymity provided by this dreamscape of the unconscious. We can understand Anderson's insistence on the parallel between death and anonymity in light of the black subjects' place in the total recall of the national imagination. Moreover, O-Dog as quintessential black male imaginary subject is produced as the object of our discontent *and* site of our pleasure and desire—although we are deathly afraid of being confronted with the mythic black man in the alley with a gun, we clamor to consume the image of him performing the same crime on movie screens across this nation.

The relationship between our national desires and the dead is concretized when Anderson, in discussing Michelet's contribution to the development of French nationalism, observes that

> Michelet not only claimed to speak on behalf of large numbers of anonymous dead people, but insisted, with poignant authority, that he could say what they "really" meant and "really" wanted, since they themselves "did not understand." From then on, the silence of the dead was no obstacle to the exhumation of their deepest desires.
>
> In this vein, more and more "second-generation" nationalists, in the Americas and elsewhere, learned to speak "for" dead people with whom it was impossible or undesirable to establish a linguistic connection. (198)

If we were to interpret Anderson's formulations liberally, then we would obviously conclude that the nation exists precisely because the dead *do not speak* or because those in power believe that conversation with the dead is "undesirable" or actually in direct opposition to the project of sustaining a working nation. The dead are further released from agency here, as they experience a second death, in the Derridean sense, for their "desires" *not* their "bodies" are exhumed for use by the state. The ability of the emerging nation to speak hinges on its correct use of the "dead" in the service of its creation. Here the dead are the most intimate "enemy" of the changing and growing nation. Should they rise and speak for themselves, the state would lose all right to their borrowed and / or stolen language.

Somewhere in the narrative of *Menace* is a profound understanding of just such a paradigm. Lost in Caine's narration of the film, we are quick to believe that he escapes the 'hood and lives happily thereafter. The smugness of this evaluation is repudiated by the film's ending— and Caine's narrative, his ability to *speak for himself,* is demonstrated in his dying. No longer the borrowed or stolen language of the state, his words reach from the place of the dead into the space of the living. He dies, but his narrative is now *his* in a way that it could not be had he lived. As intellectuals and consumers of popular culture we are left to think very differently and deeply about what meaning a narrative-in-death has for black subjects *and* representations of blackness in the popular national imagination.

Holding the Dead Hostage:
A Survey of Medicine

In no other place has the state's anxiety over its stolen discourse been so rapidly policed as in the relationship between the dying patient and the hospital doctor. In this liminal territory the national discourse and the people's discourse collide as the dying body is imposed on, again and again, in the service of the nation's prevailing treatment of death. Anderson is not the only twentieth-century critic to equate perceptions of the dead with the formation of the nation-state. In his ruminations on war and sovereign power Michel Foucault observes that

> wars are no longer waged in the name of a sovereign who must be defended; they are waged on behalf of the existence of everyone; entire populations are mobilized for the purpose of wholesale slaughter in the name of necessity: massacres have become vital. It is as managers of life and survival, of bodies and the race, that so many regimes have been able to wage so many wars, causing so many men to be killed.[23]

In fact, what Foucault notes is a shift from notions of death as a public menace to notions of death as "private," as the "most secret aspect of existence" (261). What allows this shift to take place is the presence of the hospital as a site of intervention and disruption.

What is fascinating here is the symmetry between Anderson's and Foucault's perceptions of the dead and the nation. According to Foucault, the signaling moment of change in some modern conceptions of death came about with the publication of Bichat's treatises on anatomy and pathology. Foucault reminds us that "Bichat did more than free medicine of the fear of death. He integrated that death into a technical and conceptual totality in which it assumed its specific characteristics and its fundamental value as experience."[24] By making death the object of medical observation, the profession transformed the popular relationship to death itself. The dead become known through the pathologist's scalpel and are therefore continually in service to the nation—keeping it alive, contributing to the *body* of scientific knowledge.

In his interpretive reading of Foucault, Simon During further explains that "the absorption of death into life means that each patient will for the first time become an individual for medicine. Now, each case has its own pattern of pathology; for instance, each organ dies at its own time rather than death occurring at a stroke. And now everyone has their [*sic*] own way of dying."[25] As Foucault ultimately suggests, the absorption of death into life and the amount of social control needed to achieve this end are not particular signs of medicine's triumph or rationality but of the state's/society's continuing neuroses about the physical body.[26] For now, science in its examination of the corpse is able to attack the defenseless, much like state policies are meant primarily to control all those (usually without substantial resources) who seek to break existing law and order in order to survive. What better way to assuage a fear or get rid of an "enemy" than to subject it to what Foucault recognizes as an extensive and unrelenting medical/state gaze? When I think of constant surveillance, I am reminded of the opening frames of *Menace* and the "looking" that triggers deadly rage. The dead are the ultimate "docile bodies"—imprisoned by the panoptic medical gaze. Moreover, the imposition of medical perusal of the dead requires that we *all* become, at one time or another, prisoners of the state. The nation is assured control over life and death in the case of *each* of its citizens.

Within this new paradigm the physician can extract medical information from the corpse and make this available to the remainder of the nation. The exhumed information can even be used as a rationale for living. For example, the dead are put on trial for their sins of the flesh and held up as a constant warning to us (especially in the rhetoric of disease prevention) to live a clean, healthy life. In a sense the strength of a nation depends not only on the strength of its army, to choose an obvious example; the strength of a nation resides in its ability to control the discourse most necessary to the people's survival. If Western discourse is composed of a series of binary understandings, then it would behoove the nation not only to be able to maintain the chasm between opposites but also to be able to manipulate the relationship between entities on either side. By monitoring and determining the relationship between life and death (by absorbing death into life), the nation continues its control of both knowledge and its dissemination, to borrow from Foucault. It also assures that the relationship is in fact no longer binary. It can define both entities in light of a single idea—notions of life and death can now revolve around understandings of death-in-life, embodied in the corpse itself. Foucault writes:

Life, disease, and death now form a technical and conceptual trinity. The continuity of the age-old beliefs that placed the threat of disease in life and of the approaching presence of death in disease is broken; in its place is articulated a triangular figure the summit of which is defined by death. It is from the height of death that one can see and analyse [*sic*] organic dependences [*sic*] and pathological sequences. (144)

But this "death" at the summit of the triangular relationship is not really a happening but merely an event, without connection to a named entity—"it is *not* Martha or John that we are examining today" but an anonymous corpse. If we return to During's observation that the dead become "individual[s] for medicine," we can see this process of individuation as nonrecognition. When one becomes an individual for someone else's use, one ceases to be anything but an instrument. According to Foucault, society can now stave off its fear of death by transforming it into something else: "the analysis of the disease can be carried out only from the point of view of death—of the death which life, by definition, resists" (144). By ensuring control of the corpse, society ensures control of its opposite, the living nation. Again, this relationship is precarious at best because it depends on the relative stability assigned to and silence imposed on the most fearsome article—death—and the ability of the physician's skill and his body of knowledge to speak for the silenced dead.

Emphasis on the body as a location of historic markings is central to Foucault's theory of how power works discursively. M. E. Bailey clarifies this observation: "Bodies are so thoroughly understood according to the 'knowledge' about them—biological, psychoanalytic—that there is no 'outside', no access to bodies (and perhaps no bodies) external to these systems of truth."[27] Within Foucault's framework all knowledge is intangible. Power is the intangible tangible—visible to everyone yet invisible to all.

Like power itself images of blackness are visible to everyone when the populace is called on to solve a national problem—like "the end of welfare as we know it," for example. Yet this same black image / subject remains oddly invisible, unseen like the anonymous dead, when the nation conjures an image of itself. Might I then be so bold as to say that there is no such thing as *power* without the fear and force of blackness, which enacts it in the first place? Perhaps because what we see around us is subject to our relentless scrutiny, no amount of societal denial can separate us from the many hauntings that circulate in the space(s) we occupy. The medical gaze not only subjects the body to constant scrutiny, but it more pointedly selects *certain* bodies for the pleasure of discovery. We have only to look at the pioneering work of Sander L. Gilman to see that the model for deviance and abnormality in the gendered body—the female body—has its roots in the racialized body of a black woman.[28] Racing the body removes the possibility of the exchange of bodies in the Foucauldian paradigm. In Bailey's estimation, "Foucault's bodies are not, then, essential, original, constant, facts; they are historical constructs, like sexuality and sex. Bodies are affected, altered, tattooed by historical circumstance—and they are indistinguishable from these effects, alterations, tattoos" (108). I would argue that some bodies are "constant" in that they are "tattooed by historical circumstance" again and again. Bodies are still marked—by sex and/or pigmentation—so they are not subjected to discourse so much as discourse is constructed around certain bodies so that others may survive, thrive, and evolve. Power is literally felt and realized differently depending on loci of race, sex, and sexuality. In this theoretical complex the dead figure as the folk with no recourse to discourse. If they have no discourse of their own, no defense, whose discourse must *they* borrow in order to speak? And if they have their own discourse, how do they move from the supposed void of death to find voice?

If a nation's existence is, as Anderson suggests, extremely ephemeral and reliant on imagined rather than concrete identities, then how this nation articulates itself in life *and* in death must also be formulated from popular imaginings. The Euro-American concept of marginal experience is typically marked by opposites, a polar balance, in the case of life and death, between what we believe is definitely living and what is most certainly dead. Dichotomy feeds the obsessive need to seek knowledge by any means necessary to fend off the disastrous collapse of such categories. French social historian Philippe Ariès observes that the dichotomy between life and death was not always so pronounced in Western attitudes: "In a world of change the traditional attitude toward death appears inert and static. The old attitude in which death was both familiar and near, evoking no great fear or awe, offers too marked a contrast to ours, where death is so frightful that we dare not utter its name."[29] He later explains that these new attitudes toward life and death arose during modernity and argues that "one must avoid—no longer for the sake of the dying person, but for society's sake, for the sake of those close to the dying person—the disturbance and the overly strong and unbearable emotion caused by the ugliness of dying and *by the very presence of death in midst of a happy life,* for it is henceforth given that life is always happy or should always seem to be so" (87; italics mine).

Ironically, death here becomes the particular charge of everyone (society) and, at the same time, that of no one at all. Moreover, if we follow the establishment of Western medicine, particularly in the United States, we observe that before allopathic medicine there were pockets of people (both male and female) in vast numbers of ethnic communities who practiced curing, healing, and attending to the sick, injured, or dying. As the responsibility for the sick shifted from curing rituals to "male" science, and what was tied to the healer became forbidden and stigmatized as "female"—the polar opposite of the proof of phallic science—the charge of these new doctors became the dying and the dead.

In modernity "Death" can no longer occur in the midst of the living, and to achieve the separation between the happy (living) and the miserable (the dying / almost dead), the hospital was created as the perfect institutional replacement for this uncomfortable meeting. Ariès concludes: "one no longer died at home in the bosom of one's family, but in the hospital alone." It is worth noting that Ariès feminizes the home, as a "bosom" to which the individual returns; this slight personification secures the transition from family to hospital as a move from the female to an impersonal space, presided over by a male entity. In that antiseptic site, an individual's death is mediated by "a decision of the doctor and the hospital team" (88).

During the Western drama of death the doctor functions as a kind of formaldehyde, warding off the powerful effects of death and distancing the family from its horror. Occupying this artificial position, the physician serves as a medium between the conscious but stricken family members and the often unconscious patient. The doctor, usually perceived as male, upsets the balance of life and death, usurping the position of women as mothers and potential mourners by becoming both center and margin and by altering a previously ungendered space and making it, via connotation, male. It is *his* opinion that will determine the fate of both family and patient, and *his* word will stand at the center of any discourse about the dying person. Women and family have become estranged in this contemporary ritual. The docile "family" is feminized by the "doctor." Foucault also recognized this subtle change in his own observations of the clinical situation:

> The hospital domain is that in which the pathological fact appears in its singularity as an event and in the series surrounding it. Not long ago the family still formed the natural locus in which truth resided unaltered. Now its double power of illusion has been discovered: there is a risk that disease may be masked by treatment, by a regime, by various actions tending to disturb it; and it is caught up in the singularity of physical conditions that make it incomparable with others. As soon as medical knowledge is defined in terms of frequency, one no longer needs a natural environment; what one now needs is a neutral domain, one that is homogeneous in all its parts and in which comparison is possible and open to any form of pathological event, with no principle of selection or exclusion. In such a domain everything must be possible, and possible in the same way.[30]

What Foucault describes is a scenario in which a sick person in a family, for example, is struck with a fever and is attended by a host of doctors, all seeking to subject the individual to a patterned diagnosis. Within the medical establishment this same family member is suffering from a fever, but this condition is interpreted in conjunction with the suffering of other patients, thus forming a connection between individuals and "pathological events." The family is constructed as unstable, relative to the "neutral" and universalizing gaze of attending physicians. In concentrating on the pain of the individual, the family becomes the true hysteric, whose inability to see the larger picture, to see disease as systematic rather than individually located, inhibits the process of healing. It is ironic that in our high-tech medical era, we have had politicians calling only a decade ago for a return to "family values" as the ultimate curative for a nation sickened by the visibility of queer peoples and the potential of affirmative action to take away every white man's job. How can there be a return to family values when our economic roots are based on the same market system that maintained a lucrative centuries-long slave trade? Our national economy functions best when the very notion of biological kinship, if we remember Patterson's words, is devalued and the nation is poised to reduce the family and its relative value to the will of the state for profit and knowledge.

In further examination of the genesis of the clinic, Foucault detects yet another shift. Empirical knowledge is substituted for the unknown and the unproved—society is able to assuage its fear of death with the complex array of information that the physician possesses. In the moment of late capitalist modernity, death ceases to exist even as a counter to life itself; rather, it transgresses the boundaries of its binary relationship with life and fuses with the body of knowledge in the hands of a male physician. The family in relationship to this newly created text or hospital ritual becomes feminized in the most simple Freudian paradigm, via its lack of what the male possesses.

Death, as an unspeakable subject in a hospital ward, is divested of its own language and is consumed by the scientific knowledge in the physicians' possession. The earlier fear of death's utterance is becalmed by the physicians' mastery of the suffering body. In another act of displacement and divestiture, death is also removed from its home in the family and given to the province of the collective of physicians. For archdeacon and critic Michael Perry this new location is aggravated by the unique intersection of place and purpose. "If death is seen as the supreme failure of the physician's art, then it is not surprising that in a place built to assert and affirm the physician's skills, death is treated as an unspeakable obscenity."[31] Because obscenity denotes aggressive and unruly behavior, death—and the dead, which are its consort—again becomes the entity the nation is unable to tame.

Obscenity, whether vocalized or practiced, is also aligned with sexual mores and attitudes; discourse around death often finds itself coupled with sexual expression. Western concepts of death depict the event as a fissure of the living and the dead; as Ariès asserts, "like the sexual act, death [beginning in the eighteenth century] was henceforth thought of as a transgression which tears man from his daily life, from rational society" (57). Ariès alludes to debates that raged throughout the seventeenth century over biblical interpretations of the Fall, sexuality, and death.[32] Foucault contends that where death and sex become intertwined, power makes itself known:

> When a long while ago the West discovered love, it bestowed on it a value high enough to make death acceptable; nowadays it is sex that claims this equivalence, the highest of all. And while the deployment of sexuality permits the techniques of power to invest life, the fictitious point of sex, itself marked by that deployment, exerts enough charm on everyone for them to accept hearing the grumble of death within it.[33]

Sex, if I interpret Foucault's intentions correctly, is no longer a site of rupture or a crack in discourse; rather, it becomes invested with a far-reaching power to transform a contested space—one in which death is present—into an approachable arena. Foucault drops this fusion of death and sex for the more interesting discussion of sex and the "deployment of sexuality" in his subsequent paragraphs. However, the idea of sex as a landscape wherein the effects of death are obscured or, conversely, made known holds potential implications for my discussion of Silko's own deployment of sexual acts in *Almanac of the Dead*.[34] In many of the novels discussed here, sexual liaison is the territory in which societal neuroses around death manifest themselves to readers. No longer is death the end result of sexual activity. Copulation, heterosexual or homosexual, embraces death to make the ritual of recognition complete. In *Beloved* Paul D's intercourse with Beloved and in *Almanac* Trigg's habitual bleeding of the homeless during oral sex illustrate the absorption of death into sexual acts.

Ariès continues with a consideration of how opinions of death changed in the early twentieth century. He proposes that "nothing had yet changed in the rituals of death, which were preserved at least in appearance, and no one had yet the idea of changing them. But people had already begun to empty them of their dramatic impact; the procedure of hushing-up had begun" (87). Ariès intimates that this changing attitude toward death emptied its rituals of significant meaning and that this process of "empty[ing]" necessarily involved a silencing. This silencing of the dead for the sake of the nation's continuance is paralleled in Anderson's observations of the dead's usefulness in creating an imaginary nation-state. As death became institutionalized, a myriad of schizophrenic contemporary coping mechanisms formed as Band-Aids for its rupture from the site of the living. Silence then becomes the primary suture. Speaking of this ultimate silence, Loring Danforth muses, "Death emphasizes the precarious, unstable quality of our lives. . . . [It] threatens the individual with a sense of meaninglessness and disorder because it confronts him [sic] with the loss of his sense of reality and identity. One's own death, as well as the death of others, inspires such terror because of its utter and perfect silence."[35]

What Danforth describes is the experience of a subject in a state of crisis, a situation caused by a silence that is terrifying not so much because the assumed loved one is gone but because, I would argue, the ability to seek knowledge in and from that *body* has ceased. The death of one body is a reminder of the death of knowledge—an end to knowing and a shift in a fundamental understanding of one's own identity in and through that particular *body* of knowledge—the body's library. The pathology of Western medicine transforms this finite situation by extracting knowledge from the dead. However, this procedure further frustrates a waiting populace because this library of material is not returned to those who grieve but is appropriated for use by the nation as a whole. The distance between the dead and the grieving is made even more finite because of the intervention of the physician's hand.

Here the artificiality of the medical apparatus becomes even more pronounced. The doctor, in the role of state functionary, is in the position to exhume knowledge from the corpse, and although s/he can explain the how of death, the why remains forever a mystery. And if discourse is confined to the how and not the why of things, then the latter category awaits attention and articulation. Where there is no discourse, there is no marginal or liminal space between life and death, or at least none that can be appropriately enunciated. Likewise, in the converse, dialogue between the living and the dead is placed outside discursive norms—any conversation at the border is considered irrational, fodder for another episode of *The X-Files*. One either lives or dies, and dialogue, in this Western morphology, is the possession of the living, silence the keepsake of the dead.

In the late twentieth century there have been several popular movements to rethink death, and toward this effort the contributions of Elisabeth Kübler Ross (*On Death and Dying* 1969), Raymond Moody (*Life after Death* 1976), and Dr. Jack Kevorkian (*Prescription: Medicide* 1991) come readily to mind. A return to serious contemplation of our attitudes toward death has prompted a number of recent texts, in particular Sogyal Rinpoche's *The Tibetan Book of Living and Dying* (1993) and Peter Singer's *Rethinking Life and Death: The Collapse of Our Traditional Ethics* (1995). Rinpoche's and Singer's work locate their discussions in the sometimes unstable realm of spiritual, moral, and ethical concerns. And these concerns rarely make their way into the hallowed territory of discussions of the literary. However, there seems to be a confluence among Anderson's idea of death's meaning to the nation, Foucault's conception of death as the site of contemporary knowledge about the self (figured through the physician's gaze), and Rinpoche's insistence that "death is a mirror in which the entire meaning of life is reflected."[36] If death is the font from which some of the deepest meanings about self, other, culture, and community flow, why is a discussion of its happening so abhorred in the West?

Rinpoche's earliest observations of Western culture point to the West's deep-seated fear of death: "I learned that people today are taught to deny death, and taught that it means nothing but annihilation and loss. That means that most of the world lives either in denial of death or in terror of it. Even talking about death is considered morbid, and many people believe that simply mentioning death is to risk wishing it upon ourselves" (7). Although modern fears of death touch on old understandings of the power of language to conflate binaries, investigating this collapse is nonetheless fruitful and engaging.[37] Perhaps we might see why the tomb of the Unknown Soldier and the anonymity of the medically perused cadaver have such importance in the modern context—they divest death of any power by submerging it in anonymity.[38] We have nothing to fear from anonymity. If we cannot recall a face that looks like our own, then we cannot fear our own death in quite the same way.[39]

This might also explain why (black) subjects are so important to the national imagination. The death of black subjects or the invisibility of blackness serves to ward off a nation's collective dread of the inevitable. Someone else bears the burden of the national id; someone else (always already) dies first. This parallel between death and (white) subjectivity might provide some rationale for the use of black bodies as opposed to white bodies in medical research during the course of early medicine—it is easier to lay open that which does not have the mark of sameness. Acknowledging the fear of death and speculating on how such fear might drive our choices lead me to provide an unorthodox example of cause and effect. Yet another hypothesis for slavery's end might be that white slaveholders, no longer able to bear seeing reflections of themselves (seeing their own children succumb to slavery's death knell), buckled under the psychic damage of the institution's chief reproductive economics and began to oil the hinge that ultimately led to freedom for their human chattel.[40]

For scholars like Singer, however, this fear of death does not stem from lack of spiritual understanding as much as it does from a corrupt code of ethics that allows a heinous system of contradictions to exist in our dealings with the dying. In Singer's analysis modern society is "solving problems by redefinition."[41] In a review of the medical cases involving euthanasia, cortical death, abortion, and persistent vegetative state, Singer observes "something absurd about all these attempts to define a precise moment at which a new human being comes into existence. The absurdity lies in the attempt to force a precise dividing line on something that is a gradual process" (100). What is remarkable about Singer's text is its tacit assertion that delimiting the precise moment a new human being comes into existence requires equal attention to defining the moment of our death. In this paradigm death *is* the absolute mirror of life, not its grotesque refraction.

According to Singer, the reflection and relationship between life and death changed irrevocably in 1981, when the President's Commission for the Study of Ethical Problems in Medicine examined the issue of death and accepted the new standard of determining *actual* death offered by the Harvard Brain Death Committee in 1968.[42] In the final analysis the commission's report, *Defining Death*, "proposed a 'Uniform Determination of Death Act' so that every state of the Union could have the same legal definition of death based on the irreversible loss of all brain function. Subsequently most developed nations redefined death in similar terms" (28). Although Singer does not venture to discuss the impact of such a decision beyond the scope of medical ethics, the findings of the commission seem so catastrophic as to require some type of response beyond the corridors of the White House and the medical laboratory. In defining death the commission thereby defined life. As Singer reminds us, humans are the only species for whom "brain death" is a legitimate criterion for death. Here, unlike the medical apparatus in the Foucauldian sense, which is marked by a gaze capable of extending itself to the perusal of the dead, anonymous body, the contemporary gaze extends itself even further by controlling the liminal body—dying, but not quite dead—and defining the life of the individual as it moves toward its fruition in death.[43]

This control over the period of *liminality* marks the moment of the catastrophic. Content no longer to extend the power of the gaze to the already dead, the nation's leadership chooses also to lay hands on the most private locations for the concept of the self—how a being wishes to relate to other people as s/he moves toward death. This liminal space, I would argue, is one of the places where the living and the dead converge, mingle, and discourse. Close cohabitation produces subjects capable of straddling the fence. By literally defining not only *how* one dies (as in the Foucauldian gaze on the cadaver) but also *when* one dies, the state appropriates absolute power. Not since the institution of slavery has this exercise of power over the body been so consistent and so debilitating. An NPR news piece on 18 May 1995 demonstrates the ultimate power of medical science (in the service of the state) to define the choices of the living. Discussing the tragic results of a boxing match, the commentator casually announced, "Jimi Garcia lies brain dead in a hospital." No longer dying or almost dead, Jimi Garcia is "brain dead," qualified as a known entity only to the science that places him in that state of suspended animation. Subjects in "altered states," the living no longer die in the literal sense but are harvested for their *usefulness* (literally, for their organs) and transformed into another way of being, as the language of "brain dead" implies.

In the face of such daunting state power and in the presence of an overwhelming national imaginary, creative writers are stubbornly discovering ways to circumvent the boundary of absolutes—to bring the subject of death and our national imaginings to the forefront. One such writer is Toni Morrison, who resurrects the "ghost" of slavery in order to let the dead speak to the living, in order to allow silence to manifest language.

2

Bakulu Discourse:

Bodies Made "Flesh" in Toni Morrison's *Beloved*

And I would call it the Great Long National Shame. But people do not talk like that anymore—it is "embarrassing," just as the retrieval of mutilated female bodies will likely be "backward" for some people. Neither the shameface of the embarrassed, nor the not-looking-back of the self-assured is of much interest to us, and will not help at all if rigor is our dream. We might concede, at the very least, that sticks and bricks *might* break our bones, but words will most certainly *kill* us.
—Hortense J. Spillers, "Mama's Baby, Papa's Maybe: An American Grammar Book"

So high you can't get over it, so low you can't get under it. Git out. . . . This is our chance, this is our chance, to dance our way out of our constriction.—Parliament Funkadelic, "One Nation Under a Groove"

Consistently hovering between "sapphire" and "mammy," black women are a danger both to themselves and their communities. Mammies if we don't speak and Sapphires when we do, black women occupy a category of being like no other self in literature or in reality. We are so malleable, so brilliantly represented as a constant within our stubborn inconsistency that we can be manipulated while remaining simultaneously resistant to all attempts at regulation. At our most dangerous moment black women serve the nation even more adequately as the instigators of black men's demise. Reviewing some of the most recent theories, black women not only sing the blues, but we *are* the blues—both its beauty and its trauma.[1] Given the permanence and permeability of metaphor, how can black women and those who read their texts theorize a way out of the quagmire of "damned if you do, damned if you don't"? If theory is so high we can't get over it, and we are so low no other subject dare be placed under us, then how do we "dance our way out of our constriction"?

Often the focus of black feminist scholarship is on bridging the gap between the academy and the community.[2] In one of the most contemporary attempts to elucidate for the academic community the particular marginalization of black women's words, Ann duCille's "The Occult of True Black Womanhood: Critical Demeanor and Black Feminist Studies" brings us back to the subject that consistently refuses to be blurred or blunted by critical inquiry or the judicial pen. For duCille the weight of black women's experience serves as a kind of "readable map" that critics utilize in the form of "translation and transference." The value of black femaleness, then, is intrinsically linked to her utilitarian purpose—her service to both the community and the academy. We make the experiences of other people more *real* to them. Period. duCille's concluding remarks point toward this crisis of representation that black women in the academy face:

> The trouble is that, as Moraga points out, bridges get walked on over and over and over again. This sense of being a bridge—of being walked on and passed over, of being used up and burnt out, of having to "publish while perishing," as some have described their situations—seems to be a part of the human condition of many black women scholars. While neither the academy nor mainstream feminism has paid much attention to the crisis of black female intellectuals, the issue is much on the minds of black feminist scholars.[3]

duCille challenges feminist scholars to perform the readings—to do the work—necessary to unground the popular image of black women. Our job is not just to say that stereotypes of black women are perpetuated by (white) feminist readings but to discover those mechanisms that hold such conventions in place. For that inquiry we need an adequate past to dismantle.

Beginning just such an inquiry in her earlier work, Hortense Spillers outlines a theory of the liminality of black women:

> Slavery did not transform the black female into an embodiment of carnality at all, as the myth of the black woman would tend to convince

us, nor, alone, the primary receptacle of a highly-rewarding generative act. *She became instead the principal point of passage between the human and the non-human world.* Her issue became the focus of a cunning difference—visually, psychologically, ontologically—as the route by which the dominant male decided the distinction between humanity and "other."[4]

Pushing her point further, Spillers remarks that "the absence of sexuality as a structure of distinguishing terms is solidly grounded in the negative aspects of symbol-making. The latter, in turn, are wed to the abuses and uses of history and how it is perceived. The missing word—*the interstice*—both as that which allows us to speak about and that which enables us to speak at all—shares, in this case, a common border with another country of symbols—the iconographic" (77; italics mine). What Spillers accomplishes in these two examples is astonishing. Black female bodies serve as passage between humanity and nonhumanity as well as the articulation of that passage. I would suggest that this border, which is no border at all but a passageway, also encompasses the terrain between the living and the dead, between the ancestral and the living community. Morrison incorporates this impossibility, and the culture's refusal to recognize it, in the return of Beloved. Beloved literally embodies the experience of being black and female, an experience that remains consistent regardless of changing times and discourses (of slavery, emancipation, and civil rights). If the liminal Beloved is the discourse and body that "allows" *and* "enables" us to speak, then black women in contemporary America are surely in trouble. Their place in the common imagination is surely beyond the invisible or the marginal. Spillers argues that they "do not live out their destiny on the borders of femaleness, but in the heart of its terrain" (95).

Elaborating on Spillers's central point in "Interstices," that "black is vestibular to culture" (76), I would like to add that this space is both material and linguistic—a chamber housing the flesh and its attending language. Beloved functions as the quintessential vestibular element in Morrison's novel. Morrison's creative endeavor calls on feminist critics, in particular, to examine the fantastic nature of such an arrangement. Reading Morrison's *Beloved* in the context of Hortense Spillers's later work, "Mama's Baby, Papa's Maybe," is to take seriously those critics like Ann duCille, who have prompted the academy to try to formulate a new understanding of signs and signifiers and their *literal*, and by "literal" I mean *felt*, relationship to black women.

"So High, You Can't Get Over It"

In the "Occult of True Womanhood" duCille cites Houston A. Baker's *Workings of the Spirit* as an example of black male criticism that tends to objectify black women's literary production. Her argument proves that when critics attempt to name what they are unfamiliar with, they fall prey to both the beauty and the grotesque power of marginal language. The culmination of Baker's trilogy of theoretical works on African American expressivity, *Workings of the Spirit: The Poetics of African American Women's Writing* struggles to align a wide range of theoretical perspectives and African American practice. A chapter entitled "Theoretical Returns" points toward a founding instant for what Baker terms "African-American women's expressivity":

> Africans uprooted from ancestral soil, stripped of material culture, and victimized by brutal contact with various European nations were compelled not only to maintain their cultural heritage at a *meta* (as opposed to material) level but also to apprehend the operative metaphysics of various alien cultures. Primary to their survival was the work of *consciousness*, of nonmaterial counterintelligence.[5]

Baker claims theory as a specific site for African American literary production, observing that Africans in the new land were "forced to construct and inscribe unique personhood in what appeared to be a blank and uncertain environment. Afro-American intellectual history, therefore, is keenly theoretical because it pays compulsory attention both to metalevels of cultural negotiation and to autobiographical inscription" (39). African American literature comes about because of a desire to write oneself onto a landscape that is otherwise seen through Baker's eyes as blank; America is the blank slate on which Afro-America will (w)rite itself.[6] Emphasis on "nonmaterial transactions" in the hands of "griots, conjurers, [and] priestesses" leads to "spiritual leadership" found in the black church—spirit flows from the nonmaterial to the institutional, giving African Americans a particular *and* peculiar ability to transform personal experience into institutional practice, to move the intangible to the tangible. In a word, Baker's Africans literally and ultimately wield more power than the state itself because our actions naturally incline toward the process of regulation, and in contrast, the state apparatus comes by this type of control unnaturally, through coercion.

Searching to articulate this metalevel of meaning *and* being, Baker posits black women as examples of the connection between the material and nonmaterial world. Their bodies give shape to a sounding of this particular theory. I will engage Baker's claims more rigorously in chapter 6. But who is given the power to both name and unname—to translate her experience into institutional practice and pass it off as community property, the voice of the people, a theory of expressivity? Who has the rights to authorship here? I would like to return to Hortense Spillers's "Mama's Baby, Papa's Maybe," which shifts both the critical gaze and what duCille astutely characterizes as "critical demeanor."

From the outset Spillers is concerned with both the interplay of gender (male/female) and ethnicity (white/black). She is also responding to a trend in feminist criticism that originated in the mid-1980s with the call to complicate the relationship between "sexuality" and "gender" in feminist scholarship.[7] During the course of the debate, the centrality of "women" to feminist inquiry also became an issue.[8] Unmaking "women" as the subject of feminism prepared the field for a decade of exploration in the territory of gender "undecidability"—where roles are always in flux and therefore undetermined; where responsibility for this indeterminacy shifts from white subjects as a category to a frighteningly nebulous and perpetually unnamed power structure; where "race" becomes as unnecessary as the "woman" who used to be feminism's primary sign. Although Spillers writes in the wake of such changes in feminist scholarship, in "Mama's Baby, Papa's Maybe" she seeks to locate gender, race, and sexuality within a historical moment and extend that moment into the present so that even tropes of feminist discourse like "mother" are rendered vacuous when all three categories intersect.

Following the psychoanalytic prescription for the condition of the female, of the "other," Spillers assesses what the black "family" seems to lack. We find that this lack is located in the inability to figure into the social order of the "New World." But how did this group become dispossessed of its familial inheritance *and* status? Spillers contends that "their New-World, diasporic plight marked a *theft of the body*—a willful and violent . . . severing of the captive body from its motive will, its active desire. Under these conditions we lose at least *gender* difference *in the outcome*, and the female body and the male body become a territory of cultural and political maneuver, not at all gender-related, gender-specific."[9] Pursuant to the conversation in the previous chapter, let us move one step further and extend the captive body into the liminal space of the dead, a place where gender difference is likewise obfuscated. The actual experience of the captive body (read captive peoples) in this new-world order is traumatic and consequently places gender difference outside the category of *being* (human) in terms of the laws of both property and possession. It is not so much that captive peoples are not allowed gendered subjectivity but that these relationships mean nothing under a legal system that sanctions the treatment of humans as property. Solidifying this observation, Spillers makes a dramatic distinction between *body* and *flesh*, using these terms as metaphors for captive and liberated subject positions, respectively.

If we as critics are going to work with the legacy of slavery, then we must engage in the "retrieval of mutilated female bodies" (68). The grossness (as quality and quantity) of the flesh—"matter" torn away from the body by mutilation *and* the society's "cultural vestibulary"—is a zone where the *marking* of culture appears on the flesh and the *making* of culture happens because of this constant abuse. Disallowed access to all culture but representative of it, black bodies become the literal containers of the power of state ideology and simultaneously live in a constant state of existential torment.

For Spillers, critics can ignore the violence of neither the pen nor the lash. As the captive bodies of enslaved peoples are literally pieced *out*, we begin to look at this "subject" in complete and "total objectification," as these bodies become living laboratories for the good of the nation.[10] But "the Atlantic Slave Trade," "massive demographic shifts," and "the mutilated body" are no longer *just* the legacy of African Americans. Spillers notes that "we write and think, then, about an outcome of aspects of African-American life in the United States under the pressure of those events. . . . In a very real sense, every writing as revision makes the 'discovery' all over again" (68–69). Spillers's theory has implications for all critics because we all have had hand on both lash and pen in our own attempts at "revision." She demonstrates how what we have come to know experientially as the "truth"—about ourselves and others—is embedded in the dangerous crevices of the father's tongue, the national language.[11]

Spillers's next section concerns itself with the process of naming and unnaming Africans—a project begun with Equiano's account, continued through the various nicknames foisted on African American peoples, and realized in the Moynihan report. This process of (un)naming is absolutely thorough, as "the dominant community seizes as its unlawful prerogative [the ability to name]" (69). Spillers argues that this brutal process is very present in the middle passage and sees that space as a liminal one, where Africans exist as "quantities," subjected to the process of being "unmade." These bodies pass into a new self, to be defined—in both destiny and legal language—by their captors. For Spillers there is a frightening pattern displayed in the naming of human cargo: a kind of "sameness of anonymous portrayal that adheres tenaciously across the division of gender" (73). What Spillers constructs here parallels the anonymity the dead enjoy in the national imagination; their anonymity so sustains the nation that calling them by name, adding specificity to their "being," would upset the balance of things—much like the appearance of Beloved at 124.

In this middle passage "the loss of the indigenous name/land provides a metaphor of displacement for other human and cultural features and relations, including the displacement of the genitalia, the female's and the male's desire that engenders the future" (73). The future alluded to here manifests itself as both progeny *and* ethnicity or "race." I would argue that this dislocation of desire, which always implies free choice of a partner, manifests itself as precisely the problem in reading and rewriting enslaved experience. Given the heterosexist paradigm of the dominant culture, it is doubly restricting to view oneself completely in a dichotomy of opposite sexual relations in order to have or "engender" a future. Desire becomes an imaginative landscape where same-sex relations signify, by their omission, a certain dead end to the future.[12] This problematic theoretical perspective is further explored in chapter 4 of this book.

Spillers then turns to the issue of "kinship" and posits that the value of an enslaved person is recognized precisely because s/he is outside the kinship system—outside the family, as it were. Here Spillers can be seen in conversation with Orlando Patterson. She seems to purposefully ghost his narrative in order to demonstrate the problematic absence of gender in Patterson's analysis. By focusing on the situation of black female bodies and by reading "kinship" in terms of the female, Spillers imperils the critical tendency to explore the master/slave dynamic as solely male.[13] Moreover, she moves on to say that the child "does become, under the press of a patronymic, patrifocal, patrilineal and patriarchal order, the man/woman on the boundary, whose human and familial status . . . had yet to be defined. I would call this enforced state of breach another instance of vestibular cultural formation where 'kinship' loses meaning" (74). The child and its family are defined at every turn by a system of property relations. Spillers notes that in the historical record "family" is the "mythically revered privilege of a free and freed community," connoting "the vertical transfer of a bloodline, of a patronymic, of titles and entitlements, of real estate and the prerogatives of 'cold cash,' from fathers to sons and in the supposedly free exchange of affectional ties between a male and a female of his choice" (74). These property relations also make homosexuality vestibular to a culture in the making, as "affectional" ties are rehearsed within the confines of heterosexual liaison.

In relationship to black females, we see that consanguinity and family complicate the project of gendering, of naming a particular self, under the violence of a hegemonic system:

> Certainly, if "kinship" were possible the property relations would be undermined, since offspring would then "belong" to a mother and a father. . . . [G]enetic reproduction becomes, then, not an elaboration of the life-principle in its cultural overlap, but an extension of the boundaries of proliferating properties. . . . To that extent, the captive female body locates precisely a moment of converging political and social vectors that mark the flesh as a prime commodity of exchange. . . . [T]his open exchange of female bodies in the raw offers a kind of Urtext to the dynamics of signification and representation that the gendered female would unravel. (75)

Even though their flesh was marked differently, both black and white females were fodder for the system of open exchange that Spillers constructs. But black subjects are not necessarily kept outside the patterns of relationship that define white subjectivity. On the contrary, I would propose that black relationships in the United States were repatterned to resemble more closely community between white subjects. Although black subjects cannot possess themselves of the word *family*, words like *bloodline* and *property* in the dominant definitions of *family* merge, making it impossible for either white or black subjects to possess the term. *Kinship*, then, as defined through property, is a "lie" for both master and slave.

For Spillers kinship does not come about naturally but psychologically, through a kind of cultivated relationship between mother and child—it is a "feeling" that has to be nurtured. Ironically, the very strength and perseverance of black women, heralded throughout abolitionist and post-Reconstruction literature, becomes a pathology of sorts—over time, the black mother becomes the antinarrative—a vestibule for all that is not family in the American mind-set. The constitution of family is rendered completely unstable for both "master's family and captive enclave," as the system of slavery undermines and throws into crisis the "lexis of sexuality, including 'reproduction,' 'motherhood,' 'pleasure,' and 'desire'" (76). Given this area of extreme flux, Spillers can maintain that the complex instability of subject positions, in particular that of the black woman's being an ungendered female, can be "invaded / raided by another *woman* or man" (77).

Spillers then concludes that for African American women the terms *mother* and *enslavement* are equal categories because each "defines . . . a cultural situation that is father-lacking" (80). If patriarchy "declare[s] Mother Right . . . a negating feature of human community" (80)—if "the condition of the (enslaved) mother shall determine the condition of the child"—then it is possible to ascertain that on two levels enslaved women and their descendants are doubly crossed: they are assigned to a matriarchy that is *both* a personal impossibility as they have no rights to their children *and* a cultural impossibility because matriarchy, as defined by the culture, is not a "legitimate procedure of cultural inheritance" (80). Given the complexity of subject positions, what, Spillers asks, *is* the "'condition' of the mother"? (79).

After working with Spillers's text, one cannot read categories like "mother," "female," "enslaved," or "freed" in quite the same manner. Ultimately, she notes that the female "breaks in upon the imagination with a forcefulness that marks both a denial and an 'illegitimacy'"

(80). As "both mother and mother-dispossessed," African (American) female subjectivity is placed "out of the symbolics of female gender," and we as critics need to begin to speak of her as "a different social subject" (80). Much early abolitionist and, subsequently, feminist scholarship has claimed an "African American" mother as its mascot for oppression. Given Spillers's discussion of "body" and "flesh," and "birth/right," feminist scholarship is charged with directing its future endeavors toward a more complex unfolding of the category of "woman"—namely, its racialization and meaning under the system of enslavement and how this system of meaning translates in the dominant terrain where "woman" is no longer the signifying category of feminism.

I can think of no better fictive representation of the complexity of African American female subjectivity than Toni Morrison's exploration of enslaved women under the lash of the Fugitive Slave Law in *Beloved*. In an irony of triple proportions, critics duCille, Spillers, and Morrison all seem to return to the seminal query yet unanswered: What *is* the "condition" of the black female (literally and figuratively)—as mother, as author of both her self, and eventually an/other? Perhaps a reading of Morrison's *Beloved* will provide us with some answers to this question, as well as supply the key to unlocking a pattern of critical and legal "invasion" that relegates black women to the anonymous "space of death."

"So Low, You Can't Get Under It"

Beloved represents one of Morrison's most profound and complex flirtations with the boundaries of language and with African American female authority. Within this linguistic hyperbole there is no black and white, just the colors in between that preoccupy Baby Suggs on her deathbed and so menace Paul D that he ends up in the cellar of the neighborhood church—exposed to the cold and disturbed by a mere apparition. Morrison wields memory so that it circumvents traditional ideas of past, present, and future. If the past in the novel is to be forgotten—a yesterday that they have had "more . . . than anybody"[14]—then Beloved/*Beloved* is about remembering, slowly, easily, and painfully.

But if it is about (re)remembering, it is also about the space where memory is constituted. Commenting on *Beloved*'s opening, Morrison remarks:

> The reader is snatched, yanked, thrown into an environment completely foreign, and I want it as the first stroke of the shared experience that might be possible between the reader and the novel's population. Snatched just as the slaves were from one place to another . . . without preparation and without defense. . . . The fully realized presence of the haunting is both a major incumbent of the narrative and sleight of hand. One of its purposes is to keep the reader preoccupied with the nature of the incredible spirit world while supplied a controlled diet of the incredible political world.[15]

For Morrison the black community at the turn of the century is occupied by both the living and the dead. Morrison's haunting in *Beloved* parallels the project of reclaiming "mutilated female bodies" that Spillers executes.

Out of the meeting between the spiritual and the political in a marginal place, Toni Morrison conjures both a novel (a history) and a character—Beloved—who becomes a blessing to those who wish to know her and a promoter of chaos to those who do not. Beloved is the "word" uttered at the beginning of a wedding (signifying adult life) and at the end of physical life (death). Morrison's *Beloved* allows the word to become flesh when a baby ghost returns to the place of the living, giving the "gray and white house on [124] Bluestone Road" (3) personality—making it "spiteful," "loud," and "finally quiet." A book of margins, Morrison's text plays with the efficacy of language itself, demonstrating how utterly powerful and powerless language is. Beloved becomes the living link between mother and child—between two states of existence in both language and subjectivity. Central in this linguistic interplay—this layered tale of multiple mothers—is that this community of women is called together to speak the "unspeakable things unspoken" into being. Tracing mother and daughter ties in Morrison's text, Deborah Horvitz claims that

> Beloved stands for every African woman whose story will never be told. She is the haunting symbol of the many Beloveds—generations of

mothers and daughters—hunted down and stolen from Africa; as such, she is, unlike mortals, invulnerable to barriers of time, space and place. . . . As Sethe's mother she comes from the geographic other side of the world, Africa; as Sethe's daughter, she comes from the physical other side of life, death.[16]

Although Horvitz's interpretation of the role of mothers in *Beloved* hits the mark, it is possible to see her positioning of death as the other side of life as antithetical to the relative *continuum* between the two that Morrison illuminates in her aforementioned comments. If the two worlds meet in *Beloved*, then this meeting might signal a rupture in the father's language and a return of power to the mother. A dose of "the incredible spirit world" is necessary to bring about the repair of the psychic damage of slavery and serves as an antidote to the beleaguered status of black women in contemporary America.

Immediately, Morrison moves us into a realm where signs, which later become words and then flesh, are inseparable. Morrison attempts to mend the rupture between a sign and its articulation that Spillers notes in "Interstices." *Beloved*'s narrator remarks that Sethe's two boys left the "spiteful" 124, "as soon as two tiny hand prints appeared in the cake" (3). Alluding, it would appear, to the footprints of Wordsworth's lost "Lucy Gray," this image signifies the narrow passageway between a living sign and the newly deceased body; in other words, a handprint becomes a memory of a fleshy presence—a sign of the distant past and the very near future.[17] The boys, Buglar and Howard, quit the liminality those tiny handprints represent—they flee the uncertainty that waits in a story to be told.

Morrison opens her novel by narrowing distances between two supposed dichotomies: life and death. The former we fully engage, and the latter is the sole object of our forgetfulness in this world. Marsha Darling argues that "Toni Morrison asks us to recognize that death is an event along an individual and communal continuum. Death matters; death is an integral part of living consciousness in African religious understanding. And in *Beloved* we are ever close to Death."[18] Morrison constructs an intricate pathway from forgetfulness to "rememory," using a return from death to emphasize her biblical borrowing—she depicts the word becoming flesh.[19] She speaks of Baby Suggs as a subject caught between words: "Suspended between the nastiness of life and the meanness of the dead, she couldn't get interested in leaving life or living it . . . she knew death was anything but forgetfulness" (4). In the tangle of nastiness, meanness, and forgetfulness is the hint of a story, and Baby Suggs's conscious forgetfulness is a part of the nastiness and meanness of African American existence that is a living death. Forgetfulness must be called out of the margin between worlds, and that space must be filled eventually with words, both spoken and written.

The ironic bartering system Sethe uses to purchase her baby's headstone is just one example of how multilayered Morrison's language is. A black woman's body is used in exchange for words, as Sethe explains: "Ten minutes for seven letters . . . that for twenty minutes, a half hour, say, she could have had the whole thing, every word she heard the preacher say at the funeral (and all there was to say, surely) engraved on her baby's headstone: *Dearly Beloved*. But what she got, settled for, was the one word that mattered" (5; italics mine). Sethe chooses a word that brings the dead back to the living and one that begins a life and ends it. The word and the flesh become intimately connected in this scene in which Sethe's body becomes the exchange for letters of a language whose words and logic have separated her from the category of human being and posited her body as a commodity, as an other. Here, the word *Beloved* is both spoken and written word, both sign and articulation. In essence, this language can be described as physical and temporal.

In an evaluation of African American women's literature, Karla F. C. Holloway registers "the propensity of this literature to strategically place a detemporalized universe into the centers of their texts."[20] Although Morrison's story focuses on Beloved, she constantly deconstructs and restructures the meaning of this invocation/character/word as the novel progresses. Morrison reconstructs a liminal space, the place where Spillers argues that African American bodies are just quantities, and adds quality through a name—Beloved—allowing the characters to act out the violence and subtlety of this process of becoming. Therefore, for example, the "rage" of the baby ghost can be interpreted as a rage against the impenetrability of language itself, as Beloved attempts to move from a spoken word, in effect to precede language into a fleshy body.

Sethe's body also serves as a mechanism of exchange in the novel's opening pages. The tree whipped onto the spine of Sethe's back is like the word etched upon flesh. It mediates between Paul D and Sethe when they first make love and serves as a road map for memory/re-memory back to Sweet Home. In this moment of touching and loving the ritual life of the text begins to unfold, for Morrison's purpose is not only to build a site of memory in the text but also to contextualize the ritual aspect of each character's journey to rememory.[21] It is apparent that for each of them the other provides the vital part of the past needed to complete a story or explain a happening. With Sethe's back as a silent road map, their physical bonding facilitates the deciphering of the code etched on her body. This quest serves a dual purpose; it unpacks the language of white supremacy and exposes the "flesh," to use Spillers's paradigm, as everything that makes us "us."

When Beloved enters the novel as a character, she arrives bringing invocations of language itself. When Paul D, Sethe, and Denver question Beloved's name, "she spelled it for them, slowly as though the letters were being formed as she spoke them" (52). Beloved appears as an utterance from the past, and it is as if language, both the speaking and the telling, takes shape and begins with her arrival. Deborah Horvitz argues that Beloved's presence at 124 prompts Sethe's memory, that this "female ghost-child teaches Sethe that memories and stories about her matrilineal ancestry are life-giving" (158). Although Horvitz does note that this presence is from Africa, she does not speculate about how specific that African tie might be. We can begin such speculation by exploring West African retentions in the United States.

Art historian John Vlach provides us with a cultural context crucial to explicating Morrison's narrative: "It is believed in lower Zaire that deceased ancestors become white creatures called *bakulu* who inhabit villages of the dead located under river beds or lake bottoms; they may return from this underworld to mingle with the living without being seen and can then direct the course of the living."[22] The correlation between the bakulu and Beloved is obvious, but Morrison's bakulu is "Thunderblack and glistening"; she attempts to bring this ancestor into consciousness so that she can speak to the living about the lives of the dead (261). Moreover, Beloved's emergence from water, her craving for honey, and her "shining" in front of Paul D all seem to point toward an origin deeper than the middle passage that Horvitz relies on as an explanation of Beloved's presence in the text.

Morrison models Beloved after the orisha, Oshun, who, according to anthropologist Migene González-Wippler, is the Yoruban "divinity of the rivers, . . . [t]he symbol of river waters, without which much life on earth would be impossible. In the same manner, she controls all that makes life worth living, such as love and marriage, children, money, and pleasure. . . . [W]omen who wish to bear children propitiate the orisha to help them achieve their desires."[23] In addition, Diedre L. Bádéjò observes that "Ósun is a woman of great beauty, wealth, and intelligence. She is the leader of *aje*, human and spiritual beings who manifest prodigious and transcendental energy."[24] An understanding of Beloved's spiritual genesis allows for a deeper examination of her symbolic function in the text. Morrison's choice of Oshun seems more deliberate than accidental when we notice that the orisha, Oshun, "controls all that makes life worth living." Spillers reminds us that achieving "pleasure," "marriage," and "children" is made impossible by the discourse of slavery, which sustains itself precisely because desire, matrimony, and progeny are constantly out of reach of white and black subjects alike.

As a manifestation of African spirit(s), divinity, and African American child, Beloved is the root from which collective desires unfold. This desire is actualized in the bizarre relationship between Beloved and Paul D. Beloved murmurs, "I want you to touch me on the inside part and call me my name" (116). Holloway interprets Beloved's beckoning as a demand "to be removed from her nothingness, to be specified, to be 'called'" (522). With the ancestral backdrop provided by Vlach and González-Wippler, we can see Beloved's haunting call as not only an invocation to claim the child / daughter / mother but also an invitation to participate in a ritual, to give praise and invoke the orisha who wishes to be recognized. Luisah Teish describes Oshun-Erzulie as "the queen of the performing arts," whose womb is "the sacred drum."[25] Here Beloved is clearly a representation of this orisha; her "coupling" with Paul D is a manifestation of this ritual taking place, and Beloved's pregnancy is evidence of her enlarged and reverberating drum. Moreover, it is customary that initiates of Oshun travel to Benin in August to participate in a ritual honoring Oshun, a ritual where sexual union is the chief mechanism of tribute. Using this West African retention as a backdrop, Terry Otten's claim that Beloved "enticed [Paul D] into spiritless sex in the cold house" is ironically reductive.[26]

Morrison's first chapters construct a narrow route through which stories of the past move slowly to the surface. Her characters are a people who appear to have fallen through the cracks in language. Finding no apparent value in dominant language except in economic terms, the people in *Beloved* attempt to re-create a collective history from the living death of a brutal language and bodily violence. Sethe's womb becomes the locus for the birth and generation of personal "herstory" as she refers to Denver as an "antelope"—from a memory of her own distant mother performing a dance in slave quarters: "And oh but when they danced and sometimes they danced the antelope. The men as well as the ma'ams, one of whom was certainly her own. They shifted shapes and became something other. Some unchained, demanding other whose feet knew her pulse better than she did. Just like this one in her stomach" (31). Denver's movement inside her womb brings Sethe back to the memory of one of the last instances in which she saw her own mother. The process of "rememory" is exercised in this scene. Sethe is able to take what has the potential to be a painful experience and *remember* it as it connects with a positive aspect of her life. Denver's birth symbolizes an incorporation of dance and language; her "dance" is curtailed by Amy's soothing language; however, her participation in the dance is not ended.

This delineation is crucial to our understanding of Morrison's thematic intentions in *Beloved*. Because so much of African American history has fallen through the cracks of dominant discourse, it is vital that Morrison provide a space where language and action meet, where *both* can facilitate the continuum of collective memory—alluded to as the "dance" in this scene. With a lived experience so bound and hampered by economic language, black women—and in the case of Amy, white women as well—in *Beloved* use a space of movement, where agency abounds. Here women can "dance their way out of their constriction."

Later, Sethe explains her own system of "rememory": "Some things go. Pass on. Some things just stay. I used to think it was my rememory. You know. Some things you forget. Other things you never do. But it's not. Places, places are still there. If a house burns down, it's gone, but the place—the picture of it—stays, and not just in my rememory, but out there, in the world" (35–36). For Sethe, even a burnt-to-the-ground place is still somehow present. In her cosmos the picture is an image that is shared. A memory, then, belongs to all those who take part in its creation; rememory is a form of making a solid connection between all those who witnessed the formation of that picture, the living and the dead, black and white. Language alone is not consistent or trustworthy enough for Sethe to count it among the things she must pass on; instead, she preserves pictures as something tangible to leave behind in the present and to call to memory from the past. Beloved, as one of these pictures, is part of a painful past Sethe would rather not remember. Sethe's journey in the novel is to recognize that this picture is not hers to possess, and as such, it must be called into significance by *everyone*.

But this is perhaps the central query of *Beloved*. How is Sethe to claim authority or "Mother Right" in relationship to her child? She appears to claim her baby as beloved postmortem. Sethe establishes herself as mother when she claims the "right" to kill—to possess this body in the literal sense of the word. She becomes a "mother" when she kills her daughter, when the local papers recognize her as the author/mother of both the act of infanticide and the birthing of her baby. Because of the violence of this assertion and the myriad of questions it produces, it is no wonder that Morrison resurrects the spirit of the Margaret Garner story to challenge the boundaries of language and the limits of mother-love.[27]

Beloved enters the novel when Paul D, Sethe, and Denver, returning from a carnival, begin to feel like family. Morrison describes the scene: "They were not holding hands but their shadows were . . . all three of them were gliding over the dust holding hands" (47). Perhaps Sethe and Paul D's early attempt to make family, to establish kinship in *Beloved*, is aborted because some other repair, as Spillers suggests, is necessary. When Beloved arrives, the shadowy scene is broken, and the tension of the novel is placed between Sethe and Beloved. Their union is described in much more menacing terms: "Their two shadows clashed and crossed on the ceiling like black swords" (48). This existence outside of the self described as shadows is further evidence of the distancing of the characters from physicality and perhaps from the tangibility of the written text. To restore the community bond between all of 124's inhabitants, there must be a journey through a rememory that places the characters' narratives side by side and reenters these tales of emergence and escape into collective history in their own voices. For this to take place characters must devise a chosen language of the self forged from the danger and power of the marginal / the ancestral and *not* from the master('s) discourse of slavery, which constantly inscribes a self always already defined as irrelevant, as outside all "being."

With Beloved's presence the members of 124 begin slowly to remember the past. In that process Sethe steps back to a memory of Baby Suggs preaching the "Word" in the clearing behind 124: "In this here place, we flesh; flesh that weeps, laughs; flesh that dances on bare feet in grass. Love it hard" (88). Baby Suggs conjures up a whole generation of a beloved people suffering under the lash of language that has no respect for their flesh—their essence. Analyzing body and flesh and their relationship to slavery, Spillers posits that "if we think of the 'flesh' as a primary narrative, then we mean its [*sic*] seared, divided, ripped-apartness, riveted to the ship's hole, fallen, or 'escaped overboard'" (67). The correlation between Baby Suggs's idea of the flesh and Spillers's conceptualization is uncanny. Baby Suggs refers to a freed body that she translates as "flesh." Spillers's idea of the flesh as "primary narrative" places the "body" in the context of captive, either by the historical process of slavery or by the linguistic acrobatics of the academy, and leaves the "flesh" in the place where "self" resides.

Morrison employs this body / flesh principle to create an interface between ways of becoming and the "word," making the state of self-actualization a serious possibility. Beloved is the incarnation of that bond between word and flesh, but at the same time she is the force that problematizes this relationship. In their comprehensive examination of *Beloved*, Wilfred Samuels and Clenora Hudson-Weems consistently refer to the lack of a ritual priestess in the novel as evidence of the ruptured relationship between women. For Sethe, "Baby Suggs alone leads her to the ritual grounds of the clearing where, as ritual priestess, she conducts the rite of cleansing that leads Sethe to the catharsis she needs."[28] Here both African ritual and Christian rites are blended; neither appears to have dominance. What appears to be at contest is the efficacy of this borrowed language (the "word")—its overall appropriateness when used as the primary communication for this ritual priestess is put into question.

When Baby Suggs's word is put to the test, she retires to her bed, realizing that "the heart that pumped out love, the mouth that spoke the Word, didn't count. They came in her yard anyway . . . whitefolks had tired her out at last" (180). Despite the concept of free land and free state, Baby Suggs's kin are still subject to the language of the Fugitive Slave Law, which considers any "escaped" black person as a (captive) body, not as flesh. Later, Stamp Paid reminds Baby Suggs that her debt to the community is to be paid by speaking the word: "You can't quit the word. It's given you to speak. You can't quit the word, I don't care what all happen to you" (177). Stamp Paid does not understand that Baby Suggs's "word" is willing so long as her flesh is able. The words of "whitefolks," written on a piece of paper calling for the return of what is left of her family to Kentucky, are enough language and power to keep Baby Suggs's mouth closed and her body captive. The dominant language, that is, the "whitefolks words," not only trespasses on what she believes is her "word" but also taints her place of worship. The intrusion on "her yard" and the power to use language to place bodies (flesh of her flesh) in bondage once more renders her words useless and potentially self-effacing.

Even more complex is the association between the metaphor of the word and its traditional meaning in the Christian faith. Morrison seems to imply that the violation in the clearing serves as a symbolic rupture in the language of the word; it is as if Baby Suggs has been told that the word she speaks does not belong to her, that Christian ministry is basically a white discourse. Baby Suggs learns the lesson of Sixo, that "definitions belonged to the definers—not the defined" (190). Baby Suggs's experience of capture in the clearing, an event that precipitates Beloved's death, parallels Spillers's conception of body / flesh relations. To prevent (re)capture of another body, Sethe takes a knife, not to save her own child but to destroy someone else's property. This act of infanticide is Sethe's *literal* coming into "Mother Right."

It is understandable, therefore, that Sethe, Denver, and Beloved's return to the sanctity of the clearing is fraught with tension. Without Baby Suggs's spoken word, Sethe is left to rememory, and what she recalls is her family and community—whole—at 124. While waiting for "some clarifying words," she lapses into a rememory thick with the soothing/strangling hands of the word incarnate. It is the first clash of shadows. The confrontation at the clearing takes place at the ritual site of speaking (one's own) language into being. Language, at this point in the text, moves into a state of transformation and is merged with pictures and, eventually, sound.

As the past begins to speak and personal herstories are told, something shifts in the narrative voice of the book. The collective voice begins to separate, and the individual "first person" narratives of Sethe, Denver, and Beloved emerge. However, the process of elimination by which this individual storytelling takes place is as elusive as Sula and Nel's dream talk in Morrison's second novel, *Sula*. Paul D enters the text and serves as a catalyst, much like Beloved, to the beginnings of a collective narrative; his chance encounter with Stamp Paid moves him into an aspect of the story that he cannot accept—(her)story is too personal, "too thick," like her love. At that point Paul D is put outside the thoughts and words of 124. Once Paul D is removed temporarily, the women begin to utter "unspeakable thoughts, unspoken" (199). The unspeakable is the "word" taken out of the male preacher's mouth and given to Baby Suggs. This word is the legacy she passes on to Sethe, Denver, and Beloved. But because of the rupture in their relationship, this word is tested, and language must develop power beyond collective experience to speak of the self.

Paul D's previous conversations with Sethe reveal that her relationship to the other men at Sweet Home was primarily one of objectification—she was the stage for the articulation of their desire. In his absence and in Beloved's presence she can begin to conceive of a personal herstory, a saga that is hers to tell and in which she has no *apparent* fixed "symbolic" relationship to its characters. Also, desire becomes here much more than heterosexual "love." It carries with it a longing for continuity and community beyond the reaches of sexuality or the dual appropriation represented by the "couple." However, the above argument is jeopardized by the congruency of both Paul D and Beloved's first perceptions of Sethe, who sparks an appetite in both that is loaded with sexual yearning. When Paul D remembers Sethe, he remembers "fucking" cows to relieve his desire for her; when Beloved watches Sethe, she is "licked, tasted, eaten by [her] eyes" (57). While both struggle to enter into herstory, the pathway to remembering is a sensual one, an attempt to impregnate the elusive Sethe with their own form of words. It is another ritual moment in the text that calls to mind Barbara Christian's aforementioned view of sensuality and ritual healing.

The three stories of Beloved, Sethe, and Denver represent a subconscious (re)memory—a kind of stream of consciousness that undermines the elusiveness of personal memory. Beloved's discourse stands out as the most complex and bizarre of the three voices heard in the second part of the novel. Beloved begins: "I am Beloved and she is mine. . . . I am not separate from her there is no place where I stop her face is my own and I want to be there in the place where her face is and to be looking at it too a hot thing" (210). Beloved's language is that of a lost child, of a slave in middle passage, and of a daughter seeking a mother's protection. Holloway suggests that "Beloved's discourse is the Derridean trace element—the one that dislocates the other two by challenging—disrupting what semblance of narrative structure or sense there had been in Sethe's or Denver's thinking" (520). Beloved's "broken" language nevertheless represents a coherent story, and the gap between sentences and thoughts signifies the crack in discourse through which she has simultaneously fallen and reentered. Ironically, dominant discourse seems to leave space for Beloved, an "other" outside discourse, to enter. Beloved reifies her own experience in the flesh and in the shadows by stating, "I am."[29] Her passage into language therefore becomes an active present experience rather than a passive historical occurrence. Here she states and creates her own genesis and return in an apocalyptic moment where both being and becoming are present. Moreover, she returns to that zero-degree of subjectivity— that liminal space of "quantities," of "flesh," and converses with us in her own poetry, materializing before our eyes as daughter, mother, ancestor, and orisha.

Both Karla Holloway and Mae Henderson approach *Beloved* with a view of the multiple layers of temporality, history, and memory that Morrison constructs in her text. Holloway writes that in *Beloved* "Western time is obliterated, space is not even relevant because Beloved's presence is debatable, and the nature of her being is a nonissue because her belonging (she is mine) has been established by her mother and sister."[30] Even coming back from the dead doesn't save Beloved from being seen as "belonging" to someone; for Holloway she reenters physical space just as she left it: with her being a nonissue because establishing possession is every bit as important during slavery as after. Although Beloved bridges the gap between spirit and body, she is still an "idea." If Beloved never achieves being and her belonging is always framed by someone else, then she is truly the sleight of hand, *the* trick of language that maneuvers her into the novel.

If Beloved holds only a debatable presence in the text, then the marginal *physical* presence must be shifted and shared by another character. Denver occupies this marginal position. In a space, to echo Harriet Ngubane's observations, that is both powerful and dangerous,[31] Denver must move through the language of Sethe and Beloved and act; it is Denver who has tasted the coming together of life and death. She remarks, "I swallowed her blood right along with my mother's milk" (205). At the novel's end it is Denver who calls in the crowd of healers who serve the curious purpose of rectifying the space at 124 and committing the words therein to a collective rememory.

Physically Denver is placed between the words and actions of Sethe and Beloved. Denver's very birth implies the betweenness of her life in the text. Born between slavery and freedom, in her mother's personal middle passage, she comes to consciousness in this literal moment in African American history. Brought into the world via the hands of a white woman, Denver also comes into a temporarily desegregated space. Therefore, she knows who Beloved is when she arrives; she cannot forget that place, that passage into which she was born. Only Denver questions Beloved about her journeying, and when Beloved answers, it is obvious that the worlds they speak of are vastly different:

> Denver scooted a little closer. "What's it like over there, where you were before? Can you tell me?"
>
> "Dark," said Beloved. "I'm small in that place. I'm like this here." She raised her head off the bed, lay down on her side and curled up.
>
> "You see anybody?"
>
> "Heaps. A lot of people is down there. Some is dead."
>
> "You see Jesus? Baby Suggs?"
>
> "I don't know. I don't know the names." (75)

Imagery is threefold in this myopic conversation. Denver is first to understand that Beloved is a manifestation of her slain baby sister. However, her conventional knowledge of life and death limits her understanding of "that place" to a life after death where she will meet Baby Suggs and Jesus. But Beloved speaks on at least two levels—to the common *individual* experience of life in the womb and to the larger historical *communal* experience of black people in the middle passage. Ironically, this latter experience is lost to Denver, and Beloved is a dreadful reminder of this lapse in historical memory. Part of one another, yet distant, Denver and Beloved converse, and their conversation points toward the larger, collective problem of the widening generation gap; here Beloved as "mother" is not empowered to relay to the child, Denver, the key codes necessary for her to unpack the meaning and ultimate gravity of what has been revealed to her. For Denver the space Beloved comes from is forever "over there"; for Beloved the space is "down there"—a place where "some is dead," and apparently others are not.

The symbolism of Morrison's skating scene also reveals Denver as the novel's marginal character. In their analysis Samuels and Hudson-Weems observe that "images of unity and wholeness that seem to dominate are subsumed by powerful images of death, the most important of which is the frozen creek on which they skate" (122). Later, they add, "the creek, a tributary to the river, is dormant, without life—dead in the midst of winter. Thus, in spite of the jubilation, images of death abound" (122). Samuels's and Hudson-Weems's observations about the undermining of unity in this scene are astute, but their reading of the "dead" creek is problematized by Morrison's representation of death elsewhere in the text.

Morrison's use of the black vernacular enables us to view the creek as "froze," not just "frozen." Where there is something frozen, there is the connotation of finality; when something is "froze," it represents a more elusive moment—a suspension of time. The familiar saying "still waters run deep" implies that there is always a flow of water underneath any seemingly frozen thing. This "treacherous" creek is as liminal as the space that Sethe, Beloved, and Denver occupy; it is the metalanguage they emit later—a symbol of their collective discourse suspended in time. As a tributary of the river, from whence the bakulu emerge, the creek is the extension of their threefold relationship. Each sits on the margin of some world—death/life, black/white, mother/daughter, sister/lover, ancestor/orisha. The moment of power in the text emerges when this strange and powerful bakulu discourse—the discourse of margins—comes together to create a space where there was none before; where multilayered discourse can exist; where physical bodies and the disembodied speak.

During the skating scene, Morrison constructs a liminal space for Denver to inhabit. In this scene there is no dialogue; the laughter is unspoken, and "nobody saw them falling." Denver symbolically shares in the physical experience of both Sethe and Beloved: "Beloved wore the pair [of skates], Denver wore one, step-gliding over the treacherous ice. Sethe thought her two shoes would hold and anchor her" (174). A shoe on one foot and a skate on the other, Denver is the child who knows both mother and sister; she literally skates in each of their subject positions. As their interior monologues will demonstrate later in the text, Denver does not share the conflation of mother/daughter/lover that Beloved and Sethe experience; this clarity allows her to transcend the disastrous clash between Beloved and Sethe.

When each speaks her own story, Denver reifies her marginal position with the statement, "Beloved is my sister. I swallowed her blood right along with my mother's milk" (205). Denver fears both Sethe and what is "outside this house." In her tale of memory Denver refers constantly to her "Daddy" and his "things." Much of her monologue is occupied by a longing for this father figure; she ultimately believes that Beloved is the sister who has returned to wait with her for her father's arrival. This male-consumed discourse posits Denver outside the woman-centered language that both Sethe and Beloved utilize. Because Denver is consumed with a traditional male presence and what is "outside" 124, it is only appropriate that she go from the private affairs of 124 into the public arena to gather a community of healers to rid 124 of what has confused it.[32]

In the beginning of the novel it is Paul D's shouting and stomping that pressure the baby ghost to reappear in the flesh. In the end another kind of sound moves Beloved back through her middle passage to her place at the bottom of a riverbed and to the spirit plane of the orishas. The women on the outskirts of Cincinnati assemble at what used to be the gate of 124 to exorcise a shadowy presence from its midst: "They stopped praying and took a step back to the beginning. In the beginning there were no words. In the beginning was the sound, and they all knew what that sound sounded like" (259). It is a sound that causes Sethe to tremble and Beloved to lapse back into a memory. It is a rewriting of Genesis, often posited as *the* seminal text of cultural begin-ning, a text whose word made it possible for them to become bodies and commodities instead of flesh. Morrison explains: "For Sethe it was as though the Clearing had come to her with all its heat and simmering leaves, where the voices of women searched for the right combination, the key, the code, the sound that broke the back of words. . . . [I]t was a wave of sound wide enough to sound deep water. . . . It broke over Sethe and she trembled like the Baptized in its wash" (261). In this wave of sound Beloved disappears—her leaving just as rumored and unexplained as her coming, sound having broken the cadence of the river water through which Beloved enters and exits, sound having dis-located language and proclaimed itself the true discourse of the mar-gin in this text.

"It Was Not a Story to Pass On"

Morrison's ending circles back to the type of selective memory prac-ticed in the earlier part of the novel. In Beloved's absence people for-get: "It took longer for those who had spoken to her, lived with her, fallen in love with her, to forget, until they realized they couldn't re-member or repeat a single thing she said, and began to believe that, other than what they themselves were thinking, she hadn't said any-thing at all. So, in the end, they forgot her too. Remembering seemed unwise" (274–275). Their process of forgetting wards off another pres-ence because remembering was the mechanism by which Beloved gained access to their thoughts and subsequently to a body that be-came flesh. Morrison's intent in the last paragraphs of the story is vague and unsettling. If a people are to forget Beloved, then that for-getting is a cruel and self-centered process as co-opting as the domi-nant language itself. The touch of Beloved's hand and the rhythm of her voice is replaced by their own thoughts. In a lecture given at the University of Michigan Morrison described the scene in *Beloved*: "no neighborhood, no sculpture, no paint, no time, especially no time be-cause memory, pre-historic memory, has no time. There is just a little music, each other and the urgency of what is at stake. Which is all they had. *For that work, the work of language is to get out of the way.*"[33] Without a language violently etched onto the body by the law of the land we are left with the flesh, with the dead and what they can recall. In this beloved story that is not "to pass on" is the sound and movement of an experience that will not be forgotten. The last lines of the novel not only reflect a herstory forgotten to future generations but also a process of "disremember[ing]" that is complete erasure.

In her closing examination of *Beloved* Holloway suggests that "the recursion of this text, its sublimation of time and its privileging of an alternative not only to history, but to reality, places it into the tradition of literature by black women because of its dependence on the alternative, the *inversion* that sustains the 'place' that has re-placed reality" (523; italics mine). In her footnote to this statement she credits Houston Baker with his observation of the "inversive symbolic modes of cognition" employed by African American writers. The ideology of inversion has metaphorical as well as cultural implications. A historian of African American art, Robert Ferris Thompson, writes of the Kongo:

> The inversion of pierced white basins and other vessels is common in many Kongo cemeteries. Indeed, the verb, "to be upside down" in Ki-Kongo also means "to die." Moreover, inversion signifies perduance, as a visual pun on the superior strength of the ancestors, for the root of *bikinda*, "to be upside down, to be in the realm of the ancestors, to die" is *kinda*, "to be strong," "because those who are upside down, who die, are strongest."[34]

Inversion is not only a matter of technique in African American novels. It also signifies ritual retention.[35] Morrison's query of death is that it is not an end point, and her inversion of Beloved's fate in the novel demonstrates that it is possible to return, to float across the slim margin between death and life and challenge the very system of linguistic arrangement that holds this distance between worlds as finite and impenetrable.

And black women consistently "return." "Sapphire," in Spillers's words, "might rewrite after all a radically different text for a female empowerment" (80). Returning to Spillers's claim at the beginning of this chapter, recovering "mutilated female bodies" might seem "backward" or "embarrassing," but this restoration is an absolute necessity. If language obscures our being in the material world and puts in its place a "portrait of the lady" that is distorted, then the flesh is the only category of representation that comes close to resembling black women as they see themselves. To find the flesh, the author and the critic must acknowledge no borders, must walk the space of death unafraid and uninhibited by a language that says such an outing is both a *physical* and *imaginative* impossibility. By inverting the most powerful paradigms of Western discourse, authors like Morrison and Silko reconfigure the imaginative terrain so that the space of death belongs not solely to the past, but to the present as well.

3

Telling the Story of Genocide in
Leslie Marmon Silko's *Almanac of the Dead*

Wherever it is shown the white society is murderous, corrupt, mad with greed and hideously perverted. Among the white characters, and quite typical of the rest, are a federal judge who has sex with his basset hounds and a reptilian homosexual who steals the baby of a drug-soaked stripteaser for use in a torture video.—John Skow, *Time*

Silko isn't keen on fairness. In her cosmology there are good people and there are white people.... This vivid, preposterous, splinter-under-the-fingernails book is guaranteed to make you mad and just as sure to make you squirm. The final irony is that only in the America that earns so much of Silko's wrath could such a flamboyant and eccentric piece of fiction come forth.—Malcolm Jones Jr., *Newsweek*

The epigraphs for this chapter sample popular reviews of Silko's most ambitious work of fiction.[1] Reviewers hover between a qualitative appreciation of the novel's truth-telling about contemporary American society and an absolute disdain for its negative characterization of whiteness. Malcolm Jones prefers to understand Silko's work as a "preposterous," "flamboyant and eccentric piece of fiction," rather than as one that presents white people as the opposite of "good." It is amazing that after centuries of marking black and brown peoples as the antithesis of the word *good*, we should be so frightened of turning the tables, even when that look at the underside of history provides us with some truth about the way things really *are* in the eyes of peoples surviving the terror brought on by the practice of genocide. So focused are we on a (black) "menace" that occupies our imaginary, we leave no room for other characters to inhabit such a peopled place. Ultimately, the separation between "us" and "them," between black and white—a separation no longer sustained in the blood—is hard to maintain if white faces appear as perpetrators of the very violence the status quo believes is carried out by those of darker persuasions.

In trying to define whiteness in the American context David Roediger concludes that

> a sharp questioning of whiteness within American culture opens the opportunity to win people to far more effective opposition to both race and class oppression. To take advantage of such possibilities requires that we not only continue to talk about race but that we pay attention to the most neglected aspects of race in America, the questions of why people think they are white and of whether they might quit thinking so.[2]

Recent developments in scholarship on whiteness have explored not only our understanding of how whiteness operates but also how different groups' experience of whiteness is life-shaping.[3] Silko's *Almanac* takes the experience of whiteness very seriously. Its exploration of the dead in contemporary America differs from Morrison's project, which is grounded in the relative safety of the past. Morrison's emphasis on the past still allows us to have a hands-off appoach to the problem of race in this nation because readers might acknowledge events in *Beloved* as beyond their ability to influence. *Almanac* operates without the cover of the past, and focus on the present erases the invisibility of (white) power, placing it in stark relief, giving it substance, and making death its constant companion.

Readers of Silko's novel confront subjects who are very much *like* the people in power in quotidian life. The novel's many vignettes (there are 208 in all) appear to be gleaned from outrageous local news reports and tabloid headlines. For the reviewers mentioned above, white subjects in *Almanac* can only be read as grotesques, as absolute disfigurations of white people. What is ironic, however, about Jones's claim of Silko's unfairness to white characters is that Silko meticulously depicts characters from *all* ethnic backgrounds as caught up in the pursuit of whiteness—(white) power and white people are two different, albeit not always separate, categories. This configuration challenges the "othering" generally associated with theories of the grotesque—as grotesque others are most often outside of normative whiteness.

Silko's earlier work centered in and revolved around Laguna Pueblo; *Almanac of the Dead*, however, reaches beyond Laguna and back again, with death as the principle *character* of a violent popular culture—one that thrives on the grotesque and the macabre. The text's focus on sexual and physical violence exposes the underbelly of American society as its topcoat. If Silko's prevailing paradigm has some validity, then readers would have to believe that this nation's diversity can only be realized through processes that stand in the way of diversity's actualization: sexual and physical violence. In Silko's hands the Americas become a territory ravaged by centuries of genocide—it is a narrative told from the eye view of native peoples—where death and destruction are not part of a hidden past but are on the brink of engulfing what is left of a beleaguered contemporary landscape. Michael Taussig's work on colonial life mirrors the environment Silko creates in *Almanac*. For Taussig "the space of death" is "where the Indian, African, and white give birth to a New World."[4] *Almanac* travels "the space of death," preparing for the reader a new text about the place we all call "home."

Memory, History, and the Grotesque

Contemporary theories of the grotesque help to unpack Silko's strange and varied cosmos. In his analysis of the grotesque in modern fiction, British scholar Bernard McElroy humorously claims, "In colloquial usage, [the grotesque] can mean almost anything unseemly, disproportionate, or in bad taste, and the term is routinely applied to everything from a necktie to a relationship."[5] McElroy argues that the grotesque predates "all schools and theories" and represents a "continuum" rather than a genre to which a specific kind of work might belong (2). In his first chapter McElroy outlines the theoretical sphere that twentieth-century grotesque fiction inhabits:

> Man [*sic*] is usually presented as living in a vast, indifferent, meaningless universe . . . [that] is alien and hostile, directing its energies to . . .

denying him a place and identity even remotely commensurate with his needs and aspirations, surrounding him on every side with violence and brutalisation ... manipulating and dehumanizing him through vast, faceless institutions, the most ominous of which are science, technology, and the socio-economic organisation. (17)

Certainly, *Almanac*'s use of the grotesque is grounded in this horror of alienation and negation that McElroy perceives. However, Silko's grotesque centers the marginal, as both corrupt officials and the "people" who wish to "take back the land" experience and wander through a maze of grotesque circumstances, couplings, and terrains so that categories of self and other, inside and outside become blurred. More than anything, it is the presence of genocide (past/present/future) that disrupts the idea of the grotesque as an abstraction, as an experience outside the norm. Genocide gives place and name to the grotesque—places like Wounded Knee, names like Ravensbruck.

Contemporary theories of the grotesque depend too often on the dichotomies of primitive/civilized as real categories of difference. Discussing Freudian theory, McElroy claims that the

grotesque transforms the world from what we "know" it to be to what we fear it might be. It distorts or exaggerates the surface of reality in order to tell a qualitative truth. . . . [It] does not address the rationalist in us, or the scientist in us, but the vestigial primitive in us, the child in us, the potential psychotic in us. This magical, animistic quality prevails in the grotesque art of the most disparate periods and cultures. (5)

What if the grotesque is no longer a hyperbole used to tell some "qualitative truth" but is instead our "apocalypse now"? McElroy points out that the creation of the grotesque occurred simultaneously with Western notions of rationalism, empiricism, and quixicism. Most important, though, McElroy observes that the "word 'grotesque' differentiates that which we want to have separate from our sense of reality, but still powerfully experience as real" (6).

The power of the grotesque is its ability to present the intangible as real and to promote alternative constructions of the self that have no explanation in the language of rational thought. Silko inverts the hierarchies of civilized/primitive, rational/irrational, and uses the grotesque as a vehicle to explore the depravity and utter disconnectedness of contemporary society, where the irrational *is* the dominant reality.[6] But she maintains that within this terrain of the grotesque is both the story of witchery and slavery and of revolution and freedom. For Silko the grotesque functions as a landscape where the trickster plays a game of conflating opposites, surviving the effects of living in the margins of several, often competing, imaginative realms. And it is this imaginative terrain that so captures the attention of Native Americanists.[7]

The pages of *Almanac* are filled with "spirits," and any reading requires a considerable suspension of disbelief on the part of the reader. Here spirits are both "alive" in language and "heard" as the voices of the dead speak to the living. Writing about the complex epistemology of Native American literature, Kenneth Lincoln finds

> Crossings of breath: every "word" translates the world we experience by aural or visual signs. Words embody reality. When language works, in flesh or print, our known world comes alive in words, animate and experiential. With more than one epistemological complex in this metamorphic process, any translator must look two ways at once—to carry over, as much as possible, the experiential integrity of the original; to *re*generate the spirit of the source in a recreated text.[8]

Paralleling Lincoln's approach by emphasizing the power of speech, Hertha Wong adds, "There is . . . a vivid sense of the powerful "medicine" of daily speech. Unlike writing, speech is wedded to breath. . . . To speak, then, is to reveal, to make manifest one's spirit. To speak one's life is to give forth the spirit of one's life, and if others join in the telling, the result is a mingling of breaths, of lives, of spirits."[9]

Lincoln believes that the critic of Native American texts must act as a "translator"; s/he must look both ways. Only then can "language in flesh or print" convey meaning. Wong envisions a living text created by the mingling of breaths, lives, and spirits in the telling of a communal story. In critical models used to discuss Morrison's *Beloved*, the flesh and the word play an integral part in articulating the experience of marginalized peoples. The same phenomenon of language and "being" surfaces in critical approaches to Indian literature. In both accounts speech and breath are endowed with the power, in and of themselves, to effect change; this is not because of the speaker's "force of argument" or "clarity of presentation," much praised in Western oratory, but because of the power of words to manifest being in the world at large.

For Silko, to live in the Americas means to witness the remaking of history and the dislocation of language from the speaking bodies. Herbert Hirsch corroborates this view: "Maintaining memory in the face of the repeated onslaught aimed at reconstruction and revision is not an easy task. . . . If memory can be facilely rewritten and new myths created, does memory or history mean anything at all?"[10] The annexing of words from their speaking subjects works on two levels: it demonstrates a collective desire to divorce the face of whiteness from the language it uses to legitimate itself, and it silences all those who might object to the status quo. To combat obliterated history and disembodied language, communities of color employ memory as a remedy for forgetfulness. The creation of "being" in the world, the release of the "spirit" of one's life, is intimately connected to memory and imagination. Silko's critical and creative works embody her changing understanding of the interplay between memory and imagination. In *Storyteller* Silko remarks, "Sometimes what we call 'memory' and what we call 'imagination' are not so easily distinguished."[11] Late in *Almanac*, one of Lecha's transcriptions of the fifth manuscript reads:

> Narrative as analogue for actual experience, which no longer exists; a mosaic of memory and imagination. An experience termed *past* may actually return if the influences have the same balances or proportions as before. Details may vary, but the essence does not change. The day would have the same feeling, the same character, as that day has been described as having *before*. The image of a memory exists in the present moment.[12]

Lecha's interpretation is reminiscent of Sethe's belief that a picture of an event hangs in the place where it occurred. For Lecha, however, the image is mired in the present moment, not lodged in a distant and forgotten past. Silko moves from a conflation of memory and imagination that *produces* narrative in *Storyteller* to a much more complex ideology of narrative, memory, *and* imagination in *Almanac*. Here preexisting narrative—a story in a notebook—takes the place of personal memory and imagination. What we imagine or remember does not fuel narrative; instead, narrative recreates itself independent of contemporary happenings. Narrative is a *direct* disclosure of events on a continuum of past, present, and future.

To this extent the writer becomes almost subordinate to the vibration of experience found in narrative. It is the essence of an event that calls it back from the past and makes it return in the present, and this dynamic depends on collective, not individual, storytelling. Wong's formulations about memory and imagination in Scott Momaday's work resonate throughout Silko's paradigm:

> To tell one's *personal* story, one must remember past events, one must recall old images, and one must resurrect previous feelings. Memory, then, in conjunction with imagination, plays a vital role in individual and collective self-narration—synthesizing differences and ordering chaos. Through memory and imagination, expressed in language, storytelling helps us to understand human experience. (158; italics mine)

For Silko this process is carried one step further, as collective memory not only "help[s] us to understand human experience" but also serves to significantly alter the course of events—those that are human, inanimate, and spiritual. If the past is a hodgepodge of memory and imagination, then the narrative that propels a people forward is a narrative that maintains an essence, a memory over a period of time. As Herbert Hirsch observes in his work on genocide:

> The present is always fashioned from materials of the past. Only the writing of history can be supersessive, and it is in this manner that paradigms of time influence the construction of memory. But paradigms of time are not the only influence upon the construction of memory; history is written to serve other, more earthly ends. Memory is also manipulated to serve political power, and the ability to manipulate memory is, in itself, a measure of that power. (22)

To tell the story of genocide necessitates a novel beginning. Memory must be animated so that it can subvert the effects of its manipulation by the nation. In *Almanac* memory becomes narrative, and no amount of personal recollection or acts of the imagination can prevent the story from repeating itself, from remaining stubbornly consistent in every life that unravels according to its logic.

Almanac: A Reading in Three Parts

Almanac spans the southwestern United States and moves from north-western Mexico to Central America with many of its characters living permanently or for periods of time in Tucson, Arizona. The events that unfold in this Indian epic are a simultaneous fulfillment and inscribing *both* of the prophecies of the Book of Chilam Balam, twelve of which have survived and remain as almanacs/manuscripts of the Maya priests, *and* the four codices of Mayan hieroglyphs housed in Dresden, Madrid, Paris, and Grolier. In an interview Silko explains:

> The Mayan people . . . believed that a day was a kind of being and it had . . . we would maybe say a personality, but that it would return. It might not return again for five thousand or eight thousand years, but they believed that a day exactly as it had appeared before would appear again. It's a view that basically denies a lot of western European notions about linear time, death, simultaneous planes of experience, and so on.[13]

Almanac is Silko's attempt to deconstruct Western European notions of binary oppositions and to create a space of simultaneity—a process supported by both the way events are told in the text and by Silko's narrative structure, where each story is not a "new" beginning but is meant to be laid beside the others in the text. In *Almanac* Silko creates a fifth manuscript, which is in the hands of twins, Zeta and Lecha; the former runs a lucrative drug trade at the U.S./Mexican border, and the latter is a clairvoyant who locates the dead. For Silko the "day" has come 'round again and the "story" has arrived in our town. *Almanac* is a text both universal and specific. It is a story that the many contribute to, but only those who view the *days* as cyclical can understand the meaning embedded in them.

The act of synthesizing differences and ordering chaos has signifi-cant implications for a reading of *Almanac*. This process is exercised in Silko's ordering of the novel's events. Its six parts—"The United States of America," "Mexico," "Africa," "The Americas," "The Fifth World," and "One World, Many Tribes"—all contain books with numerous subheadings. The effect is often to blur the borders between states and countries, as "Africa's" books are named "New Jersey," "Arizona," and "El Paso" and could easily belong to the first part of *Almanac*, "The

United States of America." Borders dissolve in part 4, "The Americas," and become "Mountains" and "Rivers"—a sense of what the land was before cities like Tucson, San Diego, or El Paso almost obliterated the importance of terrain by imposing the primacy of boundaries through naming on the land. "The Fifth World," where the Pueblo people believe we are now, is a world of "Foes," "Warriors," and "Struggle," and "One World, Many Tribes" is joined by a single book—"Prophecy."

While "synthesizing differences," Silko constructs a powerful story in which the voices of the living and dead speak to one another; she also builds a disturbing, and often problematic, sexual terrain at this juncture of discourse at the margins. Sexual acts serve as metaphors for the horrors of a continent ravaged by Europeans, foretold by the Maya and come round again in the present *day*. It is a place of the fusing of contradictions and gross violence, where intercourse often reflects the exploitation of the body/land of the Americas. *Almanac*'s graphic passages depict the human body as a thing to be fragmented or split; often the sexual act is a mechanism by which the body is dismembered, and the directives of the dominant culture are inscribed on it. Human beings become natural resources to be exploited and mined like the uranium at Laguna Pueblo, used in the 1940s to make the bombs that devastated Hiroshima and Nagasaki.[14] By any means necessary Silko brings the terror home. As Joy Harjo remembers, "England, France, Greece and other western European cultures can only form the boundary of the space defining America. This amnesia of both mythical and historical origins explains the arts in this country. This indigenous awareness informs the root of Silko's novel-ing. Her work transforms the abyss; it becomes a shining sacred thing that sees all, knows all" (207).

I. The United States of America

Much like the opening of Toni Morrison's *Beloved*, Silko's beginning of *Almanac* places the reader in medias res. The novel's largest section, "The United States of America," opens in Tucson with the subheading "Unanswered Questions." In a remote ranch house, inhabitants, some of them related, gather in the kitchen. Silko immediately undermines any of the reader's assumptions about family, hearth, and home, thus setting the tenor for the whole novel:

> The old woman stands at the stove stirring the simmering brown liquid with great concentration. Occasionally Zeta smiles as she stares into the big blue enamel pot. She glances up through the rising veil of steam at the young blond woman pouring pills from brown plastic prescription vials.
>
> Another old woman in a wheelchair at the table stares at the pills Seese counts out. Lecha leans forward in the wheelchair as Seese fills the syringe. Lecha calls Seese her "nurse" if doctors or police ask questions about the injections or drugs. Zeta lifts the edge of a sleeve to test the saturation of the dye. "The color of dried blood. Old blood," Lecha says, but Zeta has never cared what Lecha or anyone else thought. Lecha is just the same. (19)

The image is of the practitioners of witchery—conjured in *Ceremony* and recorded in *Storyteller*—complete with cauldron and two old women, but the aesthetics are contemporary. The dye, the color of "Old blood," serves as a reference point of conversation at the kitchen table, and Silko alludes to Zeta as a participant in Lecha's drug use with the words "[she] lifts the edge of a sleeve to test. . . . " While she tests the dye, the implication is that she is preparing, as is Lecha, to inject a drug into her own veins. Moreover, this opening image is ambiguous: are we supposed to be reminded of the witchery practiced in *Ceremony* and view this gathering as a convergence of contemporary witches, or is Silko trying to test her reader's threshold of moral tolerance?

Continuing, Silko offers:

> Lecha abandoned Ferro, her son, in Zeta's kitchen when he was a week old. "The old blood, old dried-up blood," Ferro says, looking at Lecha, "the old, and the new blood." Ferro is cleaning pistols and carbines with Paulie at the other end of the long table. Ferro hates Lecha above all others. "Shriveled up," he says, but Lecha is concentrating on finding a good vein for Seese to inject the early-evening Demerol. (19)

Ferro repeats Lecha's words as if they were a chant; at this spontaneous gathering a ritual of blood, albeit somewhat warped, is taking place. Seeing no connection between himself and his "mother," Ferro intones "shriveled up"—an image of an addict's over-used vein, a flaccid penis, or an umbilical cord long severed. A bit later Seese observes:

> The kitchen table is littered with paper wrappings from sterile bottles or rubbing alcohol and boxes of disposable syringes. Tiny bottles of Demerol line the dairy compartment of the refrigerator. Lecha gets chatty right before the dope makes her dreamy. She laughs and points at all of them together in the same room. No food anywhere. Pistols, shotguns, and cartridges scattered on the kitchen counters, and needles and pills all over the table. The Devil's kitchen doesn't look this good.
>
> Sterling the hired man is standing by the dishwasher studying the instruction book. Sterling is in training for a special assignment. All of them are in the kitchen because of recent developments. Sterling has been told very little; Ferro is coiled tighter than a mad snake. . . . Ferro says the needle slips in like a lover's prick and shoots the dope in white and hot. That's why Lecha wants them all to watch her get off, Ferro says, but he doesn't watch junky orgasms not even for his *own* mother. Zeta shakes her head, her lips tight with disgust. Ferro laughs then jumps up from the table with the 9mm in its holster and bolts out the door to the garage. (20)

It is a world void of sustenance, where food is replaced by Demerol and codeine and, in Seese and Ferro's case, cocaine, marijuana, and alcohol. More important, the "dairy compartment" becomes the repository for drugs instead of eggs and milk, all "products" derived from the female.[15] Distanced from his mother, Ferro seems to maintain that the people here are gathered for the explicit purpose of witnessing Lecha's grotesque ritual of injecting her evening hallucinogen. But this ritual is made more grotesque by his own metaphor of penetration and ejaculation, a metaphor he seems to disown with his angry laughter at the scene's closure. The beginning of this passage is tinged with humor, as Lecha muses, "The Devil's kitchen doesn't look this good." Each character's laughter mirrors the other's and parodies the unfolding drama.

These opening images have a direct correlation to the kind of palimpsest that genocide creates. Genocide is the act of expunging a people (along with their memories and their history), from the planet; it is counter to all forms of procreation, human or otherwise; and it is an act of systematic rage and blind contempt, beyond the scope of any theory of rationality. The story of the Americas from the perspective of indigenous peoples cannot be told without a complete inversion of everything we envision as part of our collective reality. So blood is no longer supple and life giving, but like dye it is artificial and fabricated, a poor substitute for the real thing. Mother's milk is absent, and in its place are semen and Demerol. There is no traditional role playing here. Women and men are equally confused and able to participate in the numbing behavior that is the aftermath of systematic removal and extermination. If we are going to travel the space of death, as Michael Taussig so eloquently reminds us, then we had better be ready to move beyond the limits of representation and into the territory of the lived experience of those imperiled by (white) power.[16]

Old blood or dried blood also serves to nourish the group at the ranch house, and Zeta's dye has obvious symbolic meaning in the text, as Silko remarks:

> [Zeta] has been dyeing everything she wears dark brown. No reason, Zeta claims, just a whim. But Lecha had warned Seese not to be fooled. *Nothing happens by accident here.* The dark brown dye stains the white grout between the Mexican tiles patterned with blue, parrot-beaked birds trailing serpent tails of yellow flowers. Lecha's mysterious notebooks have drawings of parrot-beaked snakes and jaguar-headed men. Leave it to Zeta to have the kitchen counters redone with these Mexican tiles only two weeks before Lecha returned to transcribe the notebooks. The first time Zeta had seen Seese, Zeta had told Lecha the white girl would have to go. No strangers around the ranch. . . . But Lecha had lied to Zeta, claiming that Seese already knew everything anyway. (21; italics mine)

Lecha's warning to Seese to take nothing for granted serves as a reminder to the reader as well that these events are not told for mere effect but are included because Silko is weaving a distinct pattern in the pages of *Almanac*. In his critical study of Native American literature, Kenneth Lincoln has remarked, "There are no accidents in the ways things happen, Indian traditionals are known to say."[17] If this is true, it is no mere coincidence that the dye that stains the white grout is, via its naming by Ferro and Lecha, a metaphor for old and new blood, for mother and son, or that this dye connects similar patterns on the Mexican tile and the ancient almanacs.

The parrot-beaked snakes and jaguar-headed men drawn on the ancient almanacs signify the presence of both Quetzalcoatl and the Jaguar priest. Anglo-Peruvian writer Richard Luxton confirms that "the Plumed Serpent [is] . . . Quetzalcoatl . . . the great shaman who can see far in front of himself, through mountains and into valleys, who can trace lost souls and remedy the world."[18] In a footnote to his translation of the *Book of Tizimin*, Munro S. Edmonson states: "The highest ranking priesthood was that of the Jaguar (Balam), who governed the entire country for one katun [twenty-year period] as the representative of the Sole God (Hunab Ku). . . . He was seconded by his Spokesman (Chilam), and together they manifested the complementarity (and friction) of variously named dualistic gods."[19] Silko's novel reads much like Rushdie's *Satanic Verses*, as she takes a bit of the sacred and mixes it with the profane.

The two "old women" serve as female counterparts to this ancient configuration. Furthermore, Paula Gunn Allen observes that the "Aztecs had . . . complementary deities: the internal or domestic god was a goddess, Cihuacoatl, Coatlique, or some similar supernatural woman-being; their external god was Quetzalcoatl, the winged serpent, who was a god of amalgamation or expansion."[20] Allen's formulation challenges the male paradigm offered by Edmonson, as Lecha, who is later described as moving around the country "from lover to lover and city to city" (125), and Zeta, who decides early in life that sex is not an activity she finds worthy of engaging in, both seem to manifest male and female attributes. These new jaguar priestesses must transcribe and inscribe the story of the new and old blood. Silko's intent in these opening pages is twofold. First, she alludes to a story that must be told and lived in a connection between old and new blood, a story in which a "stranger" like the "white girl" Seese is not going to be separated from the magic being made. Second, this road map conflates and blends a myriad of indigenous cultural iconography and symbols— where Itza, Aztec, and Mayan almanacs and prophecies lend themselves to the shaping of this new sanguine order.

As Book 2 opens in San Diego, we move back in time to an abandoned and grieving Seese, who remains in a drug dealer's penthouse after the kidnapping of her six-month-old son, Monte. Floating on a watery sea of dreams and memories, Seese uses marijuana, whiskey, and cocaine to get numb and to stay that way; remembering her dreams prior to Monte's disappearance alerts Seese to the problems of translation, meaning, and memory:

> She remembers having the nightmare only twice before she had the baby. Both times it was the night before a math test in college. . . . [S]he could imagine any number of possibilities from all the signs and symbols. She read many things into them. . . . Now she knows that all of it is a code anyway. The blue sky and puffy clouds seen through the deadly jade water of the nightmare pool was a message about the whole of creation. The loss of the child was another, more final message, or at least that was how it was translating—she was only just finding out that this was a translation, that the last morning she had held little Monte in her arms . . . that had been an end too. When the drugs affected her in a certain way she was able to study the message calmly. (43)

For Seese memory functions as dream-vision, where the connectedness of signs and events is inherent rather than artificially constructed. With the help of unlimited quantities of drugs, she devises a way of seeing wherein "the whole of creation" is depicted in the "lines and equations" of mathematical formulas and in the event of her loss of a child. This is a Seese who proclaims earlier in the section that "she is determined to be the first not to forget. One of the few for whom the memories never dim" (42).

This way of envisioning and remembering prepares Seese for the encounter with the TV talk-show psychic:

> According to the show's host, the woman finds missing persons. . . . The old woman's face fills the screen. She is smiling but her eyes are not friendly. Her eyes know many things never meant to be seen. The contents of shallow graves. The thrust of a knife. Things not meant to be heard; the gurgling cough a victim makes choking on his own blood while a calm voice on the tape recording narrates exactly how the execution must be performed. Her eyes said, plenty of women have lost

babies and small children. They die of dysentery and infections all the time. They starve, get shot, bombed, and gassed.

Seese was crying, but like the television, she seemed to make no sound. (46–47)

In this encounter there is no sound but a connection through vision. What Seese sees is a story told in the eyes of Lecha, the "Mexican Indian woman [who] seems to be *speaking* only to her" (italics mine). *Speaking* is translated into a vision that they share. Even though this visionary sequence is filled with the bodies of the dead, Seese finds something living within it and moves to Tucson, seeking Lecha, who might locate her lost child. But this image of hope, of finding the living, is corrupted by the only words that seem to penetrate the silence: "The dead rest just fine—it's only your mind that keeps them alive and lost" (47). These comparable visions end with Silko's assertion that to be alive is to be lost and that to be dead is to rest. In *Almanac*, living means to participate in a universe constantly numbed by substance abuse and economic horror, where the only hope is memory, which creates a vision two women share. In keeping with my earlier observations, memory here is not personal but collective.

On her flight to Tucson Seese remembers the suicide of her friend Eric. "She had not actually seen Eric's body. Only the photographs. David's photographs, but somehow that had been worse. All she knew was that something had happened to her eyes, something had diminished her vision" (53). In the Chumayel manuscript one prophecy reads, "At the end of our loss of vision and of our shame, everything shall be revealed."[21] Seese appears to be moving toward that moment in the telling of her own text—a moment where she will have to make something living from a vision of the dead. Later, when Seese recalls the interrogation by the police, she notes "that her own words sounded thin, and the details of her story did not seem convincing even to her anymore" (112). Silko constructs a space where words no longer seem viable or able to tell a story, a place where vision becomes reality, at least for the time being. What Seese travels toward is an eventual inscribing of her own story; however, at this point in her tale she is marginal to language itself, and the primacy of vision makes remembering a place of transcendence, where two eyes speak to one another and where there is power in thoughts, memories, and images.

Journeying into the past, book 5, "The Border," opens with a scene from Zeta and Lecha's childhood at a moment when the old woman Yoeme returns to Potam, a small Yaqui Indian town on the southwestern coast of Mexico. Silko writes that Yoeme "did not understand . . . how her own children, conceived and borne in pain, could behave so shamelessly to their flesh and blood mother. Yoeme had said 'flesh and blood' so everyone inside could hear" (115). The whole family fears the "she-coyote" Yoeme, who is grandmother to twins, Zeta and Lecha; as Yoeme narrates her own life, it becomes clear that their fear is a measure of their fear of flesh and blood that ties the family to a Yaqui past and to Yaqui resistance. Yoeme's loud annunciation of flesh and blood brings us back to the interplay of old and new blood in the novel's opening pages. Yoeme shares with Zeta and Lecha stories of their individual as well as collective ancestry. The girls are told that Yoeme left her children because of an argument over trees, specifically the cottonwood trees that shaded the family house. The twins understand that the family has disowned Yoeme because she is an "Indian." But Yoeme offers a more comprehensive story:

"The fucker Guzman, your grandfather, sure loved trees. They were cottonwoods got as saplings from the banks of the Rio Yaqui. Slaves carried them hundreds of miles. The heat was terrible. All water went to the mules or to the saplings. . . .

They had been killing Indians right and left. It was war! It was white men coming to find more silver, to steal more Indian land. . . . Guzman and my people had made an agreement. Why do you think I married him? . . . . To watch, to make sure he kept the agreement." (116)

Yoeme and Guzman serve not only as actual grandmother and grandfather to the twins but also as links in a chain of cultural history. In Yaqui tribal history *Yoemem* is the name for the Yaqui, and it simply means the "people."[22] In turn, a shortened version of *Yoemem, yoeme,* translates as "person." On the other hand, Guzman is an anglicized version of Gúzman, and Silko possibly alludes to Diego de Gúzman, a notorious Spanish slave trader who first encountered the Yaqui in 1533.[23] Therefore, Yoeme's insistence that her marriage to Guzman is more political exchange than love has special resonance; it is a marriage of the people and the oppressor, an act signifying the miscegenation that brings about the subsequent generation and makes the continuing genocide against Indian people a form of self-annihilation for the colonizers.[24] Whiteness is reconstructed as a state or space in constant erasure as two cultures begin to merge. She remembers that "Guzman had been only a sullen walking corpse, not a real man. . . . It was time that I left. Sooner or later those long turds would have ridden up with their rifles, and Guzman would have played with his wee-wee while they dragged me away" (177). This bizarre image of Guzman playing with his "wee-wee" is paired with the very real horror of lynching; Yoeme sees her clanspeople swinging from the branches of the cottonwood trees, and she decides to leave, but not before she instructs the gardeners to cut down six of the trees. She is damned by Guzman, not because she has left her children but because she "butchered all the big cottonwood trees." His words echo soundlessly with the silence of dried flesh and bones that hung in those same trees not long before—butchering here is loaded with bittersweet irony.

Earlier, we learn that Guzman loves what he can construct and that he transplants the cottonwoods from their place by the river, exclaiming, "What beauties!" because he can *create* them anew—he can establish an artificial relationship with them—and play the role of both conqueror and creator. Yoeme remarks that the cottonwood "suckles . . . on the mother water running under the ground . . . [and] will talk to the mother water and tell her what human beings are doing" (117). There is a subtle implication here that Guzman is another Frankenstein as he sidesteps the necessity of female reproduction by placing himself in that capacity. From Guzman's perspective, the trees that he lovingly plants around the house are precious, and the human bodies used to transport them into their new space are as expendable as Yoeme is to her family, as the mother water is to life and vision itself.

Zeta and Lecha remember a father who is described much like Guzman. A failed geologist and silver miner, "suddenly the man had dried-up inside, and although he still walked and talked and reasoned like a man, inside he was crackled, full of the dry molts of insects. . . . [S]omewhere within him there was, arid and shriveled, the imperfect vacuum he called himself" (120). Yoeme concludes that the "white man had violated Mother Earth, and he had been stricken with the sensation of a gaping emptiness between his throat and his heart" (121). Their forefathers, known as "that fucker" and "the white man," still survive in Lecha and Zeta, and the references to old blood and new blood that open in "Tucson" become expanded and reshaped in "The Border"—as well, the blood / dye that flows between the kitchen tiles has some of its story told in this space. In *Almanac* all generational stories have some kind of explicit reference to sexual functions or organs. After a time these references no longer seem grotesque but become normative to the narrative. Normalizing the grotesque and continuing to play with categories of generational ancestry allows Silko to recreate an imaginative terrain befitting the space of death, terror, and chaos. This consistent normalizing places the obscene or the absurd within the context of quotidian life—there is a place for the narrative of destruction in an American imaginative landscape, a way to recognize how whiteness has acquired being in the world.

Before her death Yoeme gives the ancient notebooks to Zeta and Lecha; Zeta discovers that the translations and marginal inscriptions don't seem to reveal much "except one old woman's madness" (135). As Zeta finishes typing her sections, Lecha arrives at the ranch to translate and type her parts of the almanac into the computer. Continuing the bloodlines of the novel, Zeta inscribes the following: "Quetzalcoatl gathered the bones of the dead and sprinkled them with his own blood, and humanity was reborn" (136). How this process of rebirth takes place is the concern of *Almanac*. Part of this intricate complex is realized as the visions move out from the written / spoken prophecies of the old priests' manuscripts to the visions, dreams, and nightmares of those living in a contemporary hell filled with the kinetic energy of creation and destruction. Lecha comes into her own vision unwillingly:

> It had dawned on Lecha—the way the darkness gradually bleeds away and the light gains momentum, much as water seeps into low places in the garden. The awareness pulsed through her day and night. When it had first broken through, she had tried little tricks . . . attempting to cut off the channel. She had sat adding long columns of figures, and although she was able to . . . do a more accurate job of adding them than she had ever done before, a part of her brain was still spinning a voice that mocked her: They are all dead. The only ones you can locate are the dead. Murder victims and suicides. You can't locate the living. If you find them, they will be dead. (138)

Lecha's awareness has all the constituents of Seese's dream/nightmare of "the whole of creation." For Lecha, however, this awareness is mocked by her inability to locate the living.[25] A living manuscript is in the hands of a woman who has lost much of her shamanistic ability—she cannot extend her clairvoyance beyond the realm of the dead; she never locates living relatives, only those who have met death, particularly in an unusually horrific way. Limitations in her sight cause Lecha much pain, and her task in the novel is to explore the meaning of this imbalance. These watery dreams of Seese and Lecha serve to moisten their arid, barren, and destitute visions; water acts as a conduit for an understanding of the intense meaning of these (in)sights.

Discovering the location of dead bodies buried in the sand by a serial killer, Lecha makes revealing observations about her own clairvoyancy. "She had suspected the concept of intermediary and messenger was too simple. . . . Lecha remembers the ragged bundles of cheap paper and the old notebooks. 'Mouths' and 'tongues' old Yoeme had jokingly called them. Now that she knew how the power worked, Lecha was not so sure anymore it could be called a gift. It was about time to go back home. . . . She had to take care of the old notebooks" (142). On a beach near San Diego she travels into the mind of the serial killer and sees what he understands to be the truth:

> He imagines the boys are trees that he must go tend from time to time. He uncovers them tenderly. They thrive best at the foot of the big dunes. Out in the flats they can't take root. Rain washes them out.
>
> He realizes they are trees while he is touching them. He fondles the boys between their legs, and a branch sprouts and pushes out. . . . He plants carefully and prays for tall trees. He dreams of towering oaks and spruce that lean and sway but do not break in summer storms. (140–141)

This account of the serial killer is strangely parallel to Guzman's perverse relationship with the cottonwoods and slaves of the Rio Yaqui. However, for this killer of little boys their bodies actually do *become* the trees; the body has become more privileged here, but the destructive impulse to dislocate an "object" from its life source and to recreate it in another space has been maintained. Lecha realizes that the power for her is no longer in the drama of finding each case but in the power of the dead, who have "mouths" and "tongues" to speak to the living; the power is located in the telling of the story itself. So she returns to commence the project of telling "about the days yet to come—drought or flood, plague, civil war or invasion" (137), events she has claimed as her own private vision but that merely manifest the collectivity of the story everyone lives as the *days* come 'round again. It is a connection that Lecha comes to understand and one that the serial killer, in his own perverse way, tries to actualize in the burial of the bodies / trees in the dunes outside San Diego. Because memory is not personal, its relentless narrative bridges the stories of Lecha and the serial killer, making them one and the same.

Lecha has this revelation confirmed in a visit to Bethel, Alaska, where she meets an old Yupik woman who "had gathered great surges of energy out of the atmosphere, by summoning spirit beings through recitations of the stories that were also indictments of the greedy destroyers of the land. With the stories the old woman was able to assemble powerful forces flowing from the spirits of ancestors" (156). The constant pain that addicts Lecha to Demerol is not caused by her powerful visions as much as by the tension created between the perverse discourse she develops with the voices of the recently slaughtered and the emerging discourse of the "spirits of ancestors"; for Lecha the power was "turning its face, and its eyes, to look toward the world that was emerging" (161). Therefore, the last vision that causes her "Sudden Retirement" is highly politicized. As she scans the TV studio audience, Lecha observes that

> she had been aware of the voice that had recently raised itself inside her; the voice also had eyes and while her eyes had been watching the audience and the host, these other eyes had been watching the mossy water of the canals of . . . the gardens of Xochimilco, with . . . [a] shopping bag floating in the dark green water. . . . Inside the bag there are two human heads, their blue eyes open wide, staring at the sky. (164)

Locating the severed heads of the U.S. ambassador to Mexico and his chief aide moves Lecha—an Indian, born in Mexico—from the drama played for the television audience to the contemporary context of a story / vision that the people are living to tell. One of *Almanac*'s truly revolutionary moments, this double vision of Lecha's allows her to see the political implications of her sight and to construct a place for herself in the rebellion of native peoples that unfolds as the novel progresses. The revolution here represents a conflation of both spiritual and political "sight(s)."

Finally, Lecha transcribes her own notebook and proclaims that her personal account is important to "understanding the old notebooks Yoeme left behind" (174). Lecha's notebook is a chronicle of her time as a locator of the dead, a chronicle wherein victim, murderer, and bereaved experience loss. According to Paula Gunn Allen, "the American Indian universe is based on dynamic self-esteem, while the Christian universe is based primarily on a sense of separation and loss. For the American Indian, the ability of all creation to share in the process of ongoing creation makes all things sacred."[26] A society that functions in terms of binaries rather than dynamics is represented in Lecha's notebook. A dichotomous society creates its own monsters—its own manifestations of the grotesque—beings whose perversity is a measure of the imbalance and sickness of a society that feeds on the TV drama of separation and loss embedded in the talk show, where someone else's pain is enjoyed as spectacle, as entertainment. To a certain extent the perversions of a serial killer are not so distant from the voyeurism of a studio audience or the grief of parents focused on the details of the life of a lost child. Part of what makes the grotesque is not only the insistence on an explicit sexual terrain but also a desire to put a face on the perpetration of terror, madness, and death.

The ending of "The United States of America" recounts the "Journey of the Ancient Almanac" and foretells the tenor of part 2, "Mexico." Fleeing north from the influx of the Spanish, four children attempt to keep themselves and the pages of the almanac alive:

> But their elders had warned them . . . because the epoch that was dawning was known by different names from tribe to tribe, but their people called the epoch Death-Eye Dog. During the epoch of Death-Eye Dog human beings, especially the alien invaders, would become obsessed with hungers and impulses commonly seen in wild dogs. . . . A human being was born in the days she or he must live with until eventually the days themselves would travel on. All anyone could do

was recognize the traits, the spirits of the days, and take precautions. The epoch of Death-Eye Dog was male and therefore tended to be somewhat weak and very cruel. (251)

During this journey, the children encounter a "hunchbacked" woman who practices witchery and eventually kills one of the children and feasts on her "liver or heart."[27] Lecha remembers that Yoeme had explained: "That woman had been left behind by the others. The reign of Death-Eye Dog is marked by people like her. She did not start out that way. *In the days that belong to Death-Eye Dog, the possibility of becoming like her trails each one of us*" (253; italics mine).

II. Mexico

This possibility is actualized in the character of Menardo, who dominates the narrative in "Mexico," part 2 of *Almanac*. Book 1, "Reign of the Death-Eye Dog," opens: "The old man was slow, lazy and dangerous. . . . Full of beer he used to get very serious, and when I was a young child, I felt frightened. It was then he bragged the ancestors had seen 'it' all coming, and one time I interrupted to ask what 'it' was, and he waved his hands all around . . . and he said, 'The time called Death-Eye Dog.' There was no one in the area who could talk the way the old man did" (257). What appears to be Menardo's first-person narrative is actually the voice of his grandfather, who "told him about the old man who drank stinking beer and talked about and sometimes talked *with* the ancestors. Menardo had loved the stories right up until the sixth grade when one of the teaching Brothers had given them a long lecture about pagan people and pagan stories" (258). Menardo's connection with these pagan stories is obscured by the presence of the Church, and most of his actions in "Mexico" are informed by this earlier wounding.

Silko's ambiguous use of *I* in the first paragraph endows the *act* of storytelling with a power that transcends the individual. Belonging to all three generations and no one at all, the story itself becomes the focal point. Individuals need only share in its experience. In this environment Menardo discovers that "around the time the others had called him Flat Nose and Big Belly, Menardo had made a horrible discovery. His grandfather's nose had been much shorter and wider than his was; the people the old man called 'our ancestors,' 'our family,' were in fact Indians. All along Menardo had been listening to the one who was responsible for the taunts of the others" (259). Menardo wishes to be "one of *sangre limpia*" and perceives that his flat nose is the obstacle to his entrance into an elite bloodline. He discontinues his talks in the garden with the old man, who dies soon thereafter, perhaps because he lacks the nourishment that the storytelling provided him. Unwilling to interact with his grandfather and the power of the stories, Menardo reduces him to the single bearer of "the evidence the flatnose was inherited"; his grandfather's death becomes the act that propels Menardo into the circles of the sangre limpia. Menardo moves on throughout "Mexico," building an insurance empire (Seguridad Universal), insulating himself and others against "unrest" and "terrorist attacks" and whenever appropriate, "stopping long enough to make a guttural sound expressing his impatience with Indian superstition" (276).

Descending into Menardo's "Mexico" is definitely a journey into a kind of hell, as his "unholy" business alliance with arms dealers from the States and corrupt government officials spirals into some of the novel's most grotesque moments. Moreover, Menardo's importance and presence in this community of thieves and speculators is as marginal as his house—built on the borders of Tuxla Gutierrez—a palace that looks out toward the city and whose backside provides a breathtaking picture through a "wall of glass and the lush green jungle vegetation outside the conservatory" (280). Menardo's *house* is situated so that it can take advantage of the light and landscape of the jungle; Menardo *himself* is allowed to attain his position so that those empowered by sangre limpia can take advantage of what he has to offer in Seguridad Universal. He does not remember the words of his grandfather, nor is he privy to the speeches of the Mayan woman, Angelita La Escapia, one of the revolutionaries in the mountains outside Tuxla Gutierrez.

La Escapia warns that the "stories of the people or their 'history' had always been sacred, the source of their entire existence. If the people had not retold the stories, or if the stories had somehow been lost, then the people were lost; the ancestor's spirits were summoned by the stories" (316). These stories also provide the reader with an understanding of Menardo and his associates' place in "Mexico." Richard Luxton records, "The Nine Lords . . . figure in Mayan thought as synonymous with the Lords of hell. They are ancient evil figures . . . warning signs which can be read at a political, economic or historical level. . . . [P]olitical coercion and private ownership of the earth [is attributed to] the Nine Lords and a previous world the Mayas had suffered."[28] Later Luxton elaborates: "In the colonial Books of Counsel there are frequent, insistent references to the Central Mexicans, associating them with the Lords of the Underworld" (191–192). Menardo's friends and associates who interact with "El Grupo Gun Club" add up to, give or take one, the number nine; they assemble at the golf range and participate in a ritual of bonding that includes mandatory drunkenness and target practice behind the course's ninth hole. In this atmosphere Menardo listens once again to an exchange of stories.

Questioning his Indian chauffeur, Tacho, about blood sacrifice, Menardo asks,

> Were there human sacrifices anymore? Not by the Indians, Tacho said, but the human sacrificers had not just been the Mexican tribes. The Europeans who came had been human sacrificers too. Human sacrificers were part of the worldwide network of Destroyers who fed off energy released by destruction. Menardo laughed out loud at Tacho. Tacho believed all that tribal mumbo jumbo Menardo's grandfather had always talked about. (336)

The conversation with Tacho leaves Menardo feeling nauseous, but it continues with El Grupo at the Club, where the general talks about "sex and blood." Menardo observes that "the more animated the general had become . . . a flush had spread up his throat to his cheeks, and Menardo had thought he saw a suspicious bulge in the general's trousers" (337). Confirmimg Tacho's earlier articulations, the general continues

> with a theory some French doctors had had: he speculated that the sight and smell of blood naturally excited human sex organs. . . .
> Here Menardo had interrupted the general to ask surely the general was referring to savage tribes—Indians and Africans—and not to civilized Europeans? But the general had laughed and shaken his head. . . .
> "No, these are the ancestors of the French we are talking about. The

cave people of France." Menardo did not recall the nuns and priests or even the high school teachers ever mentioning that the early ancestors of the French had lived in caves eating raw meat. But the general was an intellectual. . . . The French doctors had further speculated that the sight and smell of blood of the castration caused the body to release chemical signals to the genitals so that in primitive times, the conquerors who had castrated their prisoners would immediately impregnate the geldings' women. . . . [T]he general was about to complete a scholarly treatise on the use of physical measures such as castration to subdue rebel, subversive, and other political deviants. General J.'s main thesis was that only the body remembered. The mind would blank out. (337–338)

General J.'s thesis seems to contradict Lecha and Seese's understanding of seeing visions and memory. Like the serial killer who mistakes dismemberment for regeneration, General J. underestimates the power of the mind, of memory (collective), to recapture bits of experience and add them to a preexisting contranational narrative.

The story that Menardo decides to accept as true, the story that he receives from the mouth of one of the figurative Nine Lords, is one that will tell the end of his days. In General J.'s theoretical construct the "deviants" are not people like himself but the subversive political elements in the society at large. The general creates a tale of homosocial behavior in a homosocial environment; detached from any sense of connectedness to his own body and his own blood, the story he weaves is straight out of the tale of witchery that Silko samples in *Ceremony*, continues in *Storyteller*, and illustrates in *Almanac*. Moreover, the general's detachment from his physical self is mocked by the erection brought on by his own story and maintained during its telling; it becomes a focal point for Menardo and serves as a parody of each self-absorption and obsession with the company of men. Again, another generational myth/story is brought about through explicit reference to sexual stimulation. In contrast to earlier mention of sexual body functions, the general's erection serves to change the tone of the book's latter half, as we move deeper and deeper into the most disturbing aspect of Silko's longest work—its focus on male homosocial behavior as the center of the sociopolitical death complex.

Menardo has been given a chance to listen to both stories, to choose between the old and the new blood; he chooses the bloodlust of the sangre limpia, and so, neither participating in the storytelling of the Indians in "Mexico" nor allowed to perform the stories (lies) of El Grupo, he stays too long in the powerful space of death and is consumed by its energy.

Wearing his high-tech bulletproof vest, Menardo dozes and dreams:

> The faces . . . he recognized as all the old people who had passed on; they called him storekeeper and asked him to sell them food on credit. Although only an infant in the dream, Menardo had been able to talk, but only Spanish. . . . He felt the greatest anxiety trying to make himself understood by the Indians. . . . *Return. We return.* He was trying to explain to them he did not have enough to feed everyone, not enough to go around, but they understood no Spanish, only Indian, which Menardo had refused to learn. (496)

Like the dream visions of Lecha and Seese this dream comes to Menardo, but he has created such a dichotomy between himself and the "Indians" that he is unable to communicate with those that return in the dream to tell him the story. This encounter translates onto a materialistic site, where Menardo becomes the Spanish-speaking storekeeper who provides foodstuffs for a people he cannot understand; providing no substance, no nurturance, Menardo looks to his bulletproof vest: "It was a matter of trust—trust of the high technology that had woven the vest fibers, and trust in those most intimate with you. Trust. Menardo had repeated the word over and over until he was asleep" (497). He opts for an understanding of the language of technology and insulates himself against what he believes is outside, but he actually protects himself from what is within, not without, and eventually the bulletproof vest becomes the fabric that soaks up his own blood; the fabric that insulates and protects serves him well in death but not in life.

"Mexico" ends with the text's vision focused on an interrogation and dismemberment. Wearing a mask similar to that of the Death Squads of Guatemala, El Salvador, and Nicaragua, the police chief prepares to castrate one of his own—an Argentinian business partner. He describes the scene: "The best way to geld a horse was to hobble it with its head snubbed tight against a tree or post. One slit and the testicle was visible inside the slippery, marbled-blue membrane. Men were not much different" (346). In the reign of the Death-Eye Dog, there is cruelty beyond measure—a cruelty marked by the violent pleasures and games of men who subscribe to a homosocial worldview wherein no manner of life is respected or affirmed.[29]

III. The Fifth World

As indicated earlier in this chapter, it can be argued that Silko's constant reference to male genitalia is excessive and that the constant explication of a character's most grotesque fantasies is overindulged. But it is important in the telling of this particular story that the reader be spared no detail. Grotesque images and actions in *Almanac* reflect on the reader as well, as we have to call our own desires into question and define for ourselves our particular place in both the stories of witchery set in motion and the stories of the ancestors brought alive by a shared telling. "The grotesque lures even as it repels, fascinates us with our own irrational dreads, and refuses to let us altogether dismiss the game even after we have played it," says McElroy (16). Both witchery and storytelling in *Almanac* can literally bring a world into being, but the question is one of quality; and Silko's use of the grotesque attempts to qualify that world, to give it a shape.

Introducing a discussion of the grotesque in *Rabelais and His World*, Mikhail Bakhtin observes: "Eating, drinking, defecation . . . as well as copulation, pregnancy, dismemberment, swallowing up by another body—all these acts are performed on the confines of the body and the outer world or on the confines of the old and new body. In all these events the beginning and end of life are closely linked and interwoven."[30] Bakhtin's statement contains all of the elements constituting Silko's opening mingling of old blood, new blood, and copulation. I would argue that the body Bakhtin refers to is a male body, and for all practical purposes, focus on the male body is sustained throughout *Almanac*. In addition, this paradigm of the grotesque is paralleled by Lincoln's assessment of the (male) trickster, who "acts out the serious play of hunting, eating, defecating, loving, gaming, fighting, civilizing, and surviving death."[31]

In "The United States of America" Silko introduces Beaufrey, who is not only the owner of the condo that Seese remains in after the kidnap-

ping of her child but also a business partner of the castrated Argentinian mentioned above. A pusher of late-term abortion films, Beaufrey,
along with antiabortion lobbyists, enjoys "watch[ing] the creatures
grimace and twist away from the long needle probes and curette's
sharp spoon. . . . [He] only laughed because he could imagine himself
as a fetus, and he knew what they should have done with him swim-
ming hopelessly in the silence of the deep, warm ocean. His mother
had told him she tried to abort herself" (102). There are a multitude of
layered images here, as Beaufrey's warm, deep ocean parallels that of
Seese and Lecha's dreams but fails to sustain him because the context
his mother provides him with strips this water of its sustaining prop-
erties. However, Beaufrey's hatred of his mother is only a manifestation of his hatred for himself—he knows "what they should have done
with him" because he feels his own thwarted abortion was a mistake.
Moreover, in this spectacle of the grotesque, Beaufrey's language
moves from *fetus* to *creature*, and we, as readers of these images, travel
from the unborn in the womb to a "creature" created by the video gaze
of Beaufrey and his clients, by a collective of men. This is a site where
the inner and outer body do meet and where the beginning and end of
life discourse with one another, as Beaufrey sees his own self in the
grotesque images he sells on the black market and conflates his birth
with the potential for his own death.

Later, in "The Americas" Beaufrey retreats to the *finca* in Cartagena
with his companion, Serlo. Sharing a blood alliance, *sangre pura*, both
envision a world that they can create without females:

> [Serlo] had studied a large body of psychological and psychiatric writ-
> ings that clearly demonstrated that even the most perfect genetic spec-
> imen could be ruined, absolutely destroyed, by the defects of the
> child's mother. [He] believed the problems that Freud had identified
> need not occur if a child's "parents" were both male. The nature of the
> female was to engulf what was outside her body, to never let the umbil-
> ical cord be severed; gradually the mother became a vampire. (542)

Replacing the "mother," Serlo undertakes "alternative earth module"
research, a project that foresees planet Earth as ultimately uninhabi-
table and attempts to design and construct orbiting colonies for the
elite that contain "the last of the earth's uncontaminated soil, water
and oxygen." The question is, who is the most likely vampire, the man

in the alternative earth module or the woman who carries the child? Serlo's objective is to transplant himself in this metaphor and to become the more efficient model of negative maternal influence that he fabricates. There is no moral universe here; the space created by genocide is also a place devoid of a sense of right and wrong. In this place there is an assumption of superiority so far outside ideas of competition between the "races" that *anyone* in the path of such a well-oiled machine is fodder for its engines.

As owner of Bio-Materials Incorporated, Trigg is in the business of selling human body parts and plasma. He subscribes to the model of efficiency that Serlo implies above, but his relationship with the grotesque operates on a different level. Silko describes his personal participation in acquiring plasma for his company:

> Trigg had never denied that picking up hitchhikers had excited him. He had thought of it as a roll of the dice or a hand of five-card draw. The winners and the discards. Discards were "locals" or those with too many kin. Trigg talked obsessively about the absence of struggle as the "plasma donors" were slowly bled to death pint by pint. A few who had attempted to get away had lost too much blood to put up much fight even against a man in a wheelchair. Of course the man in the wheelchair had a .45 automatic in his hand.
>
> Trigg had paid extra if the victim agreed. Trigg gave him a blow job while his blood filled pint bags; the victim relaxed in the chair with his eyes closed, unaware that he was being murdered. . . . Trigg blames the homeless men. . . . He doubted any of them could hope for a better death. They were human debris. Human refuse. Only a few had organs of sufficient quality for transplant use. (444)

Unlike Serlo, Trigg fuses sexual pleasure with death and material profit. Trigg's point is not to erase the female figure but to take what is created and recycle it for sale to the highest bidder; in effect, he is *the* pimp of body parts in Tucson. Moreover, there is a direct parallel between Trigg's "sex" with the hitchhiker and his sexual relationship with Leah Blue, who is in the process of taking various Pueblos to court to usurp their water rights. Her goal is to build a town in Arizona, called Venice—complete with canals. Both in their own way participate in dismembering the land and the people who depend on it for survival. Again, the sustaining water of Seese's and Lecha's dreams is used up, diverted, placed in service of the construction of a false town.

Whereas the Leahs and Triggs of the novel turn huge profits from this "hands on" exploitation of the land, the Beaufreys and Serlos of *Almanac* perform some of the most stupendous mental feats in order to circumvent all necessity for creation itself; at least Leah and Trigg still rely on some kind of *source* for their materials—Serlo's objective is to eliminate the source altogether. My first inclination was to see Silko's portrayal of Beaufrey, Serlo, and the other men who have contact with them, sexually or professionally, as disturbing and homophobic. However, the absence of the equally threatening lesbian vampire (except in Serlo's imaginary) placed the masculinist paradigm that Silko attempts to explore in *Almanac* in greater focus. Like the pathology of medical practice, all female presence in *Almanac* is obfuscated by a Frankenstein-like insistence on the possibility of (pro)creation without female participation. The space of genocide is sustained by a type of homosocial behavior that could lead to the earth's total annihilation. However unsettling this same-sex standard appears, I do not think that her goal is to depict queer intimacy negatively. I think that her primary point here is to expose the danger of a masculinist perspective from every angle. As Janet St. Clair claims, "Silko's focus of attack is explicitly the misogynistic, arrogantly hierarchical, and egocentric traditions of Western individualism."[32]

This focus on the grotesque in Silko counters Bakhtin's illustration of what the grotesque signifies in society. Bakhtin outlines a connection between the cosmos and bodily "eliminations":

> We must here stress that it was in the material acts and eliminations of the body—eating, drinking, defecation, sexual life—that man [*sic*] found and retraced within himself the earth, sea, air, fire and all the cosmic matter and its manifestation, and was thus able to assimilate them. Indeed, the images of the material bodily lower stratum have a prevailingly cosmic connotation.[33]

This might hold true for the trickster paradigm, where connectedness between bodily functions and earthly activities is a matter of survival and thus reaffirms the fortitude of the people in the *days* that they live;

but this pattern does not hold for Beaufrey and Serlo, whose grotesque actions have no potential for transformation but exist solely for their *own* reification—their *own* survival in a space of their *own* creation. A transformation, maybe, but one that reifies the space of death as genocide rather than as rebirth. The Serlos and Beaufreys of *Almanac* see all living subjects around them as part of one large horror show —the grotesque of the theater rather than the grotesque of cosmic transformation.

Prophetic in Deed

The last lines of *Almanac* proclaim, "The snake was looking south, in the direction from which the twin brothers and the people would come." In the aftermath of Chiapas (January 1994) *Almanac*'s last words seem prophetic indeed. Writing from the vantage point of an observer of the rebellion that rocked Mexico, Paco Ignacio Taibo ends a descriptive piece in *The Nation* about the Zapatistas with "for now we're walking on shadows, disturbed and filled with hope. We are waking up with the distinct feeling that we slept among phantoms."[34] Much like Morrison's ending to *Beloved, Almanac*'s closure puts the vision of the future in the hands of a spiritual symbol, knowing that it is the people who will (dis)remember first that we are the witnesses who wake "with the distinct feeling that we slept among phantoms."

A novel of epic quality, *Almanac* insists that we view things in the Americas as they are. Its stark realism borders on the fantastic because the lived experience of genocide is so marginalized in the culture at large that the system that keeps it in place remains largely unobserved. When it is revealed, we are struck by the brutality just beneath the surface of quotidian life. Silko's challenge to existing paradigms—narrative, memory, history—in *Almanac* raises serious queries about the future of a literary discourse that has very little room for maneuvering outside of what constitutes the real and the tangible. It is the task of contemporary literary theory to move into marginal space and to converse with those authors who cross boundaries between living and dead, silent and vocal. Silko also reminds us that our personal history is shaped/distorted by a primary and unchanging narrative—so much so that even when we proclaim a narrative as distinctly ours, we are in danger of replicating the very structures that we intend to obliterate. Such a narrative maintains itself even when dead bodies are queer subjects, even when such subjects try "to dance their way out of their constriction."

PART TWO

Dead Bodies, Queer Subjects

I is heard people all my life tell 'bout seeing ha'nts and spirits, but I don't believe one word of it. They just thinks they sees them. I know I ain't ever seed even one, and I has lived much longer than them what tells those tales. I has seed many people depart this life what has been mistreated terrible, and if they don't come back to do something 'bout it, 'tain't nobody going to come back.

—Reuben Fox, from *Bullwhip Days: The Slaves Remember*, ed. James Mellon

4

(Pro)Creating Imaginative Spaces and Other Queer Acts: Randall Kenan's *A Visitation of Spirits* and Its Revival of James Baldwin's Absent Black Gay Man in *Giovanni's Room*

Someone once said that if man is but a figment in God's mind then the characters in men's imagination are no less real than we are. Perhaps. No one can say for certain. But we cannot deny the possibility.

Consider the demon. Regard him with awe and loathing, for he is what men despise. Or think they despise. Themselves.
—Randall Kenan, *A Visitation of Spirits*

At the end of heavy breathing
for the price of the ticket
we pay dearly, don't we darling?
Searching for evidence
of things not seen.
I am looking
for Giovanni's room
in this bathhouse.
I know he's here.
—Essex Hemphill, "Heavy Breathing"

Bringing back the dead (or saving the living from the shadow of death) is the ultimate queer act. My observation of this fact is informed by the powerful political slogan from the early days of ACT UP's fight against

AIDS: "silence = death." More than two decades of political activism and academic theorizing has revealed a plethora of silences in the national discourse on sexuality. Still, it is prudent here to engage the conundrum "silence = death" in yet another conversation. For the "war" is not won, and AIDS most certainly is not the last frontier.[1] There are those who remain "dead" to political and theoretical national musings about sexuality—about the removal of silence from the space of death. The disciplines of feminist, lesbian / gay, and African American studies have imagined for themselves appropriate subjects to be removed, at least theoretically, from such a contentious space into the place of recognition. These bodies / subjects are either white, but not heterosexual, or black, but not homosexual. In the crack between discourses the black and queer subject resides. The task of this chapter is to devise a means by which "black" and "queer" can speak to one another.

My first reading of Randall Kenan's *A Visitation of Spirits* in the fall of 1992 illuminated the problem and provided a way to force emerging queer theory and African American discourse to converse. I knew that I wanted to write about Kenan's novel—to make the pain and experience of that novel become somehow tangible for me. I also knew that writing about this book involved an intense personal need to have the tradition—the African American literary tradition, to which I had directed my life's work for the last ten years—acknowledge and embrace Kenan's novel as hopeful progeny in a long line of sons and daughters. But complicating this desire was a recognition that there was no precedent, almost no place for the wounded black gay youth (Kenan's Horace) who kills himself in the bosom of the South and returns as a ghost, much like Beloved's before him, to witness his own story because others cannot, or simply will not, speak his name. The lesbian / gay canon, with its consistent emphasis on white bodies, was not an adequate resource from which to glean a possible approach to *this* particular story, and no appropriate precedent appeared to prepare the way for theory. I then returned to Baldwin's *Giovanni's Room*, and the tradition unfolded itself in a queer configuration of black and white.

In evaluating the intricacies of both novels and the critical attention paid to *Giovanni's Room*, in particular, it is clear that the word *tradition*, in the African American sense, encompasses all that is surely black and procreative. Robert Bone's *The Negro Novel in America* contextualizes *Giovanni's Room* both in Baldwin's personal canon and in the "tradition" itself:

> *Giovanni's Room* is by far the weakest of Baldwin's novels. There is a tentative, unfinished quality about the book, as if in merely broaching the subject of homosexuality Baldwin had exhausted his creative energy. Viewed in retrospect, it seems less a novel in its own right than a first draft of *Another Country*. The surface of the novel is deliberately opaque, for Baldwin is struggling to articulate the most intimate, the most painful, the most elusive of emotions. The characters are vague and disembodied, the themes half-digested, the colors rather *bleached* than vivified. We recognize in this *sterile* psychic landscape the unprocessed raw material of art.[2]

We can recognize how the tradition can police manifestations of its own desires. Bone is in a powerful position, enabling himself to define not only the tradition itself but what is useful within that tradition. The passage is filled with sublimated sexual references. Bone's homophobic fears are palpable, but his lack of an appropriate critical context is even more noticeable than his latent fear / desire. Not only is *Giovanni's Room* not worthy of Baldwin's other novels, professes Bone, but it only counts as a first draft of what Bone later terms "a failure on the grand scale," Baldwin's *Another Country*. However, Bone constructs a contentious cast of players in this assessment: the themes are "intimate" but "half-digested," the characters "vague," but "painful." What appears as his most stinging criticism of this book is its bleached and sterile (translate, white and gay, respectively) landscape, fit only for the raw (as in meat) and undigested stuff of art. Bone defines for the tradition what can and cannot take place within it; moreover, in a tradition rich with signification, tropes, and simple back talk, this novel, he asserts, merits no critical attention.

Bone's one noteworthy perception about *Giovanni's Room* is that it "simply transposes the moral topography of Harlem to the streets of Paris" (226). Basically, these are black characters in whiteface. I believe the accusation is somewhat true, but the simplicity of this statement undermines the creative and emotional energy of Baldwin's novel. If we are to take this as fact we would also have to digest, however raw the knowledge, that gayness does exist under the mask(s) of blackness. I want to first ground this discussion as a response to the absolute nightmarish fear of homosexuality figured both in the African American imagination and mirrored in the contexts of each novel. Critic and poet Charles I. Nero has broken ground with his essay "Toward a Black Gay Aesthetic: Signifying in Contemporary Black Gay Literature" by presenting a chronicle of the presence/absence of black gay men in African American literature. The purpose here is not to reproduce Nero's study but to produce a context for reading (critically?) between Baldwin's and Kenan's novels.

Often critics approach Baldwin's work with ambivalent and/or hostile feelings toward his gay characters or, on the other hand, endeavor to place Baldwin within a tradition of black struggle that completely decontextualizes the importance of his portrayal of sexuality. In assessing Baldwin's contribution, critic James Oliver Horton writes:

> Baldwin's message and even some of his words echoed antebellum debates among black intellectuals, writers and political leaders who, in their time, provided a voice for many of their fellow Afro-Americans during earlier stages in the struggle for racial justice and the power of self-defined identity. It also reflected many of the values of those who voiced, through their actions, clear statements of their *dreams for themselves and their children*.[3]

Horton places this movement toward self-determination in the site of a procreative dream—an imaginative project that implicitly views itself as sustained, at least in this scenario, by a black family defined in the most narrow and heterosexist terms and supported by a dangerous allusion to the ideology of American "values," at once a nebulous and realistic destructive force pitted against the very black family it is invoked to rescue here. Even noted critic Houston A. Baker Jr. subscribes in part to this earlier genre of interpretation. In novels like *Invisible Man, Native Son,* and *Go Tell It on the Mountain,* Baker recognizes that "the arts, institutions, and leaders of black America are normally lauded for their role in insuring the survival and growth of a culture and in providing maturation and *value* for its artists."[4] Again the word *value* is given mythical meaning in the development and definition of a still-emerging literary tradition. The meaning of a specifically "black" literary product is encased in the relative "value" attached to both the product and its cultural fodder, signifying a masculinist discourse (in which Baldwin is certainly guilty of participating) and a heterosexual paradigm.[5]

Tracing the intersection of the African and the pagan in gay black literature, David Bergman offers evidence that another contemporary critic, Henry Louis Gates Jr., does not escape the trap of using a heterosexual paradigm to explicate black literary production. In using the figure of Esu-Elegbara as a signifier of African American literary expressivity, Gates "somehow [loses] the polymorphous perversity of Esu . . . and the continuum of African thought [is] reduced to the [male/female] binarism of western ideology."[6] It is not so much that contemporary scholars haven't politicized the gay and lesbian presence in the African American *community* but that the gay, lesbian, or bisexual (sub)text of critical and literary endeavors, and therefore the African American *canon*, is somehow treated as secondary to developing a literary project emphasizing its procreative aspects. The relegation of queer subjects to the unproductive end of black literary production places them in a liminal space. Such disinheriting from the procreative process contradicts a communal desire to bring back (all) black subjects from the dead, from the place of silence. The African American scholarly discussion of itself as a canon lays bare the attempt to manifest blackness, to bring it back from the dead, with the attending agenda of normalizing whiteness. In her assessment of this tradition, Cheryl Clarke observes: "I realized that the major contradictions between Blackness and lesbianism were the sexist and heterosexist postures of the Afro-American (bourgeois) community."[7]

This is not to say that critics completely ignore the intersection of tradition and homosexuality found in Baldwin's works. At the outset of his discussion of *Giovanni's Room*, Horace Porter reminds his audience that the novel "is as significant among Baldwin's works as it is in Afro-American literature in general. And we can certainly argue that if *The American* reasserts itself throughout James's career, so *Giovanni's Room* has played a similar part in the complex continuing drama of Baldwin's life and work."[8] In fact, Porter argues that the novel's focus on homosexuality is what primarily "distinguishes [Baldwin] from among his influential literary forebears" (146).

Historically, the heterosexual paradigm in African American culture was nurtured primarily by the black Church, and it is impossible to launch a critique of Baldwin or Kenan without some attention to this most profound of forces. In an essay entitled "Some Thoughts on the Challenges Facing Black Gay Intellectuals," Ron Simmons chronicles the extent of homophobic sentiment in African American literature and its relationship, both direct and indirect, to religious ideologies from the traditional black Church and the Nation of Islam. Simmons notes that scholars and religious figures like Farrakhan, Asante, Madhubuti, Baraka, and Staples often "equate homosexuality and adultery with rape and child molestation" and interpret religious and critical texts to fit this equation.[9] More important, Simmons distinguishes between motive and method in his analysis of homosexuality in the black community, writing that " 'homophobia' is not so much a fear of 'homosexuals' but a fear that homosexuality will become pervasive in the community. Thus, a homophobic person can accept a homosexual as an individual friend or family member, yet not accept homosexuality" (211). This distinction has special meaning for the trajectory of this chapter.

People in the queer community often assert that people of color are more sensitive to lesbian/gay concerns than their white counterparts. Simmons dismantles this myth by sharpening the differentiation between accepting and tolerating. As well, the fear of the "pervasive[ness]" of homosexuality is clearly equally a fear of the potential pollution of a sacred project—the construction of a black intellectual ideology steeped in a Judeo-Christian tradition—by the spread of the dis-ease of black gay subjectivity.[10] In essence, the black imaginative project can embrace difference but only in small doses, and most strikingly, it appears to mirror its white counterparts in feminist and queer studies whose work also clandestinely maintains that blackness in small doses demonstrates diversity but ultimately impedes the critical process. As Nero so eloquently reminds us: "Many . . . [black] intellectuals would also argue that the Judeo-Christian tradition is a major tool of the Western-Eurocentric view of reality that furthers the oppression of blacks. Paradoxically, by their condemnation of homosexuality and lesbianism, these intellectuals contribute to upholding [such] an oppressive Eurocentric view of reality."[11]

There is evidence that the mantle of oppression encompasses lesbian subjectivity as well. In reading a copy of Nikki Giovanni's now out-of-print *Gemini: An Extended Autobiographical Statement on My First Twenty-Five Years of Being a Black Poet*, I came across this incredible passage:

> I couldn't decide between school and an agency job and it must have been on my mind because I had a really terrible dream. There was a university chasing me down the street. I turned the corner to get away from it and ran right into the mouth of an agency. It gobbled me up but it couldn't digest me. When it tried to swallow me I put up such a fight that it belched me back into life. *As I hit the street there was the university again, waiting for me like a big dyke with a greasy smile on her lips who has run her prey into a corner. I woke up screaming. Both of them would destroy me!* And furthermore, what did I need with a master's degree?[12]

The ambiguity of the antecedent *them* makes it hard to tell whether Giovanni's worst fears are the agency and the university, as is originally posited, or the dyke and the university. It is as if in the revolutionary mind-set of black power ideology, the prospect of being consumed by the sexual love of another "sister" is as dangerous as the threat of serious consumption at the hands of mainstream institutions. Most intriguing is the position the "dyke" serves in this "terrible dream." She becomes the metaphor for the university—the agent that makes it tick, the driving force behind one revolutionary's oppression. In this scenario Giovanni's real fears are submerged under the code of a metaphor, and the dyke has no real physical presence in the dreamscape like the university or the agency; she is literally a product of its existence. As Simmons observes, "heterosexual brothers and sisters . . . often think of homosexuality as one more problem caused by white oppression."[13]

A contemporary complement to Giovanni's metonymic nightmare is the spectacle referred to by Shahrazad Ali in the infamous *Blackman's Guide to Understanding the Blackwoman*, where she states that the "lesbian Blackwoman [*sic*] . . . just as male homosexuals . . . overdoes it and makes herself a spectacle that is not welcome among civilized people. . . . She needs a special exorcism."[14] Both writers allude to the lesbian as a manifestation of a life in direct contradistinction to the creative project—both enigmatic and communal. Furthermore, the exorcism of Ali parallels the nightmare of Giovanni in that Giovanni's dream work is the unconscious process by which she attempts to exo[/e]rcise the specter/spectacle of the lesbian from her evolving imaginative project; a project that is, according to Ali's contemporary mapping, much in need of an old-fashioned cleansing in the tradition of the black Church.[15]

This envisioning of black gay or lesbian subjectivity as a product of white institutions is a relatively old phenomenon. In terms of the African American literary imagination and its attendant aesthetic, evaluating same-sex behavior and attaching to it a negative value can be traced back to Du Bois's stinging reply to Claude McKay's *Home to Harlem*. Although Nero has done an excellent job of explicating this reply, it is still necessary to recall that Du Bois's particular interest lay in defining what constituted a national literature, and black gay presence is named as not only outside this shaping tradition but also as a "product" of whiteness. It is hard not to see the parallel between Du Bois's feverish criticism of McKay and the recent recruitment of the black Church by the Conservative Right in the fight against the passage of lesbian/gay civil rights.[16] On both accounts, the need to claim ownership of a particular tradition, be it imaginative or legal, moves us into territories where power is utilized in its most "traditional" form.

Paying tribute to James Baldwin, Nigerian playwright Wole Soyinka remarks that in Baldwin's work there is "this near-evangelical commitment to the principle that rules all being—love sought, denied, waiting in the wings or hovering on the wing, a veritable deus ex machina, lacking only a landing permit from a blinkered humanity that hesitates at the door of salvation."[17] Although I do not doubt that Soyinka's insight is gleaned from Baldwin's own testimony about his novels and the centrality of love and the human condition (especially in *Giovanni's Room*),[18] I would argue that viewing Baldwin's works filtered through this sophomoric conceptualization occludes the prominence and problematic of sexuality and especially "homo"sexuality in his novels. It is precisely in Kenan's imaginative revisioning of Baldwin's most maligned and forgotten novel that we can sense the importance of *Giovanni*'s most persistent and haunting images.

Kenan's *A Visitation of Spirits* signifies upon Baldwin's earlier text and attempts to recreate an imaginative place for black gay experience in the African American tradition. In his examination of Kenan's novel, Robert McRuer places Horace in the space between discourses:

Horace Cross, as a black gay teenager, always finds himself at the inter-section of contradictory identities: in his own family, he is "black," but not "gay"; at the community theater where he works, he is openly "gay," while his "blackness" is rendered invisible, particularly by the production itself, which is about the history of the Cross family (the *white* Cross family) in North Carolina; with his "alternative" and white high school friends, he is neither "black" nor "gay."[19]

McRuer poses no challenge to existing African American literary stud-ies; rather he concerns himself with the obsessive "regionalism" found in queer studies, where "big city" experiences are continually privi-leged over cultural work performed in the marginal space of rural America. However, McRuer's placement of Horace is useful in that it envisions a black gay Horace who is everywhere but nowhere. At the time of my study, there were few critical essays written that attempted to explicate Kenan's first novel, let alone to envision a place for it in the present terrain of the new African American Renaissance. This omis-sion obviously results from the uneven critical response to the pres-ence of gay men in African American literature. Kenan's novel at-tempts to rewrite the space of blackness to include the presence of a black gay male—even if that presence is deceased. If the deceased is, in the vernacular, no longer with us, then Horace's speaking from the dead becomes a way to force a community to see what it has left behind.

Stay Down, Brown; Git Back, Black

In the opening pages of *Giovanni* Baldwin's narrator, David, recalls his simultaneous affair with Giovanni and his fiancée, Helen. Trying to reconcile himself with past mistakes, David muses that "these nights were being acted out under a foreign sky, with no one to watch, no penalties attached."[20] However, in a few paragraphs we learn that Da-vid's flight to Paris is but a flight from himself, a self that sleeps not only with a man but with a "brown" one at that. The palpable panic af-ter a grade-school affair with a boy named Joey is with David through-out *Giovanni*, reminding him that although he assumes there is no one to watch, no penalties attached, he has repressed the powerful fear and hysteria his coupling with Joey has left on his *imagination*. Conjuring the memory of his first homosexual experience, David remembers that "the desire which was rising in me seemed monstrous. . . . I saw suddenly the power in his thighs, in his arms, and in his loosely curled fists. The power and the promise and the mystery of that body made me suddenly afraid. That body suddenly seemed the black opening of a cavern in which I would be tortured till madness came, in which I would lose my manhood" (15). Here Baldwin constructs a dual hell for David—one in which he has the distinct pleasure of experiencing his own self mirrored in the physiological sameness of their bodies and the difference marked by the making of a black cavern. David remembers this moment as a "sweet disorder," and it assumes almost nightmarish proportions, a steady reminder of his brush both with a queer and a black identity.[21]

Later this encounter becomes fodder for David's own imaginings. Each homosexual act brings him closer to a recognition of his own whiteness, his own gay identity and its conception fostered in connection with a brown body. "The incident with Joey had shaken me profoundly. . . . I could not discuss what had happened to me with anyone, I could not even admit it to myself; and while I never thought about it, it remained, nevertheless, at the bottom of my mind, as still and as awful as a decomposing corpse. And it changed, it thickened, it soured the atmosphere of my mind" (24). Like the bakulu of Morrison's novel, the brown body in David's mind is a dead being that resides at the bottom. In *Giovanni* Baldwin displaces the tension of queer presence in the black community by involving a white character in a significant struggle with both his "manhood" and the "atmosphere of [his] . . . mind."

This displacement does little to dispel the parallel reality of this same struggle occurring in the traditional landscape of the African American novel—somewhere below the Mason-Dixon line. For David, mere contemplation, albeit forfeited by his own denial, is masked by a most horrible death. It is a parasitic death that internalizes the black cavern alluded to earlier and prompts David to make a decision, literally in Joey's bed, that he would "allow no room in the universe for something which shamed and frightened me. I succeeded very well—by not looking at the universe, by not looking at myself, by remaining, in effect, in constant motion" (30–31). Fleeing to another country, avoiding introspection, and remaining in constant motion reiterate David's privilege, alluded to in the novel's first lines, of being both American and white: "My ancestors conquered a continent." The attendant imaginative project—manifest destiny, bootstrap diplomacy—actualized through the machinations of colonial enterprise, is of little use to David outside his familiar territory. Traditional tools do not serve, to borrow a phrase from Audre Lorde, either "to dismantle the master's house" or, in this case, to function as its superficial signifiers.[22]

As the opening chapter ends, it is quite clear that Baldwin intends in part to use David's flight as a trope for a larger issue. David closes his primary flashback with the following observation:

> Perhaps, as we say in America, I wanted to find myself. This is an interesting phrase, not current as far as I know in the language of any other people, which certainly does not mean what it says but betrays a nagging suspicion that *something has been misplaced*. I think now that if I had had any intimation that the self I was going to find would turn out to be only the same self from which I had spent so much time in flight, *I would have stayed at home*. (31; italics mine)

When Baldwin writes "something has been misplaced," it is difficult to review this paragraph and not read it as a clue to the veiled attempt in *Giovanni* to deal with both the imaginative and physical effects of embracing a very black and gay identity. Moreover, the passage expresses David's desire to escape from America as both home and institution; "America" even though "conquered" is tainted by a queer act with a "brown" body. This leaves the possibility of viewing David's retreat as a curative to the "homosexual" behavior caused by or springing from the place that is "America," now soiled. Europe offers David another space of privilege and becomes a new symbol of whiteness.

As my reading of the opening section of *Giovanni* makes perfectly clear, escape to another country is an imaginative "out" for those who, like David, fear their queer acts will somehow divest them of their whiteness. David's flight is entirely possible because the world has been given to him as a territory to be explored and conquered—a landscape on which he can work out his fearful imaginings, avoiding responsibility and consequence at leisure. Because of his age, sex, and blackness, Kenan's protagonist in *Visitation* has none of these advantages. As if refusing to camouflage the importance of having both a black and gay subjectivity, Kenan places Horace's struggles in a changing South, at the table of not only a black family but also one with a churchgoing legacy to fulfill. These realities serve to shift much of Baldwin's "misplaced" project onto the landscape that engenders it, challenging notions of blackness and bringing the imaginative project back "home."

Unlike *Giovanni*'s opening, we are not told until much later in *A Visitation of Spirits* that the cause of Horace's pain is his misgiving about his homosexuality. We are first introduced to Horace as he contemplates an impossible but necessary transformation. Inverting the flight of Baldwin's protagonist, Kenan has Horace specifically state that "he could not see transforming himself into anything that would not fit the swampy woodlands of Southeastern North Carolina. He had to stay here" (11). Moreover, the resulting object of Horace's transformation is a bird—an obvious allusion to the dominance of birds as both grotesque and sacred figures in Baldwin's novels. As the first pages progress it becomes clear that Horace *is* the black cavern that David imagines in *Giovanni*. Contemplating his own sanity, Horace is haunted by a dual identity:

> Had he gone mad? Somehow slipped beyond the veil of right reasoning and gone off into some deep, unsettled land of fantasy? . . . Of course, he was not crazy, he told himself; his was a very rational mind, acquainted with science and mathematics. But he was also a believer in an unseen world full of archangels and prophets and folk rising from the dead, a world preached to him from the cradle on, and a world he was powerless not to believe in as firmly as he believed in gravity and the times table. The two contradicting worlds were not contradictions in his mind. (16)

And it is quite apparent that Horace has inherited this particularly black imaginative landscape but is denied access to it nonetheless. In Horace's cosmos the notion of "folk rising from the dead" is normative, and he sees his own suicide as a rebirth rather than as a death. Seeking salvation from his gay identity through the rough science of the occult, Horace believes that he can transform his material essence into something *other* with the aid of an imagination fostered in the understanding of the duality of existence. This duality is also present in

Baldwin's universe. As critic David Bergman argues, Baldwin's relationship to a distinctly African past is complicated by his understanding of a black gay identity coupled with the pronouncements of a Pentecostal heritage.[23] Reevaluating the struggle of gay Pentecostal Reverend James Tinney, Bergman notes that "one of the more difficult problems faced is how African a Black Christian Church can be before it descends into paganism."[24]

The irony of Kenan's novel is that it attempts to demonstrate—through Horace's use of paganism to transform his gay, African self into "another" (88)—the problematic of fostering a procreative black imaginative terrain that renders black gay subjectivity invisible. As Simmons suggests:

> While it is critically important to rebut homophobia and heterosexism, the most crucial challenge . . . is to develop an affirming and liberating philosophical understanding of homosexuality that will self-actualize black gay genius. Such a task requires a new epistemology, a new way of "knowing," that incorporates the views our African ancestors had about the material and the metaphysical world.[25]

Simmons's claim is made manifest in Horace's failed project of "transformation"; he undertakes this experiment as an intended act of complete self-possession, as an act of self-determination.

Horace awakens at the close of the novel's first section in the company of "aberrations like himself, fierce and untamed" (28), believing himself born again and beckoned by "The voice." For the remainder of the novel a nude Horace, clutching a gun and smeared with mud and dust from his fireside ritual, performs a visitation, like some Dickensian figure, to his recent and painful past. It is significant that this opening section is entitled "White Sorcery" and that the following is called "Black Necromancy." While the obvious difference between sorcery and necromancy is that the former solicits the help of flagitious spirits for the purposes of divination and the latter involves the conjuration of ancestors for both divination and manipulation of current events, Kenan implies that black magic is just as harmful as white incantation. By placing Horace at the mercy of white magic in the novel's opening pages and having him bear witness to the playbook of black necromancy, Kenan challenges the community-wide notion that black gay identity results from the horrors of slavery or is evidence of pollution by white culture. The sanctity of the cultural product—essential and essentialized blackness—is interrogated in these first chapters.

Witnessing the past, Horace journeys to the First Baptist Church of Tims Creek, which is both his place of baptism and his family's inheritance. He becomes an eyewitness to a scene of his own humiliation as the Reverend Mr. Barden preaches on the sinfulness of homosexuality:

> They was talking about men and women, men and men, women and women—help me, Jesus—living together in sin. Like it wont nothing. Normal. Tolerable. Righteous. Lord, yes, it was on TV in between "Little House on the Prairie" and "The Waltons" so your children, my children could have been up watching this filth, as if it were as natural as a horse foaling or a chicken molting. But, dearly beloved . . . it ain't. (78)

It is not so much the indignity of the mention of homosexuality during prime time that is outrageous to Barden here but its tainting presence in the midst of *Little House* and *The Waltons*—two programs that promote the mythology of the white family as the repository of moral righteousness in America. In contradistinction to Morrison's effort to name the Beloveds, to bring them back from the place of silence, Barden's reference to the congregation as "beloved" places queer subjects in the space of the unnamed. Not only is Barden's black jeremiad undermined by his allusion to white families, but it is also shadowed by Horace's visitation. Later Barden intones, "Satan and his demons, they come around to taint the soul, to make it unfit, O yes he does, he come, come on in and he whispers . . . in your ear, and he tells you— ha-ha—to do wrong" (80).

This fantastic scenario is actualized by Horace's ghostlike presence in the company of "his devilish crew [and] surrounded by fiends" (28); but Kenan reminds us that demons are conjured and not merely self-manifested. For Barden, homosexual presence, as stated in the Bible, is evidence of the vanity of the imagination. Barden gives the young Horace a sermon borrowed from the same source used to justify slavery while simultaneously labeling any imaginative project with a homosexual genesis as demonic and nightmarish. Faced with Barden's empty rhetoric as fodder for his own creative genius/genesis, Horace is forced to envision an alternative creative project, a dream of transformation:

He found himself seduced by this new world. . . . It all called to him, the numbers, the governments, the history, the religions, speaking to him of another, another, another . . . though he could never quite picture that other, the thing that called him so severely. Yet he labored and longed for it; as if his very life depended on knowing it; as if, somehow, he had to change his life. (88)

Unfortunately, Horace's creative project, his search for "another," is futile. How can he find an image of gay subjectivity, a mirror for himself, when this particular presence has been erased from the body of knowledge or given to him as a manifestation of the depraved inducements of Satan? Horace therefore attempts to become that which he knows himself to be—the grotesque companion of a multitude like himself, a figure suggested not by the dominant society but given to him in a preacherly text. The *source* of black gay identity is not white *sorcery* (and I do think that Kenan intends this play on words) but the subtle manipulation and command of a "white" text in the black pulpit.

Kenan's concentration on the refiguration of a grotesque image is most likely suggested by Baldwin's use of the grotesque as a prototype for David's own self-hatred. On the night of his first encounter with Giovanni David remembers that

someone . . . came out of the shadows toward me. It looked like . . . something walking after it had been put to death. . . . It glittered in the dim light . . . the eyelids gleamed with mascara, the mouth raged with lipstick. The face was white and thoroughly bloodless with some kind of foundation cream; it stank of powder and a gardenia-like perfume. The shirt, open coquettishly to the navel, revealed a hairless chest and a silver crucifix. (54)

Confronted with the specter of himself, David sees a nightmarish figure, a "zombie" painted white and marked with a cross of salvation, which it later uses tauntingly to signify David's own ignorance and descent. Toward the conclusion of his own personal salvation/transformation, Horace encounters an uncannily similar figure:

He was a black man, dressed in a sun-bright costume, orange and green and blue and red, like a harlequin's. As Horace looked into the mirror, the face appeared more and more familiar, though it was becoming obscured by milky white greasepaint. He realized. Saw clearly. It was him. Horace. Sitting before the mirror, applying makeup. Of all things he had seen this night, all the memories he had confronted, all the ghouls and ghosts and specters, this shook him the most. Stunned and confused, bewildered, he could only stare at his reflection, seeing him and him and him. (219)

David's nightmarish image is reconstructed in Kenan's text. Horace recognizes himself—the white paint becomes a masking of his self, a self that becomes, because of its generational legacy through his grandfather's church, the signifier of salvation itself and the heralding of whiteness as the genesis of queer identity. The "another" that he begins his imaginative quest for is reduced here to "him and him and him." Left to himself as both source and resource, Horace decides that a movement from his human form to that of a vertebrate will complete a creative project that he does not want to abandon. This transformation also signifies a belief that his humanity is not synonymous with his gay identity; the new "body" is better suited both to his creative expression and his self-actualization. Moreover, in a racist society, becoming a bird completely separates Horace from the problems associated with phenotypical arrangements. The parallel between Baldwin and Kenan here is in the ultimate erasing of black subjectivity in order to actualize a queer project.

(Im)Proper Objects and Misplaced Queers

In her introduction to the special double issue of *differences*, "More Gender Trouble: Feminism Meets Queer Theory," Judith Butler outlines the pitfalls of relegating *gender* to feminism and *sexuality* to lesbian and gay studies. Tracing a trajectory of feminist inquiries into sex/gender/sexuality from Gayle Rubin's "Thinking Sex" (1983) to the editors' introduction to *The Lesbian and Gay Studies Reader*, Butler argues that "to restrict the proper object of feminism to gender, and to appropriate sexuality as the proper object of lesbian/gay studies, is either to deny this important feminist contribution to the very sexual discourse in which lesbian and gay studies emerged or to argue, implicitly, that the feminist contributions to thinking sexuality culminate in the supersession of feminism by lesbian and gay studies."[26] In the impending turf war between feminism and lesbian/gay studies, Butler ultimately believes that the battlefield involves an inherent invalidation of both projects.

Butler also observes that for the editors of *The Lesbian and Gay Studies Reader*,

> Lesbian and gay studies will be derived from feminism, and yet, the editors argue, there will continue to be important communication between the two domains. . . . How is it that this framing of lesbian/gay in relation to feminism forecloses the field of social differences from which both projects emerge? In particular, terms such as "race" and "class" are ruled out from having a constitutive history in determining the parameters of either field. (6)

But in her own analysis "race" and "class" refuse to intersect with feminism or lesbian/gay studies. Where they do overlap is in the margins of her work, where she highlights Biddy Martin's influence on her thinking in "Against Proper Objects." Butler footnotes Martin's "Sexualities without Genders and Other Queer Utopias" and surmises that "she claims as well that there are problems with theories that tend to foreground gender at the expense of sexuality and race, sexuality at the expense of gender and race, and race at the expense of sexuality and gender. . . . [T]hose very theories are weakened by their failure to broach the complex interrelations of these terms" (22 n. 1). In contemporary feminist discourse the conversation between race and feminism most often occurs in the future or in the footnotes.[27] In my view it is not feminism's or lesbian/gay studies' ownership of the categories of gender and sexuality that matter to the future of feminist and/or queer theory; it is the fact that neither field wishes to interact with its African Americanist counterparts. This lack of cross-pollination is ironic, given that the development of African American studies programs provided an institutional foundation for establishing subsequent programs with "minority" interests.

And this lack of interaction, of conversation, has had devastating effects on all fields, as evidenced here in my reading of black gay presence in the midst of the African American canon. Although it is true that to some extent African American studies has paid attention to feminism, it is abundantly clear that there is no room in the closet for discussions of sexuality that move beyond a heterosexist paradigm. With African American studies having chosen its "proper object" of inquiry, and with feminism and lesbian/gay studies debating about what theirs should be, there is ample room in *all* fields for a ghosting of certain black bodies. Black queer subjectivity is the body that no one wants to be beholden to. Like Horace and his countless rituals for transmutation, in order to speak, queer black bodies have to search in outrageous places to find voice—they have to come back from the dead to get the recognition they deserve.

In all respects feminists and their theoretical allies have ignored the first sexual revolution in this nation that, I would argue, was more intriguing than the second. The first "outrage," to borrow from both Morrison and Faulkner, occurred during slavery, when white subjects experienced an unprecedented period of sexual revolution—a space where black bodies opened to them under the lash, in the fields and sometimes even in bedrooms.[28] Would not an interplay of sexuality and gender find a remarkable stomping ground in the field of relations during slavery? Critics like Hortense Spillers, as Butler suggests, have already broken ground with similar observations. It is not that race needs to be added to the equation; rather, it is that race cannot be excised from it; the question, as Morrison reminds us, is not "why" but "how."[29] And why is it that the proper object of feminism is reduced to the terrain of gender and sexuality? What will it take for theorists to begin to move across critical boundaries? Why are certain black subjects such dead weight in feminism, in lesbian/gay studies, in African American criticism?

In Butler's piece race is, to borrow from Spillers, "vestibular" to feminism and its lesbian/gay allies. And if race is vestibular to discussions of sexuality and even gender, then we have some tacit explanation for why black queer bodies are so absent in the founding paradigm of African Americanist discourse. If lesbian/gay studies or feminism is not having a conversation about race, why should African Americanists reconfigure their own work to narrow the distance between points? Black (queer) bodies never get to determine the way discursive boundaries are organized. Like the countless understudies who know all the lines but rarely get to perform, they constantly wait in the wings for the appropriate time to be *somebody's* proper object.

For example, in her analysis of the social and the symbolic, Butler notes, "The symbolic is understood as a field of normativity that exceeds and structures the domain of the socially given" (19). She later asks, "How ought the relation between the social and the symbolic . . . be reconfigured?" (19). Perhaps the space of reconfiguration exists where whiteness and blackness intersect. Perhaps we might begin asking not only if the lesbian has appropriated the phallus (dildo?), but we might be so bold as to inquire about what that phallus looks like? Given that owning the phallus, or at least a replica, is as easy as a trip to my local Good Vibrations shop, and given that sales of "colored" dildos outstrip those of "white" ones, then asking the question "What does the phallus look like, what 'color' does it own?" might be outrageous, but it is absolutely the only queer act left to those seeking a conversation at the margin—those seeking to bring back the dead from the space of silence.

This book began with the intention of putting critics in conversation with one another. My work here is proof that some of these connections are important to revitalizing a terrain seemingly evacuated of its conversational value. A conversation at the borders among African American, lesbian/gay, and feminist studies might be especially dangerous because focus on race, sexuality, and gender threatens to catapult us into a past we prefer to remain ignorant about. If looking at black bodies (and white bodies, for that matter) through the lens of slavery dissolves gender difference, to remember Spillers's assessment, then the place of contact among three fields of inquiry is revolutionary indeed. As Spillers maintains: "Under these conditions, we lose at least *gender* difference *in the outcome,* and the female body and the male body become a territory of cultural and political maneuver, not at all gender-related, gender specific."[30] The central query here is whether we still labor "under these conditions." We might ask if we have reclaimed the space of difference in fewer than 140 years after emancipation.

In the confrontation between fields some things will most certainly be lost. The loss of *gender* difference could prove dangerous to an African Americanist position solidly entrenched in its masculinist posturings *and* thoroughly destabilizing to a feminism reputed to herald gender as the determining norm. But feminism ought to cease grieving over the residual effects of coalition building, and African American studies ought to challenge itself to look beyond the gender/sexuality binary it has borrowed from feminism.

Robert McRuer comments on the placement of queer bodies in *Visitation*, arguing that Tims Creek, North Carolina, is

> not the most conducive atmosphere for the expression of queer desire, certainly. But as liberal gay and lesbian thought likes to remind us, "we are everywhere," and rather than conceding that "everywhere" *actually* means New York and San Francisco, I'm interested in what (perhaps more radical) cultural work can be done when that "everywhere" includes such an apparently marginal and inhospitable place.[31]

McRuer moves on to discuss the extent to which Kenan's novel is a "veritable treatise on the unstable opposition between sameness and difference" (227). Indeed, there is another place that Kenan travels to in the novel in order to have Horace circumvent the problem of apparently marginal and inhospitable places. Kenan allows Horace to narrate the story of his own death in much the same way the Hughes brothers position Caine in *Menace II Society*. Although all black people experience the inhospitable racial climate that is America, Kenan's return of David/Horace to a black South challenges our critical placement of black (male) subjects (like Horace and Caine)—one gay, one straight; one barren, one procreative—at opposite ends of the spectrum of blackness.

Narration from the grave, or the space of death, prepares these characters to consider a conversation with one another in the context of a figurative death that we all share. In all of the spaces he occupies, there is no space in which his many (queer) selves exist. Horace's answer to this is to escape the harsh fact of his life for the more pleasant, and therefore agreeable, realization of (him)self in death. By relocating Baldwin's tale of first encounters in the black South, Kenan allows a twofold project to emerge: a commentary on the community that engenders Horace's macabre answer to his own life and a mechanism, or back door, through which blacks, hetero- or homosexual, can speak and be heard. In their deaths we see the stories of Horace and Caine as tragically aligned—without their bodily demise we would be unable to see any parallel in their narratives.

In a sense Kenan's use of Horace's suicide escapes the triviality of queer theory's obsession with sameness and difference—death marks the point of absolute difference, and it is a sameness that we would rather not recognize. Although Horace's psyche is embattled with competing pictures of his sense of belonging and being recognized as belonging, we find an end point to this internal and external bickering in his suicide. By crossing the line into (an)other space Horace comes alive, in the flesh, for the first time. Like Beloved he appears naked and visible and haunts our imaginative attempts to erase him from our fruitful landscapes, and canons, if you will. Horace's suicide—his journey through the space of death—challenges our attempts *not* to read him as the "proper object" of African American, feminist, and/or lesbian/gay critical endeavors.

5

"From This Moment Forth, We Are Black Lesbians": Querying Feminism and Killing the Self in Consolidated's *Business of Punishment*

If something doesn't fit the story, it just gets left out. Until it sneaks back one day, suddenly appears amid the other memories, and the simple narrative line is wrecked, the neat explanation no longer works. If there is a truth at all in this world of overlapping subjectivities, it sometimes seems too complicated to hold in my head.
—Marion Winik, *First Comes Love*

A black lesbian with a nose ring studying literature by the disabled—that would get you a job.—disgruntled white male job seeker quoted in *Chronicle of Higher Education*

Much hard-core popular industrial/thrash and rap music conforms to an impressive list of "isms" too frightening to list.[1] Musicians in these genres also tend to flirt with death, wishing it on themselves and various others, from the local police and heads of government to rival bands. When a friend first introduced me to the music of Consolidated, she explained that they were an eclectic thrash band—"white boys" who mixed it all up, creating a pastiche of rap, rhythm and blues, and industrial music.[2] Add lyrics denouncing all forms of fascism, homophobia, jingoism, and vivisection to the driving beat and you have a sure sell for committed radical lefties all across the country. I later learned that the San Francisco–based band consists of three members: Adam Sherburne (singer), Philip Steir (drummer), and Mark Pistel (bassist). Getting their start on the local park concert scene in 1978 and releasing their first album, *The Myth of the Rock*, in 1990, the group headlines the politics of the radical left, especially those pertaining to women's political, economic, and reproductive rights.[3]

I went out and bought their then popular third CD (*Play More Music*) mostly because I could not believe that such a band actually existed and, secretly, because I wanted to prove my friend wrong. I would (inevitably, as with most thrash and industrial music) find something that she missed and punish her for it, as we on the left are known to do to one another. I listened to the CD, waiting to be insulted. But it didn't happen, and I anxiously awaited their next release. When *Business of Punishment* arrived in stores, I bought it and played it nice and loud. *Business* represents the band's last album with a large record company (London Records), and several of the fifteen tracks on the album highlight the band's sense of being fodder for the corrupt politics of the record industry. The album is an eclectic blend of musical genres, with some of its most narrative tracks like "Woman Shoots John" borrowing melodies from Sly and the Family Stone and others conjuring memories of soundtracks from blaxploitation films. Its title song is classic Consolidated; Sherburne drones on with a nonsensical reading of crime and punishment: "for those who're casting pearls to swine someone profits from the crime . . . punishment. and then seal off the neighborhood a brand new prison for their own good yesterday's executioner becomes today's victim they must remain sick so we can continue to treat them lock down prison riots for anybody doing time we've been witness to the crime . . . punishment." The music for this second track is as irritating as the vocals, the flatness of Sherburne's delivery and the awkward, even dissonant, musical arrangement creates a new kind of syncopation. The remainder of the album is less morose, and I especially appreciated the band's return to its roots in industrial/thrash on track 9, with its driving technoindustrial beat, audience commentary ("if you don't like abortion, get a vasectomy!"), and the refrain, "if you don't want a nazi in your house don't let one don't know a fundamentalist 'til you've met one if you've memorized your civil rights don't forget one if you don't want an abortion don't get one." When I got to the last track—a sampling of open-mike responses during their live performances—I was stunned when in response to the question, "Why aren't there any women in your band," one of the members responded, "From this moment forth, we are black lesbians."

They had stepped beyond the boundaries of good taste and personal politics. Didn't they know that I, the *black lesbian* listening to their music, was the truly authentic, speaking subject? Isn't subjectivity earned rather than stated, lived over a period of time, as opposed to attained in an instant? As a participant in their moment of self-revelation, I had to ask myself, Is the speaker *really speaking for me* when he shouts, "from this moment forth we are black lesbians"? Is this an act of solidarity or pernicious co-optation? Does radical politics happen only when solidarity and co-optation occur in a kind of voluptuous simultaneity? And does this space of desire and pleasure, co-optation and solidarity, always constitute death for one subject and life for another?

Shocked into my own personal theoretical conundrum, I was forced to rethink my understanding of "identity," "subjectivity," and, for that matter, feminism. I began to contemplate the preternatural relationship among the three and the cultural moment that allows for a blurring of the boundaries separating them. For the purposes of this discussion, I would like to keep to a general definition of *subjectivity.* Regenia Gagnier has produced an extremely cogent explanation of the subject writing itself in her book, *Subjectivities.* In the introduction she observes that "granting the subject's social embeddedness, an embeddedness most pronounced when one begins to write, one must also grant—at least this study has taught me to grant—the subject's mediation (i.e., transformation) of structures and systems, including systems as large as language or the state."[4] Gagnier's caution extends not only to the subject speaking for itself but also to the "embeddedness" of the author reinventing the person or persons under the pen.[5] This reinvention is always an act of appropriation, no matter how politically correct our motivations. Moreover, Gagnier's parenthetical use of *transformation* in regard to the interaction between speaking subjects and existing structures anticipates the premise of this chapter—a premise that begins with three white male subjects *subjecting* themselves to constant erasure until, ultimately, they reach the "end" of the black/white (if black can be seen as an end point, and white can be seen as a beginning) binary itself, pronouncing themselves black, lesbian subjects. Subjectivity is used here not to transform existing social structures but to perform a dramatic remaking, or killing, of the self. Staging a variety of queer acts, Consolidated's music presupposes that identity equals subjectivity—to say that you are someone else is to become that person. With each new identity—from sex worker to HIV teenager to black lesbian—band members die a little, tinkering with the desire in us all to manifest being in mere utterances. However, if whiteness *is* social structure, or at least how it is *read*, then Consolidated's final act of self-erasure can constitute both a change of self and a change in existing structures.

Whereas whiteness has the leisure of reinventing itself as other (in blackface, for example) in the popular imagination, blackness is truly embedded—it is indeed a mark on the body and the mind, like no other—surpassing sex and sexuality or, depending on your theoretical perspective, embodying and therefore consuming both. For example, a woman identified as a "black lesbian" might choose to change her sex *and* her sexuality, but s/he will always be a black subject *making* those alterations. And such transformations, of desire and organs, will be interpreted most likely as having been arrived at under the static regime of blackness.[6] Perhaps this is why the black lesbian is so important as the primary but invisible subject of feminism. She is the last resort, the end point, if you will, of feminism's attempt to assert itself in the public arena. Noticing the enabling presence of black lesbians to feminist discourse, Evelynn Hammonds issues the following challenge: "White feminists must refigure (white) female sexuality so that they are not theoretically dependent upon an absent yet-ever-present pathologized black female sexuality."[7] I will have more on the end point of black lesbian subjectivity and its relationship to feminism, in particular, toward the end of this chapter.

Listening to Consolidated's music requires the attending critic to adjust the distances between centered and marginal subjects. Group members consistently take on the identities of the people they sing about—ultimately claiming to transcend their whiteness and maleness as they become women in the sex industry, people who are HIV positive, and finally black lesbians. In their attempt to deal with prevalent social issues and government responses to them, they explore the feminist concept of the personal as political and attempt to divest themselves of their own white privilege. Consolidated fans represent a diverse assembly of postmodern youth, many of whom are sampled on the album, conflating the static distance between performer(s) and audience(s). Why haven't we created a theoretical paradigm appropriate to the multiple crossings performed in Consolidated's text, let alone a comparable model for the transformation of existing ways of speaking about personal politics, feminism, or whiteness?

It is not my intention to let Consolidated off the hook here. I understand the long and tired history of white performers "borrowing" black style and sometimes black rage for their own profit.[8] However, there are more immediate concerns I would like to focus on. Consolidated's presence in a marginal subgenre of the music industry is simultaneous with a nexus of academic work and popular political reform focusing on and restructuring marginal identities and subjectivities. And it is this simultaneity that I would like to tease out in the following pages. Consolidated does not appear in a vacuum, and this chapter is most concerned with the cultural and critical moment that *produces* Consolidated rather than the cultural and theoretical material that they reproduce.

It is paramount to keep in mind that one of the chief critical moments that informs Consolidated's manifestation is the shift in intellectual scrutiny from black subjects to white subjects.[9] Consolidated puts whiteness in the spotlight by forcing us to ask if whiteness can be transcended, if whiteness in the popular imagination takes on the same kind of embeddedness as blackness. Or, to amend the question, can whiteness and maleness be transcended in the face of an overwhelming oppositional subjectivity—blackness and lesbianness? And if so, *what* are the politics of, or at least *how* can we theorize about, this activity? Of the many subjects that Consolidated raves about, I focus specifically on three: feminists (a stand-in for white women), white men, and black "wommin."

While attempting to answer these questions, I want also to keep in mind aspects of pleasure/desire that constitute the *experience* of listening to Consolidated's music and function to keep the three subjects in play with one another. This same relationship of desire and pleasure is outlined in George Cunningham's "Body Politics," an examination of black male images:

> Triangles of desire chart the contours, textures, and structures that unite race and gender as an embodied and subjective experience. . . . I am interested in examining the ways in which this paradigm of trian-

gulation structures the often contradictory possibilities of resistance and complicity in racial and gender hierarchies. I argue that the subject positions available to black men are intimately entwined with those available to white men, black women and white women.[10]

Cunningham's articulation of the enmeshed relationship among all three subjects emphasizes the incredible interdependency of subjectivity. Such interdependency not only enlarges the field of subjects at play (and at pleasure) but also cautions the critic against the usefulness of a dysfunctional oppositional paradigm. Whereas several (post)modernist theorists have attempted to cut across various social narratives and the subjects they produce, popular music places such queries in full view—challenging the limits of critical intervention. For example, at least for the compact disk consumer, Consolidated's physical ventriloquism—their becoming black lesbians—can be achieved. For the listener there is no body boundary to move past. There is just the knowledge that the people speaking might not *look or sound* like black lesbians, but there is no guarantee that they cannot *be* black lesbians, at least politically. If being a black lesbian is always already a political state of existence, does "being" only tell us who we are as social subjects, sans the narrative that creates the gerund in the first place?

It is precisely this last query that highlights the importance of the place of feminism in Consolidated's transformation. Having already established themselves as "good," even "radical," feminists by their attention to abortion, reproduction, pornography, and corporate greed with songs like "Butyric Acid," "Born of a Woman," "No Answer for a Dancer," and "Worthy Victim," respectively, Consolidated's feminism is seemingly above reproach. In defense of themselves as such, they resort to "being" black lesbians as the ultimate cover for their lack of diverse membership. On the album they *are* every (feminist) woman, and their invocation of the black lesbian as a knee-jerk defense of feminist privilege demonstrates wonderfully the continued disinheriting of blackness within feminist discourses, as well as the ironic (powerful?) place that it holds as feminism's last resort.[11] Specifically, Consolidated's ownership of feminist discourse demonstrates the need to historicize popular interpretations of feminism. To illustrate this need, we would have to go back to feminist beginnings—to the struggles of the early Second Wave to encompass the subject positions of women of color or lesbians in their revolutionary tracts before the rise of academic feminism.[12]

Second Wave Feminism: The Lesbian Divorce

As a daughter of feminism I cut my teeth on the work of the early Second Wave, under the brilliant eye of Lila Karp, a member of one of the first feminist groups in New York in 1968.[13] In literature denouncing contemporary feminist practice, critics often reduce the history of feminism to one moment rather than treating its rise to popularity as a series of events, all worthy of our attention. We forget that our quarrel with Second Wave feminism is not with what it was but with what it became. We especially forget that early feminist groups such as Cell 16 and the New York Radical Feminists had black women like Florence Kennedy, Cellestine Ware, Margo Jefferson, and Patricia Robinson either in their ranks or writing some of feminism's most powerful ideology.[14] Black women contributed both to the early radical ideology of the feminist movement, short-lived though it was, and to its publications.[15] As the radical "no more fun and games" feminism of 1969 quickly gave way to the "a woman's place is in the house *and* in the senate" campaign of liberal feminism, it lost some of its early strident critiques of capital, state-sanctioned racism, and institutions such as marriage.[16] Some feminists, dismayed by the mainstream voice of liberal feminists, began to focus on "women's culture," and from this emphasis cultural feminism was born. It is this later brand of Second Wave feminism that nourishes the very problematic feminism of New Age America. What the "new" feminisms left behind was not only radical politics but also black subjects whose situation in America could best be addressed through that lens. In light of this premise, some attention to the rift between radical and cultural feminism might be appropriate here.

As left politics began to embrace and encourage the essentialism coming out of groups like the Black Panthers and US (Ron Karenga), women became a distraction to the central goal of masculinist revolution.[17] As women defected from the left, they also took with them the destructive politics of vanguardism so that each group, from Cell 16 to

The New York Radical Feminists (NYRF) to The Feminists to Women's International Conspiracy from Hell (WITCH), had to put forth the most radical posture to prove that it was the vanguard of the new movement. In fact, in one of the founding pieces of cultural feminism, ex-politico cum feminist Jane Alpert signaled a radical rereading of Firestone's influential *The Dialectic of Sex*. In her 1973 piece, "Mother Right: A New Feminist Theory," published in *Ms.* magazine, she writes: "The unique consciousness or sensibility of women, the particular attributes that set feminist art apart, and a compelling line of research now being pursued by feminist anthropologists all point to the idea that *female biology is the basis of women's powers*. Biology is hence the source and not the enemy of feminist revolution."[18]

According to Alpert, Firestone's work misfired in two directions: its reliance on technology to free women from biology and its insistence on biology—as defined by men—as a determinant of social roles. Alpert's insistence on biology as aiding female agency contributed to the growth and popularity of cultural feminism, much like African American studies' clandestine procreative project boosted its acceptance in the academy. However, to rely on biology, one also has to rely on machinations that sustain such an organic system—one of which is procreation. In essence, Alpert's pronouncement signaled not a turning away from maleness as biologically determined and therefore disruptive to essential female identity but actually a gradual embrace of "maleness" as the countering principle, albeit in absentia, to the female principle. How can one herald biology as providing the parameters of women's space and expression without simultaneously naming the heterosexual liaison it entails as necessary to ensure the survival of the species?

Other feminists were coming to similar conclusions, even before Alpert's landmark 1973 letter to *Ms.* magazine. In her 1971 "The Fourth World Manifesto" Barbara Burris proclaimed somewhat cautiously that "the split between the male and the female will only be bridged and a fully human identity developed . . . when the female principle and culture is no longer suppressed and male domination is ended forever."[19] For this group of feminists the desired end point to feminist intervention would be a recognition of male and female cultures, in place of the hierarchy in which the male principle and culture dominated.

Gone from the agenda is any attention to focusing feminist activism and ideology against a dominant culture; absolutely present is a commitment to look inward to the self for sources of feminist resistance and cultural resilience. Alpert fingers consciousness raising as one of the key factors in women's individuation. She explains that "we began to be able to define ourselves as individuals and as women. . . . What we discovered in each other was the pulse of a culture and a consciousness. . . . [G]aining confidence in our thoughts, feelings, resentments, desires, and intuitions as attributes that we shared as a people and which were therefore valid—became the basis of beginning to trust ourselves as individuals" (90). This process of individuation is directly linked to a recognition of what Alpert calls a "female" culture. Moreover, to adhere to this new direction, and therefore this "new age" (94) that Alpert heralds, seekers must "raise the issue of the interconnection between female biology and religious and secular power" (92). She ascertains that the power attributed to matriarchal culture might parallel the kind of power lodged in the "soul" of feminist art and the power that women begin to feel in the process of defining themselves as separate from men.

This redefining proved to be the straw that broke the camel's back, as a rising cultural feminism had to deal with the specter of vanguardism that haunted the male left. Cultural feminists had to ask themselves, who in this new age model would be more able to lead the movement, women who were still tied to men sexually or women who were more liberated and chose sexual relations with other women? This rather new development coincides with other kinds of separatism voiced in the black power movement. Constituent to the transition from radical to cultural feminism is the specter of black power—and its attendant masculinist perspective—that informs the move to a female-centered female culture, composed mostly of white lesbian bodies. Each band, whether lesbian separatist or black nationalist, holds as sacred some biological principle; whether this sacredness is identified as male or female, its biology makes it a prime candidate for both an elevation to the status of religion—and therefore an ideology not to be questioned—and the reconciliation of male and female in the act of procreative desire. Much like the African Americanist project outlined in chapter 4, the new lesbian feminist platform imaginatively ensnares heterosexuality.

The move from radical to cultural feminism forced this new age of feminism to relate to blackness in ways similar to the dominant culture. Cultural (lesbian) feminists mimed their desire for black subjectivity as they played out their own vanguardism through heralding lesbianism as the quintessential element of being feminist. In a wonderful harangue that becomes almost self-satirizing, lesbian feminist Jill Johnston proclaims:

> And biology is definitely destiny. The woman in relation to man historically has always been defeated. Every woman who remains in sexual relation to man is defeated every time she does it with the man because each single experience for every woman is a reenactment of the primal one in which she was invaded and separated and fashioned into a receptacle for the passage of the invader and that's why every woman is a reluctant and a fearful bride.[20]

What better way to keep women's liberation at the vanguard of radical politics than, at the precise time that "black liberation" was being declared as the quintessential (à la the Weathermen) center of left politics, to declare from within the women's movement a cadre of folk oppressed within the larger push for female or feminist liberation? Early feminist critiques of the male left found a palimpsest in the rhetoric of the black left, as "The Fourth World Manifesto" made clear in its deconstruction of the anti-imperialist discourse of Franz Fanon.

Alpert's philosophy found its most solid stronghold in emerging lesbian separatism. An example from the 1975 anthology *The Lesbian Reader* parallels Alpert's original findings and fulfills her predictions:

> We have lived by our wits, as an oppressed and helpless people, for centuries. But we have not, despite massive and brutal conditioning, forsaken our Mother Nature; and she has not forsaken us. It took four hundred years to wipe out the last large concentration of evolved women (the witches, the wise women) but some of them survived the Burning Time and their genes have traveled through time to us. And we feel it; we know it. We are beginning to see into the past and into the future, to heal and create again, to be aware of our own strange abilities.[21]

The embrace of this new feminist principle paved the way for cultural feminists to leave behind a more outspoken politics for the safe harbor

of what Andrew Ross observes as "offering a weak vocabulary of social responsibility somewhat removed from the politics of class, race,
gender and sexual preference waged by the post-sixties left."[22]

What I find here, however, is that cultural feminism, and the lesbian
separatism it engendered, moved more toward the politics of reconciliation between the sexes than its philosophy would suggest. Under the
mother's right, in this new age of feminism, practitioners had to come
to grips with the fact that men would want to partake of the new fruits
of the evolving movement and that the "spiritual" or "new age" dimensions of their cultural feminism left women no option but to open
the "circle" to include men who recognized the power in Mother Nature. The new age provided the perfect palimpsest on which to repair
the damaged relationship between white men and white women.
Feminist politics were rerouted to accomplish this repair over the bodies of the many radical women who would have abhorred any such
transition. The move toward reconciliation, simultaneous with an
abandoning of radical politics, also left the space open for men to form
their own "political" groups. In the last decade we have witnessed
such a possibility in the Million Man March (a day of atonement), the
Iron John movement, and the Christian right's Promise Keepers.

If anything, we as (radical) feminists must take a hard look at representations of the new age because in them we can find evidence about
what really went wrong in 1973. Two relatively recent books, Alice
Echols's *Daring to Be Bad* and Judith Grant's *Fundamental Feminism*,
both have as their subplots a subconscious reluctance to name the politics of early lesbian feminism as the most likely contributor to what we
now know as the New Age.[23] No matter which direction feminists
ran—to the sweat lodge or to the ivory tower—their anxieties about biology and destiny consumed them. For example, we would not have a
Judith Butler worrying about the fixity of sex, gender, and the subject
of feminism if it were not for those tiresome, New Agey, biology-is-
destiny, proud-to-proclaim-themselves-as-"feminists" feminists in
the community holding sacred circles and looking to what is behind
their navels for inspiration. More appropriate to this evaluation, we
would not have Consolidated mimicking the competitive vanguardism displayed during the reconstruction of early feminism. Consolidated continues to mime the dance of reconciliation between fem-

inism and its feared opponent and sometime friend—masculinist discourse, masculinist posturing. If the band members have appropriated feminism and become its subject(s), then this act is not an anomaly. Read through the historical trajectory outlined in this section, the band's appropriation falls neatly into the popular terrain that feminism mapped for itself in the early moments of its reincarnation. What Consolidated performs for us is not a new and extremely fluid postmodern subjectivity. Instead, they mimic a feminist vanguardism that sees black subjects as fodder for the machinery that sustains relationship between white male and female counterparts. Women of color have been particularly frustrated with the ghosting of whiteness in feminist criticism. What I have tried to argue here is that ghosting is not only a result of feminist preoccupation with white bodies but also a complex rendering of the heterosexual relations buried in the discourse feminism created in its second evolution.

Judith Butler, Kobena Mercer, and the Slippery Subject of (Radical) Feminism

Many practicing feminist theorists would not describe their work as a product of the historical tensions outlined above. I would argue, however, that much of the attempt to inject more theoretical rigor into the canon of feminist inquiry stems precisely from the popular belief that the feminist movement has been rerouted by New Age spiritualism and somehow gone soft on its examination of feminist categories of sex, gender, sexuality, and experience. Consolidated seems aligned with the call for a return to "rigor" as they mix in the jargon of postmodernist theory on cuts like "Woman Shoots John." In the midst of recounting this story of female vigilantism, they drone "the extreme form of power is all against one the extreme form of violence is one against all," and "does power grow out of the barrel of a gun or is it that power and violence are opposites where one rules absolutely the other is absent?"[24] Consolidated's claim to rigor in their feminist politics allows them free rein with the identities and subjects they play on stage.

A return to the "continued disinheriting of blackness" in the territories of critical theory might be helpful as a backdrop for understanding what produces Consolidated's reproductions of feminist sound bites. Therefore, I turn for a moment to a similar slip in subject(s) that occurs in theory as well, a moment when a tension between the implied and the stated subject belies a kind of perpetual fault line in the practice of feminist theoretical inquiry.

In the first chapter of her now widely read *Gender Trouble: Feminism and the Subversion of Identity,* Judith Butler observes that

> within feminist political practice, a radical rethinking of the ontological constructions of identity appears to be necessary in order to formulate a representational politics that might revive feminism on other grounds. On the other hand, it may be time to entertain a radical critique that seeks to free feminist theory from the necessity of having to construct a single or abiding ground which is invariably contested by those identity positions or anti-identity positions that it invariably excludes.[25]

I find this one of the most powerful and disturbing statements about the direction of feminist inquiry in the late twentieth century.[26] In the last sentence Butler mentions her own attempt to "entertain a radical critique," "free[ing] feminist theory" from a "single . . . ground," already "contested by those . . . it invariably excludes." She appropriates radical politics as if feminism, in its various incarnations, has not contemplated any such notion, and she places radical politics in service to theory rather than practice. What this maneuver accomplishes is profound because Butler is able to circumvent naming the multiple voices in feminism. She is able to destabilize "women" as the subject constituent of feminist identity without having to examine when and where this destabilization occurs. There is absolutely no politicized point of entry here, no causal relationship; feminism is assaulted from all sides by invisible antagonists.

Kobena Mercer offers a more precise articulation of what happens when radical critiques meet what Butler calls a single or abiding field of inquiry:

> Just now everybody wants to talk about identity. As a keyword in contemporary politics it has taken on so many different connotations that sometimes it is obvious that people are not even talking about the same

thing. One thing at least is clear—identity
it is in crisis, when something assumed to
is displaced by the experience of doubt an

For Mercer, identity is only destabilized w
queried. I am interested here in the apparent
tion in Consolidated's response to an audie
tity as a profeminist band is momentarily un
to such a crisis is to call in the heavy artillery—
embody the ghost of feminist discourse—the v
in black lesbian subjectivity. I am also intereste ___ ... butler's reluctance
to *name* the forces that act on feminist theory so that it (is forced to) be-
come(s) a discipline that excludes.

In all fairness it is true that Butler and Mercer have different theoretical agendas, but I would not say that they have different politics. Butler reminds us, "In the course of this effort to question 'women' as the
subject of feminism, the unproblematic invocation of that category
may prove to preclude the possibility of feminism as a representa-
tional politics. . . . What relations of domination and exclusion are in-
advertently sustained when representation becomes the sole focus of
politics?" (5–6). Although it is absolutely appropriate and theoretically astute to declare that representation need not be the sole focus of
feminist politics, it is somewhat more complicated and therefore dangerous to suggest that in the ensuing complex of competing identities
there is *no* subject of feminism that can be held accountable for what
appears to be its simultaneous demise and slow reconstruction. In this
political matrix those who rage against the original machine go unnamed, and those who maintain a central place in that machine have
identities so fluid that they become nonsubjects when the formal inquiries and accusations begin. A perfect parallel is Consolidated's
shift from white males to black lesbians. Although representation
ought not to be the sole focus of politics, it is difficult to *have* politics
without some discussion of what is actually being represented.

Mercer differs from Butler in naming a politically charged identity
for those individuals who cause a crisis in leftist thinking. Mercer's political agenda is circumscribed by the following statement:

The ambiguity of "identity" serves . . . as a way of acknowledging the
presence of new social actors and new political subjects—women,

lesbian and gay communities, youth—whose aspira-
ot neatly fit into the traditional Left/Right dichotomy. How-
am not sure that "identity" is what these movements share in
mon: on the contrary, within and between the various new movements that have arisen in postwar, Western, capitalist democracies,
what is asserted is an emphasis on "difference." (260)

Ambiguous identities work in an entirely different way for Mercer; his paradigm seeks to center Marxist/socialist discourse, proving that identity and difference converge in the most contested spaces. For Butler's inquiry to work, the multifarious subjects of feminism would also be its representatives; they would have to be, at various times, the ancestors *and* authors of feminism's current dilemma. We know from experience that this is not true. For example, a black lesbian subject, in the popular or academic mind, has never held the coveted position of being *author* of the feminist discourse that Butler now finds imperiled.

A possibility in language does not make for a possibility in practice, especially if that avenue forecloses the very discussion necessary for such a change to be universally accepted. But contemporary feminist theory so relies on this potentiality and obfuscation that followers in both academia and the lay population—and even a group like Consolidated—can grasp the paradigm, thus absolving themselves of their (white male) identities and claiming a new set of clothes in each creative endeavor. However, their killing of the self, or miming of marginal experience, ultimately proves that radical politics cannot take place without attention to the experiential life of those subjects who are necessary to a revolutionary rethinking of archetypes and identities.

Consolidated: White Anger, White Angst

Claiming both a feminist *and* a radical stance, Consolidated performs the complicated politics of maneuvering among identities. I would like to switch gears again and read the necessity for Consolidated's trespass in the context of other national events. Because of Consolidated's roots in the Bay area, it might be wise to use recent California politics as a palimpsest for understanding the simultaneous *rage* and *ap-*

propriation that the band utilizes for their radical politics. Historicizing this claim more fully, I turn to the work of Tomás Almaguer. In his epilogue to *Racial Fault Lines: The Historical Origins of White Supremacy in California*, Almaguer observes:

> What stands out most clearly from this comparative history is that European Americans at every class level sought to create, maintain, or extend their privileged access to racial entitlements in California. *California was, in the final analysis, initially envisioned as a white masculinist preserve.* It bears recalling that the European American editors of one of the territory's first English-language newspapers, the *Californian*, proclaimed in 1848, "We desire only a white population in California. . . ." While this study has explored these issues in historical terms, only the most politically naive would deny that we continue to live this history in very fundamental ways. . . . *California remains a contested racial frontier* and the site of continued political struggle over the extension of this society's most cherished civil rights and equal opportunities to all cultural groups.[28]

The passage of Propositions 184, 187, and 209 in California indicates the deep racial divide in the state.[29] It is difficult to grow up and create music in California and not be deeply affected by its climate of what Almaguer calls "racializing discourses." More important, as magazine reporter Peter Schrag reminds his readers, "Where California goes, the nation is usually not far behind."[30]

It is no mystery that this nation has seen a plethora of political movements led by white men since the mid-1980s.[31] It is also noteworthy that these movements emerged simultaneously with the critical dismantling of the monolith of whiteness that began earlier in the decade. Interesting also is that just when affirmative action and decades of civil rights work began to bear fruit came a national outcry that the interests of the minority culture have somehow overshadowed those of the majority.[32]

ACT-UP activism is the perfect example of the pallet on which a white masculinist and heterosexist preserve gets remixed and redefined.[33] During the 1980s, white gay males active in the fight against HIV/AIDS felt the particularly painful conundrum of being white in America but at the same time subject to a hatred and fear reserved for more marginal subjects of the state. This difference did not keep some men from maintaining their white privilege. As Leo Bersani recalls, men active in early HIV/AIDS activism "had no problem being gay slumlords during the day, and in San Francisco for example, evicting from the Western Addition black families unable to pay the rents necessary to gentrify that neighborhood."[34] Bersani's statement demonstrates that in the midst of radical politics, there is still business as usual. Again we seem to have another moment when popular discourse feels the pressure from academic/theoretical discourse—when the *political* acts of white male subjects reassert their dominance in the public realm as if to stave off an impending divestiture in a whiteness that enables them to purchase land, become landlords, and thus benefit from a booming market economy.

The political fallout from HIV/AIDS is that gay white men who saw themselves as oppressed within the larger white culture had to think about aligning with people whose lot they considered themselves immune to. The "crisis" of white male subjectivity began when white men who thought they had divested themselves of their own supremacy found themselves unwilling to let go of that particular ideology in the face of *becoming like* their colored counterparts. Perhaps the crisis was just as much the dis-ease within their own group as it was the disease with which they approached coalition building with other marginalized peoples. The white male anger expressed in anti-HIV/AIDS protest and telecast via satellite to major cities all over the world triggered an avalanche of public response, one of which was the return to "family values." This return can also be read as a reinscription of white male heterosexuality as the more legitimate force in a growing display of white male rage.[35]

As if in answer to the request "will the real representative white man please stand up," a surging mass of conservative and sometimes Christian white men advanced to denounce homosexuality altogether, at the same time asking the government for many of the same things demanded by minorities and gays (at least theoretically): governmental accountability, preferential treatment in light of the crisis (declining family values or HIV/AIDS, for example), and increased representation from political constituencies.[36] From this middle group, the various Christian-based coalitions, has grown an even more radicalized contingent—militia groups—bent on achieving all three ends by any means necessary.[37] The parallels are chilling, but if we are to move against and beyond dichotomies, we must at least be willing to entertain not only the possibility of a parallel, at least theoretically, but also the potential for meaning in any relationship between these divergent displays of white male angst.

More than anything else, the media attention to white male anger not only reopened the popular discussion of white subjectivity but also fundamentally changed the nature and definition of white masculinity. The question I want to consider is that in the shadow of a resurgence of mostly extremist, sometimes brutal, white masculinity, how does any white man move to speak against a subject position designed for him by the media? The media depiction of white male anger has made it difficult for white men to substantiate their own forms of protest distinct from already established avenues of public *and* political expression. Consolidated might be the perfect pill for the crisis of white male subjectivity, but the group members' inability to voice their own rage and therefore their own subjectivity, in response to what they believe is a neofascist movement underfoot these days, demonstrates their continued silence under the shadow of other expressions of white male anger. Why is it that they constantly cross-dress to get their point across? Is it because white male protest has been so delegitimated that to launch their own protest they have to wear someone else's clothes? Perhaps their own rage against the machine is not a matter of what has been done to us (black lesbians) but of what has been done to the collective image of white masculinity.[38] Ultimately arguing that white male rage is impossible without an act of appropriation to legitimate its presence, and following in the footsteps of Eric Lott's theorizing of white male desire and black bodies, I'd like to end with the assertion that white male rage is always an act of desire for the other, and in Consolidated's case for blackness specifically.[39]

Black Lesbians: The Perfect Answer to the Problem of Feminism

In the midst of this national reexamination of white masculinity and expression of white rage, there is Consolidated's stating that "from this moment forth, we are black lesbians." In a 1994 *Rolling Stone* interview announcing the debut of Consolidated's fourth release, *Business of Punishment*, Adam Sherburne comments, " 'In the past we made calculated decisions to go with concrete ideas because these ideas have been obliterated in post-modern, post-subjective culture.'"[40] Sherburne's words parallel his actions. If indeed we are in a "post-subjective" culture, what better way to demonstrate this phenomenon than to state that what you see is not always what you get.

What is remarkable about Sherburne's definitive statement, "From this moment forth, we are black lesbians," at the end of *Business* is its total collapse of the categories of subjectivity and identity. If, in Butler's cosmology, the subject of feminism is endangered by the various struggles among the identities that it chooses to embrace and/or reject, then Consolidated's music would provide the perfect example of such intense conflict. Consolidated obviously performs the postmodern crisis of feminist subjectivity by explicitly engaging several marginal identities. This kind of engagement thwarts the notion of a beginning for the feminist subject. Sabina Sawhney writes that "the notion of an essential self—a self presumed to have its origins in a specific culture, ethnicity or nation—is debunked by the performative and discursive configurations that participate in the production of these selves. These instances direct us to look beyond the stubborn linkage of 'origin' and 'essence,' forcing us to confront the political, historical, and discursive origin of identity."[41]

During the course of the album, band members *never* sing about what it might be like to *be* a black lesbian. This experience is ghosted much like the provocateurs that destabilize feminism(s) in Butler's chronicle of feminist posturing. On the album every other marginal identity gets represented, but black lesbian female identity is simply *stated*, transgressed into so easily because of its accessibility on the menu of politically correct mantras. Furthermore, band members support this conclusion by producing the declaration "From this moment forth, we are black lesbians" as an end point. The crowd's loud affirmation of their pronouncement demonstrates that this change in subject positions is enough of an answer to the accusation of sexism— "Why are there no women in your band?"—brought by a member of the audience.

This chapter began with a series of questions about Consolidated's unorthodox closure to *Business*, and many of the potential answers take us in equal and opposite directions. On the one hand, the band's statement can be seen as another co-optation, another successful expedition to the terrain of the marginalized; on the other, it can be quite revolutionary for three white men in an age when white male anger is soaring, and continually legitimized, to relinquish, if even for a moment, their own subjectivity. If subjectivity is based on an individual's experience of the world, then Consolidated's band members have only the experience of (an)other to constitute theirs.

I would like to focus on the possibilities that the latter statement opens. Consolidated's resistance to self-representation is evident in another place on their album, and it is to that space that I now move. Although the story of "being" a black lesbian is never articulated in Consolidated's most recent work, her rage is appropriated for use in yet another moment. In a diatribe against William F. Buckley, Ted Nugent, and Rush Limbaugh, band members along with comedian Greg Proops detail the appropriate ways in which each of these figures can be killed. During the song "Consolidated Buries the Mammoth" they reserve a particular punishment for Clarence Thomas: "One of the most appropriate ways for Clarence Thomas to expire would be, he goes to a conference called, 'The Black Women for Power League,' and he's gonna speak there and he thinks that he's gonna get a lot of chicks. But when he gets there it's all black lesbians [and] they lock the doors and fuckin' kill him with cocktail forks" (track 11). Again, the particular power of black lesbian presence is enlisted to provide an end point—to produce a deadly end in this case.

What intrigues me about Consolidated's choice of assassins is how it remarks on black feminist politics surrounding the Clarence Thomas/ Anita Hill hearings, which took place in October 1991.[42] Dismayed by both the result and the spectacle of the hearings, black women from across the country contributed to a campaign called "Black Women in Defense of Ourselves." Spearheaded by Elsa Barkley Brown of the University of Michigan and others, the campaign focused on the publication of a full-page advertisement in the *New York Times* with the names of black female contributors superimposed on an Africanist silhouette of a black woman's head. A symbolic gesture at best, the campaign served to unite black (and white) women in an effort to comment on the invisibility and subsequent denigration of black women in the culture at large. For many people the advertisement was just a small step, not nearly enough needed to generate the long-overdue discussion about black women and race in this nation. Consolidated must also have seen this demonstration as ineffectual in the grand scheme of things.

I read their killing of Thomas as the *perception* of a failure in black feminist politics. If black lesbians hold the masculine position of (angry) escort to feminism, then the anger of straight black feminists is not enough. The retaliation for such a public disgrace of black feminist politics needs to be much more severe, and for this work you need the appropriate (angry) subject of feminism—the black lesbian—and black female heterosexual anger is certainly not sufficient. In fact, the proof of this is in the demeanor of Anita Hill during the October proceedings. As Karla Holloway insists,

> My grandmother was right, nice girls did not wear red, I thought—and Professor Hill had clearly been raised as a nice girl. She was properly mannered, neatly attired, softly spoken, and in every dimension certainly a "credit to the race." Professor Hill was clearly what my grandmother had in mind when she encouraged me and my sisters to carry ourselves well, to speak with precision and care, and to bring honor to our families. However, although all of the same behavioral codes from my private, family-centered education were being remarkably emulated in Professor Hill's polite demeanor, the occasion was nonetheless a serious challenge to the weightier directives I had been urged to follow in public situations. For all the frank talk about sexual harassment, pubic hair, and pornography, Professor Hill may as well have worn red.[43]

Regardless of how black women carry themselves or ask to be addressed, certain codes of conduct, Holloway suggests, are employed so that black female subjects appear as always already wearing red, as always already unruly subjects.[44] Like Anderson's dead in service to the nation and like O-Dog, who is our worst nightmare, black women reside in the place of constant anonymity and yet maintain a recognizable usefulness. If straight black women were to unleash even legitimate anger, it would divest them of their ability to inhabit the category of women. But black lesbians are never portrayed as afraid of such a loss, for they have stood in for the male in feminist discourse for so long that they embody him; they have *never* been considered as decidedly *female* in the first place. Observing Hemingway's use of the black female body in *To Have and Have Not*, Morrison notes: "The strong notion here is that of a black female as the furthest thing from human, so far away as to be not even mammal but fish."[45] In a sense Consolidated's ritual killing of Thomas with cocktail forks alludes to the false "femininity" that black lesbians possess—the weapon they use here is sheer absurdity in the face of the murderous rage being released.

We have to ask ourselves difficult questions here. Why is Consolidated's reading of *this* particular subject of feminism so accurate? Why is the perfect escort of contemporary feminism, and queer studies for that matter, the (enraged) black lesbian? I suggest an even earlier point of departure for our ruminations on the place of the black in feminist and, subsequently, lesbian (queer) studies.

In "Black Bodies, White Bodies: Toward an Iconography of Female Sexuality in Late Nineteenth-Century Art, Medicine, and Literature," Sander Gilman traces the place of the black female body in relationship to the study of female reproduction and in the service of the burgeoning eugenics movement.[46] His scholarship reveals the absolute connection between racist nineteenth-century scientific thought and the construction of "deviant" sexualities through lesbianism and prostitution. It appears that the words *lesbian* and *black* are forged in blood, in physiognomy, and ultimately in racist science. The link between lesbianism and the black body cannot be obfuscated, yet within queer studies not much has been made of this connection.[47] Such a deep psychic connection provides ample territory for a discussion of the racialized lesbian body. Can we think of a lesbian without thinking about her origins? Is a lesbian, therefore, always inscribed, written, identified as black *first*, becoming white through a series of transgressions, through the theorist's pen?

These questions are important because they help to realize a relocation of a politics of the lesbian and feminist subject, as well as to provide an explanation for the scandalous paucity of written work on the black lesbian as the (angry) subject of feminist discourse.[48] Obviously, this construction of the black lesbian is so prevalent that even casual readers of radical feminism—Consolidated—can see the appropriate place of the black lesbian feminist in the paradigms of feminist discourse. Black lesbian subjects and their women-of-color allies have always haunted feminism's attempt to articulate itself, putting themselves in the position of challenging the racial inclusiveness of feminist theory and practice and at the same time pushing a developing lesbian/gay studies to describe the face of its constituency. The place of the black lesbian within queer studies has been defined by decades of use value as the heavy hand of feminism, as Judith Roof so cogently argues: "In 1985's proliferation of feminist literary critical anthologies, the myriad differences among women are often reduced to the formula 'black and lesbian.'"[49] She also later surmises, "This is just another version of the power analogy; feminist critics battle male theory and have again enlisted diversity on their side" (229). It was a good thing that poststructuralist postmodernism came along, or the claims of racism in both feminism and lesbian/gay studies would have begun to appear well founded.[50] But now that the "subject" and/or authors of feminism have no names, no faces (or at least interchangeable ones), we cannot hold either discipline accountable for the actions of a de-faced host(ess), even though the actions of people of color began the political unrest that made each field of inquiry possible.

The killing of Clarence Thomas in *Business* suggests that there is something extraordinarily menacing about a black man who, because of his relative wealth and social/political connections, escapes the usual wrath of a system specifically designed to enmesh him. Such a man is dangerous, and in the example of both Clarence Thomas and O. J. Simpson, the miscarriage of "justice" can only be rectified through the assassination/murder of the escapee from the penal colony. In my conversations after the hearings and trial, respectively, I heard many people call for the death of either as a quick solution to such brilliant escapes. What is most powerful about a similar call to arms in Consolidated's work is the utilization and/or threat of black lesbian bodies as the ultimate defense against an accusation of sexism. Flaccid feminism is no match for the phallic power of the quintessential black lesbian.

If anything, Consolidated's reading of black lesbianism should provide, however obscure, a wake-up call for academic feminism, for its complete failure in addressing and therefore dismantling the myths about female sexuality and lesbianism. Such a failure requires a new approach to feminist discourse—one that names the people, places, and events that continue to gnaw at a concept of centered feminism. It is time for queer studies and its feminist allies to address the culpability of its major figures in the "battle" against a winning patriarchy.[51] For if the ultimate goal of feminism is truly, in the words of the Second

Wave, to "obliterate the patriarchy," then more of our attention should be focused on how that patriarchy has managed to escape our attention, to mask itself, and to survive.

Saying that there is no unified subject of feminism, or any other discursive field, will not stop the police from singling out black subjects at the corner of University Avenue and Bay Road in East Palo Alto, California; nor will it prevent a university advisory committee from dismissing the importance of black feminist scholarship. Such acts merely demonstrate that there are some subjects who always appear as targets in the sight of a triumphant patriarchy. I am not advocating the discontinuance of stimulating intellectual discourses on the subject of the body and fluctuating identities, but what I would like to see is a suspension of the pretense of "politics" in the course of this discussion. As one woman pronounces during the open-mike session at the end of Consolidated's CD: "The politics stop, man, when the sexism stops, when the fucking bullshit that women deal with every day of their lives—when *that* fucking stops man, then the politics can stop."

Performance Problems

Evaluating black female sexuality, Evelynn Hammonds remarks, "Nor are black queer female sexualities simply identities. Rather, they represent discursive and material terrains where there exists the possibility for the active production of speech, desire and agency."[52] Much of this energy, in the popular and theoretical terrain, has yet to be released. I have tried to demonstrate here that removing black queer female voices to the space of silence, to such an inarticulate space, might not be solely a result of our own racism. Rather, such inattention can stem from a variety of paradigms so entrenched that they go unrecognized even to the trained critical eye. When the critical eye fails to see, it is sometimes popular culture that places a magnifying glass over the missed area, enabling all to see a piece of the problem.

Introducing a collection of theoretical essays on performativity and performance, Andrew Parker and Eve Kosofsky Sedgwick conclude:

These essays strikingly refrain from looking at performativity / performance for a demonstration for whether or not there are essential truths or identities, and how we could, or why we couldn't, know them, as *a certain stress has been lifted momentarily from the issues that surround* being something, an excitingly charged and specious stage seems to open up for explorations of that even older, *even newer question of how saying something can be doing something.*[53]

Parker's and Sedgwick's opening remarks cast a deep and similar shadow over the kind of exploration of identity and performance I have been conducting here. When we do switch from *being* to *saying* something, and therefore *doing* it, a new avenue of critical work opens. If we are not carefully attuned to and responsible for the kind of specious stage we have stumbled into, however, we most likely begin to perpetuate the very behaviors we are trying to eradicate. This chapter does not pretend to have all the answers, but asking the right kind of questions can take us in a myriad of directions. We are always in the position of *being* something to or for somebody, and the present challenge is not to eclipse the distance between saying and doing but to qualify the ways that "being" enacts itself in the (post)modern terrain.

6

Critical Conversations at

the Boundary between Life and Death

It's a hell of a thing to live in the world being called the impossible real—being called the traumatic, the unthinkable, the psychotic—being cast outside the social, and getting named as the unlivable and the unspeakable.—Judith Butler, interview

If the deaths of Michel Foucault and Paul de Man have taught the academy anything, it is that what you say is just as important as what you do.[1] In his analysis of the impact of Foucault's work on the modern academy, During writes: "Obviously those who take Foucault's contribution as seriously as it deserves will feel the demand to elaborate and move past it, but perhaps its real challenge lies in the question: 'can it continue to be used to break down the limits of academic professionalism?'—and that requires real changes in our methods and topics of study" (23). Indeed, the hesitancy with which literary critics approach the subject of real death, as opposed to literary death(s), indicates the extent to which the physician's art has failed tremendously in conquering our societal fears. Because these societal fears are pervasive, discussions of death, and notions of the dead, have the potential to dissolve barriers between communities. Speaking about death and the dead necessitates that critics move beyond familiar country and into liminal spaces. These liminal spaces are present whenever a scholar moves between the borders separating nations and communities, disciplines and departments. Moreover, use of the dead in discourse is not necessarily a creative sleight of hand but a critical maneuver as well. For the purposes of this chapter's inquiry, the silence of the dead is mapped onto the literal and figurative silence of the excluded and marginalized. How do critics wake the dead with discursive interventions? What kind of playing field do critics construct when they move about divisions that are more porous than they appear?

Feminism at the Margins

This book began with a brief examination of Josette Feral's concept of marginal experience. In the margin/center debates that raged in the mid-1980s critics fastidiously crossed the line between communities, and contemporary discursive space was won, mapped out, roped off during these displays of critical muscle. Much of the margin/center debate materialized because of the powerful and dissenting discourses of feminist criticism. Within this context Elizabeth Meese's work fits well with the overarching concerns expressed here over subjects meeting at the sometimes translucent borders of difference. In a comprehensive study of various feminist theoretical perspectives utilized during the 1980s, Meese begins her project by questioning the validity of the margin/center dichotomy: "Feminist Literary Criticism . . . has always represented itself as having a substantial cast in the 'margins,' but perhaps if this identity is to persist, we should consider how it might designate a space figured as 'all margin' in the interest of disseminating the center and transforming the place of knowledge into a free space."[2]

Meese offers an excellent formula for redefining the peopled place of the margin while simultaneously disseminating the center. She also turns feminist criticism in on itself and demonstrates how this particular academic power can and does appropriate "dominant" strategies for use in its own "liberating" discourse. This formula, however, still places the center in an empowered position because the focus of those people in the margin is to move against this historically unyielding force. Here feminism still operates as liberating, and dominant criticism retains its place at the center by maintaining its unanimity; much like the unknown soldier and the anonymous cadaver, master discourse is both the tomb at which we pay our remembrance and the body offered up to us for examination. Feminism remains a marginal voice, opting out of its place at the center. The marginal place of feminism in the critical landscape has changed substantially since the publication of Meese's assessment; feminism now maintains a place of dominance in articulating the relationship of subjects (both male and female) to notions of identity.

The trajectory outlined by Meese assumes that the life force (or the life) of feminist criticism is not constituted by one individual (or singular) discourse; however, she also notes that to move away from that life force (for many) would surely entail a figurative death of feminist inquiry. Meese echoes this fear among writers of traditional feminist criticism by noting that "tensions foreclose extensions and lead to exclusion, like occlusion—'To prevent the passage of; shut in, out, or off.' The project ends. The subject dies" (24). It is unclear whether these tensions that prevent extensions in discourse are evident within the established discourse of feminism or whether this taut arena is caused by the collective voices of critics of color whose *noise* creates unwanted reverberation along its margins. Meese foresees an actual death for feminist criticism if it cannot negotiate and sustain a multivocal site of difference. Given my evaluation of recent feminist theory by Butler and others, the "multi-vocal site" of feminism seems to have disappeared.

I would argue that feminist debates, regardless of any inclusion of lesbian/gay/bisexual, native, black, or Latina voices, cannot tremendously change the *living* conditions of this country's working poor, a disproportionate number of whom are women.[3] But when women of color speak, are they speaking from a "feminist" platform, or are they speaking from a different place altogether? Are they ever really, to borrow from Judith Butler, the subjects of feminism, or are they instead constantly subjected to feminist perusal? Throughout the introduction to her work, Meese continually privileges and centers feminist perspective; her ideas of multivocality always have their source in the products of feminist theory. What happens to those critics who would like to speak from a varied place of subjectivity? Do they become always already dead to the *listening* and established subject—feminist criticism? I think that the answer to this question is a definite "yes" and necessarily so if the critical space is to be constructed in its traditional garb, familiar to us all. As if in answer to my query here, Meese continues by arguing that critics need to continue debating tough questions concerning the power of language, one's own as well as that of others, to say more and less than it intends, the capacity of feminism to represent the materiality of women's lives, as they are figured through language and in the daily paper, popular fiction, and traditional literature and criticism by women and men, the imbrication of theory and praxis in the political role of feminist intellectuals. (24)

Meese urges feminist critics to embrace the materiality of women's lives. What hinders Meese's effort is her general construction of marginality and its relationship to discourse. She states that "the challenge to re-figure the politically and intellectually powerful relationships between *language and life*, as they are played out in the identity struggles of race, gender, ethnicity, class, and sexual orientation, could easily encompass the future work of both feminism and deconstruction" (25; italics mine). If speaking/language is associated with life, and if, to echo a powerful message from the lesbian and gay movement in this country, "silence equals death," then what becomes of speaking from the margins or, for that matter, discourse in the margins? Aren't marginalized subjects always speaking from a place of silence—from the space of death? Is this dual way of being always dichotomized?

There is an intriguing continuity of metaphor in Meese's opening chapter. Much of her project appears to be posited as a matter of life and death. The subject—feminist literary criticism—is in danger of suffering a premature death, and it is her job and ours to revive it, to bring it back to life. Meese ultimately challenges her feminist audience to transcend the confines of the "word"—to ask what it means "to say that power is always mediated in/through language" (25). This is a pronouncement that collapses on itself because any move to speak to the center implies a *use* of its vocabulary. There is no change here unless centered *and* marginal discourse can exist and speak in the same space, which, historically, has proved impossible. Therefore, the process of expanding and "(ex)tending" previously marginalized discourse(s) is lost in the ever-present dichotomy of us vs. them, center vs. margin, language vs. silence, illusion vs. reality. This marginal place is still highly artificial and rigid and is almost never held sacred or finite by the writers discussed in this book. As Meese suggests, we need to

make this space happen, but how it comes ak
making. The feared intersection of the knowr
within a discourse makes it nearly impossible fc
points to exist simultaneously. In the remainin;
plateau, or theoretical site, on which a series of ii
bates occur at or in the "margin" in order to den
speak to one another and how authorial subjects-
at times indirectly, with language, silence, life, anc
contentious and dangerous space. My intent is to c
tween disparate critics, to move into that space where subject positions are honed, silences are exposed, and critical dialogue is haunted
by a constant ungrounding.

Movements across Porous Boundaries

Examining the authority of centeredness and the power of canonical
categories, Arnold Krupat surmises:

> The author-ity of the author . . . derives not from his [sic] predecessors
> and their productions, nor from his contemporaries and theirs, but, in-
> stead, from his personality, his imagination or . . . from his individual
> genius which transcends the society that would seek to constrain it.
>
> This particular mythology never developed in Native American cul-
> ture, where the individual who spoke only for himself spoke, there-
> fore, for no one else; where the individual could not in any positive
> way be imagined to stand outside or against his society . . . where, of
> course, there was no writing—and so no authors.[4]

I seriously doubt that Krupat's latter announcement would serve as a
universalizing truth for all native peoples in North America. However, Krupat's analysis, despite his distancing employment of *he* as a
universal signifier, provides another perspective on Meese's implied
assessment of marginality *and* power as both relate to the centeredness
of feminist critique or the authority of feminist voices. Meese certainly
does not argue for an authoritative or definitive feminist criticism; she
seems to move toward the type of collective theorizing and speaking
that Krupat outlines in his study of Native American literary practice.

In a later theoretical journey, *Voice in the Margin*, Krupat discusses is-on formation and its intersection with Native American lit-. Krupat traces those moments in the history of literary theory when critics have attempted to write otherness and, for that matter, "nativeness" out of the canon with an implicit assertion that "American" literature was to be a reflection of "American" culture; in defining oneself, therefore, the critic defined a culture and a literature in one sweep—in this formula, the converse is also true. Krupat painstakingly elucidates a period in the formation of an American canon when whiteness and maleness become definitive constituents of American culture. Somewhat ironically, Meese's *(Ex)Tensions* also moves into the territory of feminist debates of "cultural crossings" (seen as marginal space), value, and canonicity in relationship to her explication of lesbian, Native American, African American, and white women's texts. Krupat and Meese concur in their examination of what is marginal to the canon; they depart one another in their attempt to write themselves into these sites of marginality.

Krupat observes that "literature is [mistakenly] taken as just another socially determined category of discourse: like 'greatness,' what is or is not 'literature' is whatever those empowered to define it say it is."[5] During the evolution of his discourse on Native American literature, Krupat relies very little on "native" American voices to engage the massive body of European thought that he calls forth in *Voice*. Moreover, he allows himself to assume a position of power in actually determining which literatures by people of color are worthy of his and other critics' attention, thereby adhering to the belief that "great" literature *is* selected and defined by those in power. Krupat surmises, "Given the increase in Spanish speakers, there is no doubt in my mind that Latino literature will soon exert major pressure on the canon, a development I look forward to with enthusiasm. Nonetheless, to the present, the cultural expression of red, white, and black people *seems to me* to have a historically urgent claim to primary attention" (54). What I take issue with here is not Krupat's right to make political assertions but his apparent ignorance of the role of power and politics in his posturing; the statement "seems to me" appears innocent enough until one takes into account that, given the constituency of English departments across the country, his critical approach will tend to be more widely read and respected than that of a Silko or a Momaday. This stance clearly rubs against his earlier remarks on authority in *For Those Who Came After*. His implied subject position in *Voice* is as important as his stated positioning; as he marginalizes himself in relationship to his own literary colleagues, he also marginalizes himself in his own text and places himself outside both mainstream and emerging criticism. This is not a position of power but of danger because neither "subject" is able to integrate with the discourses being conjured here. In his work even the margin is static and co-opted by the megalomania of the center.

Therefore, when Krupat moves into a discussion of a Native American "critical response," he takes all the baggage and tools of the master, thus grossly misconceptualizing one Indian author's intent. In a section entitled "Native American Literature and the Canon," Krupat scrutinizes the movement of a vast number of American poets in the 1960s to turn from "European models and sources to acquaint themselves with Native American models and sources—as they also turned to the cultural productions of Afro-Americans and women" (120). Footnoting a comment by one of the American poets (Louis Simpson) in this generation, Krupat observes:

> Simpson continued, "I was writing with sympathy and an historical sense of feeling, but to write about Indians you should in a sense become an Indian." Leslie Silko has quoted Simpson's remark to criticize "the unmitigated egoism of the white man, and the belief that he could 'in a sense become an Indian.' "
>
> Unfortunately, for Silko's "attack," Simpson had gone on to say, "you have to know how they think and feel. *And that I know I could never do, so I wouldn't even bother trying.*" . . . Not to quote Simpson to this effect is simply dishonest on Silko's part. (121)

There are a number of problems with Krupat's approach to Silko's comment, the most paramount being his relegation of such an important exchange to the footnotes of his own text on "marginal" discourse. Silko's remarks were made in a 1979 article, "An Old-Time Indian Attack Conducted in Two Parts." The irony and humor in the title cannot be overlooked when one attempts to explicate the article's content as well as the author's general intent; Silko is obviously appropriating signifiers from the dominant culture with each word choice—how can an "old-time" (traditional) Indian "attack" be conducted in "two parts," as if it were naming itself using the nomenclature of the colonizer, as well as organizing itself following the military structure of the cavalry? It is Silko in the role of a very clever trickster, for she chooses an approach to the work of poets Louis Simpson and Gary Snyder that mirrors Western critical methodology and coincidentally implicates the violence inherent in its structure.

Krupat labels Silko's legitimate anger "dishonest," thereby making her valid criticism of Simpson appear intellectually bankrupt. In this process of devaluation Krupat substantiates his own argument while making hers appear hysterical. But an example of Silko's "attack" indicates that her critique implicates not only poets like Simpson and Snyder but also critics such as Krupat:

> Ironically, as white poets attempt to cast-off [sic] their Anglo-American values, their Anglo-American origins, they violate a fundamental belief held by the tribal people they desire to emulate; they deny the truth; they deny their history, their origins. The writing of imitation "Indian" poems then is pathetic evidence that in more than two hundred years, *Anglo Americans have failed to create a satisfactory identity for themselves*.[6]

Having established an ambiguous identity for himself as simultaneously marginal to dominant discourse *and* part of its center, Krupat's positioning in his own text wavers at the crack between poetry and rhetoric.[7] Krupat's endeavor to create a space where Western and therefore dominant theoretical *discourse* can converse with Native American *literatures* is frustrated by his own whiteness, his own maleness, as Silko's attempt to critique the motivations of poets like Simpson is aggravated by the inadequate intersection of Western and "Indian" modes of critical expression. Indian subjects don't enter the discursive space, which is given preference in Krupat; they only produce literature that is available, like reservation land, to be mined by those wielding the power of the pen.

Krupat's effort is particularly hindered because the space he creates is not a meeting where one discourse speaks to another but where *discourses* meet *literatures*. Ultimately, it is a place where Krupat seeks to tease out some similarity in native literature to the forms and codes of Western theoretical discourse, where new historicist analysis meets

Native American autobiography, where an established discourse meets a marginalized literature. Krupat notes: "As the textual representation of a situated encounter between two persons (or three, if we include the frequent presence of an interpreter or translator) and two cultures, Indian autobiographies are quite literally *dialogic*" (133). It leaves the scholar to wonder if there is a Kiowa word for what the Kiowa poet is trying to do or if there is a Laguna word for what the Laguna poet is trying to do. If we take Henry Louis Gates's *Signifying Monkey* as an example of using West African contexts to explore African American literature, there most certainly is a distinct cultural naming for what goes on in any body of ethnic literature.[8] The use of cultural archetypes in literary theory is not without its problems; however, it is important that the critic move into those marginal spaces of contention. Anytime a *discourse* meets a *literature*, there is a place of contest. Like the dead, who are supposed to have no discourse with the living, native voices are silenced in Krupat's analysis of Native American literature and canonical discourse.

Whereas Krupat seems at crucial moments unaware of his own subject position, Meese, in her approach to Silko's *Ceremony*, is constantly vigilant of hers. Because of her "marginal" status as a woman, Meese shares an identity with Silko, but her tools of interpretation are those of a feminist inquiry that is highly contested at every discursive juncture. Meese admits that the

> value of [Silko's *Ceremony*] rests for me in the fact that *today*, right now even, I can read it (in my position as a white feminist scholar and teacher in the U.S.) as a lesson in crossing cultures, another set of (canonical) boundaries. I can read . . . lessons about my subject position . . . which might equip me for moving in the "between," for participating in the affirming gestures of reciprocal exchange, a fragile, genuinely anxious participation in giving and receiving, in this precariously constituted global village. (36)

Meese approaches *Ceremony* with two purposes: to discover aspects of the novel that can tell her more about herself and to tell the reader more about several planes of marginal consciousness at work in the novel. It is a process of equal exchange and, I would argue, the beginning of a discourse in the margin, albeit a fragile one. She sets for herself a rigorous task—one in which she hopes to return "to the idea of use value, to stipulate the proper use of use, the way in which feminist literary critics make texts useful to us in order to avoid the oppressive dimension of an inevitable reterritorialization" (36).

However, any journey toward an exploration of self in the Western dialectic naturally entails a negation of an other seen as outside the self. But Meese wisely sidesteps this dangerous ground in exchange for a more useful voice—one that posits that "the value of Silko's text resides in the *imbricated* figuration of writing and ceremony" (40; italics mine). Her choice of *imbricated* as a descriptive term for the relationship between writing and ceremony mirrors her subject position in her own piece. Because *imbricate* connotes those objects "overlapping at the margins," it is more than appropriate that she finds this site between the act of writing and telling as comfortable territory. The power of experience *and* language to tell and to write leads Meese to offer a reading of *Ceremony* inclusive of an ideology of the margin rather than exclusive of it, as with Krupat's analysis of Native American autobiography. Seeing these territories as overlapping allows Meese to come close to an internalized concept of the margin. Bringing her sense of marginal experience and recognizing Silko's position within her own community create a space of equality where Meese is not necessarily presenting her own experience as central; rather she sets her narrative beside Silko's as a point of difference and strength for critical coalition building. Here the margin is transformed. No longer in rigid dichotomy with the center, marginal space is lucid and conversational, and those subjects that are "othered" in the process of critique are figuratively brought back from the dead, from the place of silence. Audre Lorde recommends this type of exchange as key to feminist process in her groundbreaking essay, "Age, Race, Class, and Sex: Women Redefining Difference." Lorde notes that "it is not our differences which separate women, but our reluctance to recognize those differences and to deal effectively with the distortions which have resulted from the ignoring and misnaming of those differences."[9] In her explication of difference, Meese finds that "while Tayo believes in the power of his curse, that his words make substance, constructing a reality which corresponds to the story he is creating, his words are without power or effect in the material world he seeks to change" (40). As a character in the margins of discourse, Tayo discovers that language—the word—is simultaneously empowered and disempowered, dead and alive.

Although Meese's critical approach to Silko is more substantial than Krupat's, she does manage to infuse her chapter with a plethora of feminist and mainstream critical methodologies. At times these opening theoretical acrobatics encumber her discussion of *Ceremony*, making the focus of attention the use of Silko's text as a metaphor for the relationship between critical subject and critic, "between giver and receiver" (38). Nevertheless, for all of the chapter's obstacles it is a convincing example of how to enlist critical strategies that constantly seek to explore, challenge, and question the usefulness of the margin at each step of the critical process.

As Josette Feral indicates in the passage cited at the beginning of this book, being an empowered subject means choosing marginality. bell hooks's career-long endeavor to examine marginal locations qualifies Feral's assessment: "As such, I was not speaking of a marginality one wishes to lose, to give up, or surrender as part of moving into the center, but rather as a site one stays in, clings to even, because it nourishes one's capacity to resist. It offers the possibility of radical perspectives from which to see and create, to imagine alternative, new worlds."[10] The marginal position is deeply personalized and internalized by hooks. She moves away from a conventional externalized margin—one placed in relationship to a center—and concentrates on the empowering/disempowering forces of her own experience. Similarly, Leslie Marmon Silko divorces herself from the Western technique of recalling an event in a linear context—from center to margin, as it were—and celebrates the possibilities for creative storytelling that a marginal position can offer: "The structure of Pueblo expression resembles something like a spider's web—with many little threads radiating from a center, criss-crossing each other. . . . [T]he structure will emerge as it is made and you must simply listen and trust, as the Pueblo people do, that meaning will be made."[11] Silko's paradigm also envisions an extremely malleable, unstable yet resilient, center with boundaries easily penetrated and open to suggestion by members of an extended community of speakers.

The production of meaning carries with it an understanding of when to keep silence and when to speak in a loud voice, when to pursue knowledge and when to prefer what is secret to what can be discovered. Laguna Pueblo critic Paula Gunn Allen notes that

> the white world has a different set of values, one which requires learning all and telling all in the interests of knowledge, objectivity and freedom. This ethos and its obverse—a nearly neurotic distress in the presence of secrets and mystery underlie much of modern American culture. Witness the John F. Kennedy murder investigations . . . the Irangate hearings . . . and the cry for full disclosure in political, personal and scholarly arenas. Indeed, entire disciplines have been developed on exactly the penchant for knowing everything possible that characterizes American ideas of adulthood though the earlier American belief in privacy is strongly at odds with this trend.[12]

This desire for knowing creates an atmosphere for the kind of arrogance illustrated by Simpson's approach to Native American poetry to flourish in literary circles. Furthermore, this exposure of secrets contributes to the vanity of a society totally convinced of the importance of its own *word*: "It is only the western Europeans who have this inflated pompous notion that every word, everything that's said or done is real important, and it's got to live on and on forever."[13] Allen's words parallel the findings of Aries and Foucault; the predominance of knowledge supersedes the body, presides over the body so absolutely that the "word" and its importance replace altogether the person either dying in the hospital ward or speaking from the dead.

The obsessive desire to know that Allen refers to as distinctly "American" is undermined when contrasted with ideas of secretness/ sacredness in Native American and African American communities. Allen states: "Among the Pueblos, a person is expected to know no more than is necessary, sufficient and congruent with their spiritual and social place. One does not tell or inquire about matters that do not directly concern one."[14] What is ironic about Allen's assessment of knowledge, community, and silence is her identity as a lesbian feminist critic within her own community, a precarious position not without its tensions but one that she does not engage at any point in *The Sacred Hoop*; this silencing allows for some of the book's more pronounced failures.[15]

Explicating the opening of her novel *The Bluest Eye*, Toni Morrison complicates this intricate web of silence, speech, knowledge:

The opening phrase . . . "Quiet as it's kept," had several attractions for me. First, it was . . . familiar to me as a child listening to adults; to black women conversing with one another; telling a story, an anecdote, gossip about some one or event within the circle, the family, the neighborhood. The words are conspiratorial. . . . It is a secret between us and a secret that is being kept from us. The conspiracy is both held and withheld, exposed and sustained.[16]

Morrison's discussion of knowledge and disclosure provides a warning for critics unfamiliar with the cultural terrain to pay attention to the fundamentally different view of how knowledge, and therefore language, is given, received, and used. This is not to contend that the critical relationship of people of color to their own literatures is not without tension. For example, the controversy that ensued after Henry Louis Gates's defense of Two Live Crew during their trial for violation of Florida's obscenity statute clearly demonstrates that all critical junctures are places of danger.[17] Again, the power in discourse is revealed here as a complex of meaning within which *both* disclosure and silence, writing and making meaning, serve as intricate systems of conversation in the territory of the margin.

Houston Baker has endeavored to qualify the relationship between theoretical and culturally derived practices. He notices that "theory's relentless tendency is to go beyond the tangible in search of a meta-level of explanation. A concern for metalevels, rather than tangible products, is also a grounding condition of Afro-American intellectual history."[18] To seek out the intangible, Baker uses African American women's voices and bodies as an example of the relationship between theory and practice: "The master discourse that carries us most effectively toward such metalevels is poetics. . . . [A]n Afro-American theorist can turn his or her autobiographical attention today to sounds of mothers and sisters. . . . Poetics, drawn from a master discourse, become the inventive site of a hearing of Afro-American women's voices" (147). The master discourse Baker speaks of is therefore reconfigured within the tropes and realities of "[our] *own* metalevels [written] palimpsestically on the scroll of this mastery" (140). The question then becomes whose text—in this (re)mastery of the master's discourse—stands as re-used and/or erased? Is this a relationship of reciprocal exchange or of constant erasure? Baker's text is informed by feminist discourse on erasure, women's bodies, and canon formation; and the *body* he conjures here is a highly contested location for this kind of literary (re)production.

Baker continues:

> The "poetics of Afro-American women's writing" signals a theory that seeks to arrive at the guiding spirit, or consciousness, of Afro-American women's writing by examining selected *imagistic fields* that seem determinative for selected texts. . . . By examining imagistic fields that compose space, therefore, we also come to apprehend values and beliefs that govern our lives. Our cultural geographies are, thus, comprehensible through images. (150)

The center of his working model shifts from that intangible unbounded arena where the spirit works to tangible "imagistic fields"—from a place of infinite possibility to a locus of absolutes. This leap is highly suspect, not only because it moves from the intangible to the tangible but also because it revives issues of power in relationship to who is allowed to assign meaning to those fields of images. In a cogent response to Baker's piece in the same collection Mae Henderson maintains that the use of "the black woman as a privileged *object* of discussion in the formulation of a poetics of Afro-American women's writing. . . . [and the] privileging of the visual image, in particular, from 'autobiographical situationality' of the male poses certain conceptual and theoretic problems."[19] Henderson chides Baker for involuntarily aligning himself with modes of discursive analysis that place him in a quagmire of representations that, in terms of African American women, have served primarily to objectify and commodify her body. I would argue that the objectification that Baker implies occurs in part because he abandons the intangible for the tangible; it is the tangible that is contested in the critical site, whereas the intangible—that which we refuse to see and are unable to "name" or give meaning to (to echo Hortense Spillers)—has yet to be scrutinized adequately.[20]

As a suggestion for change, Henderson presents a critical approach that stems from a feminist perspective in which "the first requirement for the critic or theorist of black women's writing must be the deconstruction of the gaze of the other(s)—i.e., an alteration of perception, or revision, in the sense of approaching the discursive subject or object from a new perspective or angle of vision" (161). It is ironic that in dismantling Baker's language Henderson ambiguously employs deconstruction (the father's discourse) but pays no attention to the implications of her own usage here. The new perspective of this literary critic should articulate, she continues, that the "power of black women's writing is precisely its ability to disrupt and break with conventional imagery" (161). Here Henderson implodes Baker's imagistic fields for a more useful paradigm, one that sees this break, this space where syncretic discourses converse, as a new "angle of vision."

Most important for this discussion is where Henderson chooses ultimately to locate this break with convention:

> We must continue to recognize and respect that dialogue is necessary to fill in the lacks and deficiencies within and among different and competitive paradigms. *In pursuing this critical dialogue, we engage not only our peers but also our predecessors.* This critical connection with both past and present is in the spirit of the Afro-American community. We are a people who have survived through recognizing and respecting each other and the ancestors. (163; italics mine)

This simultaneous dialogue among peers and predecessors appears as a locus where critical space *is* a dialogue between both the living and the dead, *as well as* between male critics and female authors. Both Henderson and Baker, regardless of differences in their theoretical approaches, see African American women's "writing"—implying both critic and novelist—as a site of discursive power, a site where past and present converge, dualities are conflated, and living and dead coexist. Henderson's formulations are central to the direction of this study.

Having placed the work, language, and dialogue of the critic in the (contested) space where living and dead converse, Henderson inverts the project of criticism at the margins postulated by Baker and Krupat, respectively. The job of the critic is twofold: to define where marginal space exists *and* to travel into the territory of those relegated to the space of death. When we participate with and move into the internal life of a community, we no longer see ourselves as marginal or centered subjects in the small universe of academia. Instead, we see ourselves as integral to the makings of theory and practice; we move beyond the rhetoric of "for and against" that holds such discourse hostage.

In the "Spirit" of the "New Age"

Use of the word *spirit* conjures an array of images for the existing critic—from the glazed stare of peddlers of popular new age psychologies to the romanticization of Native and African American ritual practices and beliefs. Karla F. C. Holloway and Stephanie Demetrakopoulos's approach in *New Dimensions of Spirituality* transports the concept of "spirit" beyond and between critical evaluation and quotidian existence. Both define *spirituality* as a practice, a system of beliefs organized around rituals and ceremonies that celebrate the interplay among worlds of discourse, those present to us as well as those beyond our reach; and that discourse is centered on the work and words of women, in critical and quotidian life. Much of the work on community and spirit, especially in the Eco-feminist tradition, emphasizes the connection of women and ritual power.

It is crucial however that we, as critics, adhere to Henderson's counsel against essentializing and privileging the female body. According to Allen, "sickness of all kinds . . . comes about because of our resistance to surrendering to the complexity and multi-dimensionality of existence."[21] Although I argue in the succeeding pages that women play a pivotal role in articulating the marginal discourse of the living and the dead, this emphasis is not meant to exclude or preclude the contributions of men to this powerful dialogue; rather, I intend to demonstrate that women are not only present and active in the forces/ discourses of life and death but are instrumental as keepers of balance between the apparent poles of male and female in that liminal space where the story and the discourse unfold as each is being made. Although I am cognizant of the effect of gender assignment in discussions of rituals surrounding death/the dead, I am also concerned that the process of unraveling this quagmire of representations goes far beyond the boundaries of this project. Mae Henderson's blueprint in Afro-American Literary Study in the 1990s for critical dialogue seems appropriate for this interaction because she suggests that critical discourse is a matter of life and death; it is a conversation between two worlds and two living discourses with only an imaginary membrane separating them. Henderson suggests that, in essence, the life of criticism incorporates what is perceived as dead (the ancestors, the black feminist critic's discourse) and regenerates it, transgressing the limits of physicality so that our discussion can encompass that which is psychic as well.

To combat the mutual exclusivity of life and death in the Western paradigm, contemporary critics have suggested new avenues of exploration and inquiry. As an anthropologist, Carol McClain recognizes there is a utility in crossing Western feminist critical discourse with theories of women's traditional roles in non-Western societies.[22] McClain, for example, makes particular mention of Harriet Ngubane's *Body and Mind in Zulu Medicine*. Ngubane provides a definition of the marginal that challenges Western paradigms:

> Among the Zulu the source of pollution is essentially a happening associated with "birth" on the one hand and "death" on the other. . . . Although "this world" and the "other world" are viewed as two separate entities, the beginning of life, whose source is believed to be in the "other world," happens in "this world," and the cessation of life in "this world" is believed to mean continuity of life in the "other world." Notionally there is an area of overlap between the two worlds. Such an area is marginal and dangerous.[23]

Unlike Western concepts of pollution as contamination, Ngubane defines *pollution* as a "mystical force" that is closely associated with women.[24] According to her study, the status of marginality is attributed to women as mothers during and after childbirth, as chief mourners, and as spiritual diviners. As primary actors in the movement of life and death, women have the ability to reach the apex of spiritual leadership as diviners who have contact with the ancestral spirits (89). It is possible to borrow from Ngubane this transformed definition of marginality and employ it not in conjunction with an established center but as removed from the dichotomizing discourse of power in the West and as placed in the designated *critical* space of the spirit—where life and death intermingle and where women often facilitate this meeting. In this realm of the spirit, Ngubane sees that "the mother and the chief mourner . . . [are] channels through whose bodies spiritual beings cross from the other world to this world and from this world to the other world, [which] applies also to the diviner, who is a point of contact with the spirits who return to this world. Through a woman the transition of spiritual beings is made" (88).

Although Ngubane does not posit her argument in an overtly feminist framework, she does allude to the institution of patriarchy as a factor in the development of ideas of pollution and women's bodies in those Zulu beliefs that she examines. In sum, she implies that dominant culture distorts the balance not only between the two worlds she speaks of but also between the perceived place of women and the relative status of men in Nyuswa-Zulu society. In comparison, Paula Gunn Allen posits that this sense of male/female equilibrium in Laguna culture is constantly in flux: "The male principle is transitory; it dies and is reconstituted. The female principle, which is immanent in hard substances . . . [like] wood, and water, is permanent; it remains. Male is breath, air, wind and projectile point; female controls, creates, and "owns" breath, air and wind . . . and hard substance from which the projectile point is shaped" (267). There is evidence in both Native and African American retentions of a cultural link between women and the combined forces of life and death. In Yoruban tradition *Oya* is, among other things, the female orisha, or deity, of the graveyard. In the Keres Indian culture "women paint their faces yellow . . . at death so that the guardian at the gate of the spirit world, *Naiya Iyatiku* (Mother Corn Woman), will recognize that the newly arrived person is a woman" (226). Providing a parallel in literature, Trudier Harris notes that in Toni Morrison's works "characters adhere to many folk beliefs, superstitions, and signs common to historical communities. This is especially true of beliefs surrounding sickness and death."[25] Cultural critics involved in these foregrounding discussions are attempting to redraw the place of "women" and "spirit" in the discourse of the margin; in their framework this discursive space is becoming shared territory, one in which a multitude of voices speak. As Houston Baker implies, this sound of the spirit is a reverberation that has no foreseeable boundary.

No other contemporary theory lends itself to a discussion of silence and death so well as postmodernism. The postmodern project relies heavily on a subject in crisis—a marginal subject between the dichotomies of life and death.[26] In the discourse of postmodernism *everyone* can participate in the "privilege" of the margin; it is made so appealing that one would "die" for the vicarious experience of this crisis that opens the gateway to multiple identities. Postmodernism is the attractive zombie theory of the academy, a place where the living travel through death and are reborn to utter the truths of such a journey. Examining postmodernism as a global condition, Michael Grosso observes that it "is a quest for reconciliation between the new physical science and the new catholicity of the world spiritual traditions."[27] It appears that in Grosso's postmodernism there is room for a dialogue between worlds. In a section entitled "Toward a Healing Vision," Grosso develops the following hypothesis:

> Scientific materialism has spawned a technology that threatens (1) to poison the biosphere to death and (2) to destroy it through nuclear war. Is there a linkage between scientific materialism's nihilistic myth of death and the threat to the biosphere? *Whatever the answer to this question*, my point is that these historically unprecedented threats to life on earth are mobilizing forces of the collective imagination. The global crisis has evoked new and profound reflections on the meaning of death. (241)

Grosso's unwillingness to answer his own question points to a larger problem with his theoretical framework. Although he utilizes, as well as redefines, postmodernism as a space that respects both science and indigenous experience, he simultaneously implicates technology in that renaming, a technology he would rather not take to task. This allows him to romanticize this "new mythology" as "like the native [sic] American Indian quest" and to leave Euro-American expansionist by-products, such as scientific materialism, to other critiques. This politics of reconciliation appears faulty at best; it is a catholic consciousness that does not take responsibility for its own by-products but dons the religious vision of a specific other as a means to promote a global solution to a problem that "someone else" created. When Grosso invokes the collective imagination—he declares that a mere wish has the power to move this crisis toward solution, a power that dislocates the threat to life on earth from the people and places it impacts to the almost scientific trappings of the mind, where it can exist if and when dominant culture would like discourse with it.[28]

To a degree, Grosso's text exemplifies the very thing he seeks to condemn because he relates to his own subject matter as a scientist would to something in a test tube; he might articulate the problem that needs to be solved, but his methodology is influenced by the discourse that he must use. Ojibwa economist and activist Winona LaDuke speaks to the same issues of technology and progress that Grosso articulates, but from a different perspective:

> Euro-Americans perceive the development of their culture as a mastery of the natural world, a prime example of the progress from primitive to civilized society. They seem to believe that this culture is either immune to ecological disasters, or clever enough to survive them. This is racism, founded on the precarious conception of the technological and mental superiority of the consumer-producer system.
>
> Racism, oppression, and death are integral components of the resource development process, and they are contained within the mining, milling and technological use of uranium. . . .
>
> There is a crucial difference between the native's mentality and the visitor's mentality; that is, the mentality of the industry. The visitor moves from resource to resource . . . *assaulting the Earth and the Earth's people, and leaving behind skeletons*. The native, nontransient population has no option to move or evacuate.[29]

LaDuke's appraisal of the same system differs drastically from Grosso's configuration. Grosso offers up postmodernism as the generating theory behind his new mythology of death as a means to distance himself from the discussion; this distancing is neither useful nor an option for LaDuke, who must live in the dystopia that scientific materialism has created. Moreover, these scholars view death from radically divergent perspectives. For Grosso death is a product of imbalanced science, but for LaDuke (as well as for Rinpoche and Tibetan Buddhism) it is an actual physical occurrence rather than a mythic happening. Grosso fails to explore the possibility or probability that "world spiritual traditions" and "physical science" might never reconcile. LaDuke's "visitor" who leaves behind skeletons is a haunting metaphor for Grosso's position as outsider and visitor to the territory he seeks to illuminate. The skeletons here are the physical remains both of a consumer-producer relationship and of those who seek to converse with Grosso's text but find little liminal space for this encounter.

The Leaning Tower of Babel

The contemporary womanist process of reestablishing, to invoke Henderson, a discourse between peers and predecessors is more than an adept critical maneuver. It is quite possible to view this process of reevaluating and repositing discursive boundaries as moving against the Western proclivity to create a rupture between what constitutes the living and what are believed to be the dead, between actual happenings and, to paraphrase Grosso, a mythic postmodern event. Meese's closure to her explication of *Ceremony* speaks to a reformulation of discursive boundaries:

> The conflict, in fact, is irresolvable, requiring that we live in the borderlands, on the frontier . . . where "illness" threatens the body and the spirit, language and ceremony, in a perpetually circulating tension between the text of desire for health, wholeness, and Identity [*sic*], and the text of dis-ease, pain, and heterogeneity. These tensions between competing categories require a particular ceremony that takes (its) place in the place of struggle and negotiates a way. (45)

For Meese, neither the text of dis-ease nor the text of wholeness can exclude one another. The borderland is a territory of conflict, change, *and* simultaneity, but she makes no move to resolve that tension; rather she is satisfied with making part of its discourse known. To negotiate a way is, I would propose, to open and explore marginal space, where the "predecessors" to any words we utter or language we use must be acknowledged. In speaking of the dead, the "eguns" in Yoruban language, Luisah Teish argues that ancestors "hold a place of affection in the hearts of their descendants. Elaborate annual rites are held in their honor, which the whole village attends. . . . In exchange for this loving reverence they offer protection, wisdom, and assistance to those who revere them."[30] For both Meese and Teish there is discourse and dialogue between the tangible and the intangible.

But connections across cultures threaten the status quo. The mixing of several points of view from people of color challenges the ideology of a centered culture and a marginal discourse. Abdul JanMohamed's and David Lloyd's experience with the National Endowment for the Humanities (NEH) illustrates the panic that ensues when this center is not paid its proper respects. The negative response from the NEH panel of reviewers to their application for funding for a conference on "The Nature and Context of Minority Discourse" reads as follows:

> A conference that would bring together in a few days of papers and discussion specialists on Chicano, Afro-American, Asian-American, Native-American, Afro-Caribbean, African, Indian, Pacific Island, Ab-origine, Maori and other ethnic literature would [not] be anything but diffuse. A Conference on ONE of these literatures might be in order; but even with the best of planning, the proposed conference would almost certainly devolve into an academic Tower of Babel. *It is not at all clear that a specialist on Native-American literature, for example, will have much to say to someone specializing in African literature.*[31]

JanMohamed's and Lloyd's experience with mainstream academic perceptions of multicultural discourse is in no way singular. To call attention to the possibility of speaking across "territories" is to create a discursive realm that threatens established ideas of a single subject and acknowledges the cross-pollination of the past and present. Moreover, this idea of contamination is having a serious impact on the discipline of ethnic studies, as programs and departments are moved to continue to fight over peanuts. Like elephants in a zoo we trample on one another to get what's coming to us, and then we have a long historical memory about which one of us did the killing during the stampede. It isn't often that we care to remember where we are or who put us there in the first place.

Intimacy among fields is considered even more problematic when discussions among communities are aimed toward conversing about the intimacies of community life—a margin perhaps more dangerous than one placed artificially alongside an endangered (white) center. It is ironic that Native American critics, according to the NEH, have nothing to say to African critics, even though, in the collective history, these peoples were experiencing each other long before Europeans found their way to *either* continent.[32] In the introduction to *Spider Woman's Granddaughters* Paula Gunn Allen claims that "the dogmatism of the Western literary position has consequences that go well beyond the world of literature, which include the Western abhorrence of mixing races, classes, or genders. Similarly, the mixing of levels of diction, like the mixing of spiritual beliefs and attitudes, is disdained if not prohibited."[33] Allen's observation that mixing levels of diction is shunned by Western critical posturing parallels JanMohamed's and Lloyd's recounting of the NEH response. To ignore the "mixing" of cultural representations and voices is to deny the whole history of this country. Attempting to chronicle the power in discourse(s) of the margin—where the living talk to the dead—gnaws away at any established center by removing the focus on *unicentered* to a *multicentered* discourse, thus creating a place that is destabilized and liminal, a margin that has a myriad of interpretive possibilities and a host of unruly subjects.

The works examined here all seek to move into the "place of struggle" and eventually into a dialogue between what are considered the living and the dead. In an interview with scholar Marsha Darling about the novel *Beloved*, Toni Morrison remarks, "The gap between Africa and Afro-America and the gap between the living and the dead and the gap between the past and the present does not exist. It's bridged for us by our assuming responsibility for people no one's ever assumed responsibility for."[34] Similarly, Paula Gunn Allen seems to speak to Morrison's claim with an evaluation of her own cultural milieu: "We are the dead and the witnesses to death of hundreds of thousands of our people, of water, the air, the animals, and forests and grassy lands that sustained them and us not so very long ago" (155). Strong evidence is presented here that there is dialogue to be had between and among cultures; that the margin does not hold its place; and that dialogue, both real and imagined, is taking place among worlds, dichotomous though they may seem. The dead truly acknowledge no boundary, and their unruly universe is worthy of critical examination—no matter how promising, such an encounter is potentially dangerous. *Raising the Dead* suggests that it is time for critics to take the lead from authors when stepping into this capricious terrain where the dead survive and clamor for our recognition.

EPILOGUE

As to black, only the mentally troubled are usually fascinated by it, though there are exceptions. Some few persons may take to the color for its sophistication, but in this preference they may attempt to hide their truer natures. They may wish to appear mysterious, but this in itself may be obvious. People who dislike black are legion. Black is death, the color of despair. In virtually all cases such persons will avoid the subjects of illness or death, will acknowledge no birthdays and never admit their ages. They loathe inevitabilities and would hold to the present forever if they could.

—Faber Birren, *Color and Human Response: Aspects of Light and Color Bearing on the Reactions of Living Things and the Welfare of Human Beings.*

"I'm in the Zone":

Bill T. Jones, Tupac Shakur, and

the (Queer) Art of Death

How many brothers fell victim to the streets?
Rest in peace young niggas, there's a heaven for a "G."
Be a lie if I told you that I never thought of death.
My niggas, we the last ones left.
—Tupac Shakur, "Life Goes On," *All Eyez on Me*

I will never grow old. My hands will never be discolored with the
spots of age. I will never have varicose veins. My balls will never become pendulous, hanging down as old men's balls do. My penis will
never be shriveled. My legs will never be spindly. My belly, never big
and heavy. My shoulders never stooped, rounded, like my mother's
shoulders are. I will never need a son to massage my arms, as my father did . . . I am not protected, remember? Old is for people who are
protected. The unprotected have to die young.
—Bill T. Jones, *Last Night on Earth*

i see you blackboy bent toward destruction watching for death with
tight eyes—Sonya Sanchez

The Quick and the Dead

In *Webster's Ninth New Collegiate Dictionary,* the primary definition of
the word *body* is "corpse." The secondary definition is "person." The
implication is startling: as the body marks space equally in death and
in life it becomes the bridge between the way others see us (science/

pathology) and the way we see ourselves. Both Shakur and Jones have challenged death, often miming its culture, sometimes playing the role of the dead.[1] In the spectrum of popular images of black (male)ness, we are constantly suspended between Shakur and Jones. We can't (or at least we shouldn't) embrace either—one black body "ailing" with dis-ease, fighting the grave with a weapon called dance, another black body too hard to break, his tattooed physique a bullet coming at you with the rage of phallic rhyme. The following examination of confluence in the work of black dancer/choreographer Bill T. Jones and rapper Tupac Shakur is the final example of how the book reads between often disparate public spheres. What I want to do in this section is to open the possibility of *seeing* and *reading* these queer/black bodies—in the same space.

Our anxiety about black subjects like Bill T. Jones and Tupac Shakur manifests itself in the countless journal articles and media attention that vilify and embrace such performers. When black artists flirt with the culture of death, or the "space of death," to borrow again from Taussig, they claim relationship to or kinship with the dead. Although Jones and Shakur represent different, if not competing, masculinities, they nevertheless speak from the same stage—each performing the event of his own death and packaging it as art. Rather than concentrating on their performance of black masculinities via their dance or music, respectively, I want to read across their bodies, to begin with the corpse, if you will, before we get to the person. What I offer here is a decidedly queer vision of performing bodies.

On 14 September 1994 dancer/choreographer Bill T. Jones premiered "Still/Here" in Lyons, France. The piece (in which Jones does not perform) has been described as "a multimedia dance spectacle about survival."[2] In the production, dancers of varied hues and body types perform while video screens display images of terminally ill people and their narratives—all collected by Jones during a two-year period in which he conducted "survival workshops" with the dying.

In her now infamous *New Yorker* harangue about Jones's "Still/Here," Arlene Croce expresses a paralyzing fear of death with comments like "Jones represents . . . something new in victim art—new and raw and deadly in its power over the human conscience."[3] Although in its next issue the *New Yorker* published several responses to the piece, they were, for the most part, parallels to Croce's reading.

Marcia Siegel's lengthy and stinging critique of Croce in *The Drama Review (TDR)* suggests that I am not too off the mark when I say that Croce's fear of death is shared by many. Siegel remarks, "It isn't [the] health [of the media images in 'Still/Here'] that bothers Croce at all, but the idea that Jones asks us to pay attention to death and dying."[4] To say that Croce is unkind to Jones would be an understatement. Her review is crushingly acidic and, for the most part, mean spirited.

Claiming that "victim art" is "beyond the reach of criticism" (54), Croce finally surmises that in such work "death is no longer the nameless one; we have unmasked death. But we have also created an art with no power of transcendence, no way of assuring us that the grandeur of the individual spirit is more worth celebrating than the political clout of the group" (59). Jones's powerful unmasking of death creates so much anxiety for Croce that her fear moves beyond Jones's dance—which she refused to see. Her personal attack on Jones indicates that her fear borders on a seething hatred of what Jones and others have done to a once-beautiful art form. I recognize this fear in Croce as another kind of recognition and unmasking. The face of death has been unmasked, and the black face staring back at Croce is almost too much to bear. This might lead me into other ruminations about the psychic life of nations—how these imagined communities, to echo Benedict Anderson, take certain icons like tombs of unknown soldiers, like black bodies to stand for both national pride and national horror, respectively. Losing either, I would argue, is a deathblow to how the nation envisions itself as a whole.

Even more interesting are Croce's two statements about Robert Mapplethorpe: "Jones and Mapplethorpe, parallel self-declared cases of pathology in art, have effectively disarmed criticism"; and "The possibility that Mapplethorpe was a bad artist or that good art could be obscene seems not to have occurred to anyone" (58, 60). That both artists remind us of the black body—Jones by being marked by his black body, Mapplethorpe by being obsessed with someone else's black body—are clues that Croce's fear is twofold: a fear of blackness and a fear of death. It is absolutely ironic that the figure—the (borrowed) black body—credited with reviving, if not engendering, modernist aesthetics is now at the center of postmodern art forms. In its "unmasked" state it is much more lethal and foreboding than even the disturbing strokes that became Picasso's signature on the canvas. The presence of this black figure—like the presence of Morrison's Beloved, "thunderblack and visible"—literally disarms an entire field of inquiry. Such a presence is pathological indeed—meaning murderous, meaning cadaver like.

Is There a Queer Here?

My desire to place *queer* in dialogue with Shakur and Jones's bodies stems from my conversations with colleagues in the field about "queer" readings and the process of "queering" bodies, public spaces, and institutions. In David Eng's essay "Out Here and Over There: Queerness and Diaspora in Asian American Studies," Eng calls for a return to the possibilities of the hyphen in the term *Asian-American*. Such a moment, he argues, might allow "scholars in Asian American studies to consider queerness as a critical methodology based not on content but rather on form and style."[5] This reinsertion of the hyphen, of the possibility of "queer," can combat what he historicizes as an overwhelmingly masculinist and therefore misogynistic and homophobic early Asian American studies. Eng's piece concludes with a reading of Ang Lee's *The Wedding Banquet* and the position of the male immigrant's "queer and diasporic status" (43). My query for Eng is whether it might have been possible to take Ang Lee's immigrant woman, Wei-Wei (May Chin), as the film's queer subject rather than the film's more obvious queer representative, Gao Wai-Tung (Winston Chao), the gay male lead.[6]

But we have to be careful of the violence we do to certain texts when we try to queer their subjects. Queering Bill T. Jones might be appropriate, as would be an investigation of Ang Lee's gay male character Wai-Tung, but what price will we pay for our looking when we venture into more sacred categories of the heteronormative and suggest that Shakur or Wei-Wei become similar proper objects of inquiry. In beginning to ask ourselves what a queer subject looks like, we might begin to see performance theory for the black hole that it is; pun intended.

In "Queer Nationality" (1992) Lauren Berlant and Elizabeth Freeman argue that "the struggle is now also over proper public submission to national iconicity and over the nation's relation to gender, to sexuality, and to death."[7] Death takes a rear seat throughout the rest of their essay, but its importance cannot be overestimated in the politics of queer expression—the nation's attitudes toward death seem not only to inform but to activate queer studies. Is it then possible to say that what makes subjects queer is their relationship, both performatively and literally, with death and that this relationship *is* of *national* concern? Our proximity to death as human beings—to cancer cells that might wage war against our otherwise "fit" bodies, to other forms of dis-ease—might mark the queer space in us all because the possibility of an impending death is something we all share.

Let me say here that I am aware of the proximity of marked bodies—black bodies / queer bodies—to the discourse of pathology, literally the study of death. However, I am much more concerned with the phenomenon of the space of death and the dead who inhabit such space in direct juxtaposition and perhaps contradistinction to our societal notions about what it means to be "living" in the first place.

The place where Shakur and Jones collide—the space where Shakur's performance meets Jones's—is a volatile one. In " 'The White to Be Angry': Vaginal Davis's Terrorist Drag," José Muñoz invents the term *terrorist drag* to describe Davis's performance of "the nation's internal terrors around race, gender and sexuality."[8] Muñoz's theory builds on his own work with a modality of performance he calls "disidentification." Using Muñoz's paradigm in the context of this work on death, I would argue that disidentification is not only about other subjects, particularly white subjects, but also about a disidentification with life. Unlike other artists in drag, Shakur is not in the midst of becoming as in Vaginal Davis's performance; he is *being*—he is in a state of complete identification, not "passing" but already gone.

In a 1994 interview Shakur reflected on his childhood: " 'All my cousins was like, 'You too pretty.' I didn't have hard features. I don't know, I just didn't *feel* hard' " (*Vibe*, February 1994, 36). Shakur finds his hardness on the other side, and his complete disidentification with life refracts our pleasure in knowing that certain bodies are in sites we'd rather not occupy. In the latest issue of *Vibe*, Karen R. Good interrupts her article on DMX to reflect: "Some black men, X men, are so absolutely scared of—or familiar with—death and its gradual approach, that they've embraced it . . . so familiar with its formidability, they call on it, challenge it, shadow box. . . . And though there is nobility in confronting fears, living to die ain't noble or fearless. It ain't living" (90). Shakur's movement across the boundary between living and dying is best explained by his own statements about his music: "My music is spiritual. It's like Negro spirituals, except for the fact that I'm not saying 'We Shall Overcome.' I'm saying that we are overcome."[9] The immediacy of Shakur's words is reflected in Jones's autobiographical statement about being unprotected. Jones reminds his readers: "The unprotected have to die young." It is no longer that the unprotected die, but they *have* to. It is necessary. Being marked for death is serious business and suggests the kind of immediacy to the situation, and the collusion between being queer and black, that is supported by one of the iconographic symbols on Shakur's body: THUG LIFE. Fans at one of his concerts recognized the tattoo and after the fact coined the acroynm: The Hate U Gave Lil Infants Fuck[s] Everybody. So THUG LIFE represents a coming back from the dead, as black youth not only recognize their relative invisibility in the culture at large but also perceive an active hatred aimed at them that is systematic (this is what the universal *U* implies). These words etched in the flesh take on a life of their own and resonate even after Shakur's death—Still/Here.

Returning to the opposition between passing and already gone that I made earlier: Let us consider the essence of queer subjectivity as stated in the prevailing understanding of the literature from the field—a subject without boundaries with the ability to travel in diverse circles, constantly un/marked, absolutely fluid. Are we saying then that reading queer subjects is to be reading whiteness (the absence of all color)? That its center/origin is a body that is always passing, unmarked at times by gender, sex, or race? If we are to expand the definition of *queer* to encompass other bodies, then we will need to do some hard work here. We will need to focus on what we really mean when we equate the queer body/subject with liminal spaces. That these liminal spaces might be so dangerous as to *become* death itself is more than frightening. It represents an apocalyptic moment for queer studies and a challenge to read "race" into the equation of its origins. Bill's and Tupac's bodies are emblematic of the queer—refusing to go away, Still/Here, coming at you soft and hard, embracing the contradiction as if it were a religion. The space of death is marked by blackness and is therefore always already queer. The convergence of language and being here is powerful and telling.

Let the Dead Speak

As I write this last piece and saturate myself with Tupac's music and Jones's dance, I think of my own brother, in boot camp—the postmodern alternative to doing real time. But the piece also brings me back to 1988 and to Greg and how we used to dance back in Detroit hopping from club to club, bringing in the morning with the rest of our friends—Brett, Emory, and Jesse. A stop off at (queer) Denny's and a sunrise drive back to Ann Arbor. Greg and Jesse were truly young, black, and, to recall the words of at least two deceased hip hop artists, "didn't give a fuck." Greg and Jesse contracted HIV at the same time, but class separated them from similar fates—Jesse at home with his family, Greg in jail with full-blown AIDS and denied access to the AZT that could have prolonged his life. At home in 1989 I write my dissertation. I no longer dance—I am a serious scholar. I have left the dying to their deaths—alone and unprotected.

Notes

Introduction: Raising the Dead

1. Several reviewers and literary critics remarked on the presence of Beloved. Reviewing the novel for the *New York Review of Books,* Thomas Edwards stated that "Morrison provides us no cozy corner from which to smile skeptically at the thrills we're enjoying. If you believe in *Beloved* at all you must accept the ghost in the same way you accept the other, solidly realistic figures in the story" (5 November 1987, 18). On the other hand, Paul Gray of *Time* concluded that "The flesh-and-blood presence of Beloved roils the novel's intense, realistic surface. . . . In the end, the implausibilities in *Beloved* may matter less than the fact that Sethe believes them" (21 September 1987, 75). And commenting for the *Nation,* Rosellen Brown observed that "We feel about this vulnerable girl [Beloved], at least at first, as we might about a benign extraterrestrial" (17 October 1987, 418). Critics also made much of Beloved's "ghostly" presence. See Bernard Bell, *"Beloved*: A Womanist Neo-Slave Narrative; or Multivocal Rememberances of Things Past," *African American Review* 26, no. 1 (spring 1992): 7–15; Emily Miller Budick, "Absence, Loss and the Space of History in Toni Morrison's *Beloved," Arizona Quarterly* 48, no. 2 (summer 1992): 117–138; Stephanie A. Demetrakopoulos, "Maternal Bonds as Devourers of Women's Individuation in Toni Morrison's *Beloved," African American Review* 26, no. 1 (winter 1992): 51–60; Gayle Greene, "Feminist Fiction and the Uses of Memory," *Signs* 16, no. 2 (winter 1991): 290–321; Deborah Horvitz, "Nameless Ghosts: Possession and Dispossession in *Beloved," Studies in American Fiction* 17, no. 2 (fall 1989): 157–167; Sally Keenan, "Four Hundred Years of Silence: Myth, History and Motherhood in Toni Morrison's *Beloved,* in *Recasting the World: Writing after Colonialism,* ed. Jonathan White (Baltimore: Johns Hopkins University Press, 1993), 45–81; Linda Krumholz, "The Ghosts of Slavery: Historical Recovery in Toni Morrison's *Beloved," African American Review* 26, no. 3 (fall 1992): 395–408; David Lawrence, "Fleshly Ghosts and Ghostly Flesh: The Word and the Body in *Beloved," Studies in American Fiction* 19, no. 2 (fall 1991): 189–201; Andrew Levy, "Telling *Beloved," Texas Studies in Literature and Language* 33, no. 1 (spring 1991): 114–123; Lorraine Liscio, *"Beloved's* Narrative: Writing in Mother's Milk," *Tulsa Studies in Women's Literature* 11, no. 1 (spring 1992): 31–46; Philip Page, "Circularity in Toni Morrison's *Beloved," African American Review* 26,

no. 1 (spring 1992): 31–40; Barbara Hill Rigby, "'A Story to Pass On': Ghosts and the Significance of History in Toni Morrison's *Beloved*," in *Haunting the House of Fiction*, ed. Lynette Carpenter and Wendy K. Kolmar (Knoxville: University of Tennessee Press, 1991), 229–235; Ashraf H. A. Rushdy, "Daughters Signifyin(g) History: The Example of Toni Morrison's *Beloved*," *American Literature* 64, no. 3 (September 1992): 567–597; Maggie Sale, "Call and Response as Critical Method: African American Oral Traditions and *Beloved*," *African American Review* 26, no. 1 (winter 1992): 41–50; Carol E. Schmudde, "The Haunting of 124," *African American Review* 26, no. 3 (fall 1992): 409–416; Deborah Ayer Sitter, "The Making of a Man: Dialogic Meaning in *Beloved*," *African American Review* 26, no. 1 (spring 1992): 17–30; Jacqueline Trace, "Dark Goddesses: Black Feminist Theology in Morrison's *Beloved*," *Obsidian II: Black Literature in Review* 6, no. 3 (winter 1991): 14–30; and Molly Abel Travis, "*Beloved* and *Middle Passage*: Race, Narrative and the Critic's Essentialism," *Narrative* 2, no. 3 (October 1994): 179–200.

2. See especially Jonathan Yardley's review of Toni Morrison's *Beloved*. Yardley comments: "These relationships are convincing enough as devices for thematic exposition, but rather less so as genuine human connections" (*Washington Post Book World*, 6 September 1987, 3). See also Margaret Atwood, "Haunted by Their Nightmares," *New York Times Book Review*, 13 September 1987; Connie Casey, "Pain Is the Stuff of Toni Morrison's Novels," *Chicago Tribune*, 27 October 1987; Stanley Crouch, "Aunt Medea," *New Republic*, 19 October 1987; Marsha Darling, "Ties that Bind," *Women's Review of Books* 5, no. 6 (March 1988): 4–5; Helen Dudar, "Toni Morrison: Finally Just a Writer," *Wall Street Journal*, 30 September 1987; Michiko Kakutani, review of *Beloved*, Toni Morrison, *New York Times*, 2 September 1987; Elizabeth Kastor, "Toni Morrison's *Beloved* Country," *Washington Post*, 5 October 1987; John Leonard, review of *Beloved*, by Toni Morrison, *Los Angeles Times*, 30 August 1987; Elizabeth Mehren, "A Haunting Death Inspires *Beloved*," *Los Angeles Times*, 14 October 1987; Mervyn Rothstein, "Toni Morrison, In Her New Novel, Defends Women," *New York Times*, 26 August 1987; Nicholas Shakespeare, review of *Beloved*, by Toni Morrison, *London Times*, 15 October 1987; and Judith Thurman, "A House Divided," *New Yorker*, 2 November 1987.

3. Marilyn Judith Atlas, "Toni Morrison's *Beloved* and the Reviewers," *Midwestern Miscellany* 18 (1990): 51.

4. Reviewing *Beloved*, Rosellen Brown proclaimed that Beloved's "astonishing presence is unlike that of any character in American fiction" (*Nation*, 18 October, 1987, 418).

5. For a more in-depth discussion of Carpentier's and Pietri's influence on the American novel, see Jose David Saldivar's *The Dialectic of Our America: Genealogy, Cultural Critique, and Literary History* (Durham: Duke University Press, 1991), 90–96.

6. Sally Keenan, "'Four Hundred Years of Silence,'" *Recasting the World*, 47.

7. Even in contemporary reviews of *Beloved*, the canon debate often influenced critics' reactions to the novel. John Leonard concludes his review of *Beloved* for

the *Los Angeles Times*: "*Beloved* belongs on the highest shelf of American literature, even if half a dozen canonized white boys have to be elbowed off" (12).

8. Toni Morrison, "Unspeakable Things Unspoken: The Afro-American Presence in American Literature," *Michigan Quarterly Review* 28, no. 1 (winter 1989): 3 (italics mine).

9. Morrison is less careful in her later publication, *Playing in the Dark*, to confine her examination of black influence on U.S. literatures to the nineteenth century. In *Playing* she tends to obscure the contribution of other peoples to a growing national literature.

10. I am thinking of the creation of whiteness studies, and the reexamination of nineteenth-century literature and its icons in the context of black agency. Eric Lott's *Love and Theft: Blackface Minstrelsy and the American Working Class* (New York: Oxford University Press, 1993) is representative of this kind of influence.

11. Michael Taussig, *Shamanism, Colonialism, and the Wild Man: A Study in Terror and Healing* (Chicago: University of Chicago Press, 1987), 4.

12. I have talked about the appropriation of American Indian cultural traditions in my earlier work. See "Humanity Is Not a Luxury: Some Thoughts on a Recent Passing," in *Tilting the Tower: Lesbians Teaching Queer Subjects*, ed. Linda Garber (New York: Routledge, 1994), 168–176.

13. Joseph Roach, *Cities of the Dead: Circum-Atlantic Performance* (New York: Columbia University Press, 1996), 52.

1 Death and the Nation's Subjects

1. Orlando Patterson, *Slavery and Social Death: A Comparative Study* (Cambridge: Harvard University Press, 1982), 5.

2. See also Joseph Roach's discussion of Patterson's work in *Cities of the Dead*, 112–113.

3. My argument is informed by Valerie Smith's reading in "Loopholes of Retreat: Architecture and Ideology in Harriet Jacobs's *Incidents in the Life of a Slave Girl*," in *Reading Black, Reading Feminist: A Critical Anthology*, ed. Henry Louis Gates Jr. (New York: Meridian, 1990), 212–226. It can also be argued that Jacobs's "loophole" represents the converse for Dr. Sands (the father of her children), who must exist under the shadow of the Fugitive Slave Law as well. For a more extensive discussion of white male subjectivity during slavery, see Joel Williamson, *William Faulkner and Southern History* (New York: Oxford University Press, 1993), 22–29. See also Joel Williamson's *The Crucible of Race: Black/White Relations in the American South since Emancipation* (New York: Oxford University Press, 1984).

4. For a discussion of the use of the term *black* in the United States, see F. James Davis, *Who Is Black? One Nation's Definition* (University Park: Pennsylvania State University Press, 1991). For a discussion of racial categorization in the colonial

period of the Americas see Jack D. Forbes, *Africans and Native Americans: The Language of Race and the Evolution of Red-Black Peoples*, 2d ed. (Urbana: University of Illinois Press, 1993).

5. bell hooks, *Black Looks: Race and Representation* (Boston: South End Press, 1992), 168.

6. By focusing on slavery I do not mean to imply that it is responsible for all contemporary racial inequalities. Social historians like George Lipsitz have always maintained that other structures of inequity have contributed to America's racial problem. For Lipsitz "contemporary racism is not just a residual consequence of slavery and *de jure* segregation but rather something that has been created anew in our own time by many factors including the putatively race-neutral liberal social democratic reforms of the past five decades" ("The Possessive Investment in Whiteness: Racialized Social Democracy and the 'White' Problem in American Studies," *American Quarterly* 47, no. 3 [1995]: 371–372).

7. Jane P. Thompkins examines the importance of Eva's death in *Uncle Tom's Cabin*, offering a reading of death that parallels my contemporary study: "In the system of belief that undergirds Stowe's enterprise, dying is the supreme form of heroism. In *Uncle Tom's Cabin*, death is the equivalent not of defeat but of victory; it brings an access of power, not a loss of it; it is not only the crowning achievement of life, it *is* life, and Stowe's entire presentation of little Eva is designed to dramatize this fact" ("Sentimental Power: *Uncle Tom's Cabin* and the Politics of Literary History," in *The New Feminist Criticism: Essays on Women, Literature, and Theory*, ed. Elaine Showalter [New York: Pantheon, 1985], 85).

8. The building blocks of existentialism are set forth in Jean-Paul Sartre, *Being and Nothingness: A Phenomenological Essay on Ontology*, trans. Hazel E. Barnes (New York: Washington Square Press, 1956), and are utilized throughout Simone de Beauvoir, *The Second Sex*, trans. and ed. H. M. Parshley (1952; reprint, New York: Vintage, 1974).

9. Toni Morrison introduced the second part of this riddle during a PBS interview with Bill Moyers; the first part was divulged by David Roediger in his paper "Studying Whiteness: An African-American Tradition," presented at the Making and Unmaking of Whiteness conference at the University of California at Berkeley, April 11–13, 1997.

10. Orlando Patterson notes Theda Perdue's *Slavery and the Evolution of Cherokee Society, 1540–1866* (Knoxville: University of Tennessee Press, 1979). For further study of slavery and the Cherokee nation see R. Halliburton Jr., *Red Over Black: Black Slavery among the Cherokee Indians* (Westport, Conn.: Greenwood Press, 1977).

11. Roach also maintains that "circum-Atlantic societies . . . could not perform themselves, however, unless they also performed what and who they thought they were not" (5). See also pp. 31 and 78.

12. For a discussion of the relationship of experience to categories like "evidence" and "history," see Joan W. Scott, "Experience," in *Feminists Theorize the Po-*

litical, ed. Judith Butler and Joan W. Scott (New York: Routledge, 1992), 22–40; I am grateful to my colleague Paula Moya for calling my attention to this essay.

13. Josette Feral, "The Powers of Difference," in *The Future of Difference*, ed. Hester Eisenstein and Alice Jardine (New Brunswick: Rutgers University Press, 1985), 91.

14. Toni Morrison, *The Bluest Eye* (New York: Washington Square Press, 1970), 18.

15. Public Enemy, *It Takes a Nation of Millions to Hold Us Back*. Def Jam Recordings, Columbia Records, 1988.

16. *Menace II Society*, dir. Allen and Albert Hughes, 104 min., New Line Cinema, 1993, videocassette.

17. I am loosely interpreting Sartre's idea of "bad faith." My usage here is influenced by the following explanation: "The basic concept which is thus engendered utilizes the double property of the human being, who is at once a *facticity* and a *transcendence*. These two aspects of human reality are and ought to be capable of a valid coordination. But bad faith does not wish either to coordinate them or to surmount them in a synthesis. Bad faith seeks to affirm their identity while preserving their differences. It must affirm facticity as *being* transcendence and transcendence as *being* facticity, in such a way that at the instant when a person apprehends the one, he can find himself abruptly faced with the other" (Sartre, *Being and Nothingness*, 98).

18. I am not the first critic to observe this beginning in Anderson's text. Michael Taussig offers this, albeit cryptic, interpretation of Anderson's paradigm: "Like the Nation-State, the fetish has a deep investment in death—the death of the consciousness of the signifying function. Death endows both the fetish and the Nation-State with life, a spectral life, to be sure. The fetish absorbs into itself that which it represents, erasing all traces of the represented. A clean job. In Karl Marx's formulation of the fetishism of commodities, it is clear that the powerful phantasmagoric character of the commodity as fetish depends on the fact that the socioeconomic relations of production and distribution are erased from awareness, imploded into the made-object to become its phantom life-force. . . . In like fashion the State solemnly worships the tomb of the unknown soldier and (many) young men are as Benedict Anderson reminds us, prepared not only to go to war and kill their nation's enemies, but are ready to die themselves. With this erasure we are absorbed into the objects' emptiness" (*The Nervous System* [New York: Routledge, 1992], 138–139).

19. Benedict Anderson, *Imagined Communities* (London: Verso, 1991), 9.

20. In his later remarks about the beauty of Suwardi's language, Anderson notes that "by the imaginary transformation of himself into a temporary Dutchman (which invited a reciprocal transformation of his Dutch readers into temporary Indonesians), he undermined all the racist *fatalities* that underlay Dutch colonial ideology" (117–118). Here death has been largely abandoned by Anderson for a return to a discussion of "fatalities" disembodied from any real

conception of death as a lived experience. Death is commodified—as is capital, as is technology; death is another entity in the service of a larger structure.

21. I realize that I am climbing out on a limb here. However, I am constantly reminded of characters in Leslie Marmon Silko's *Ceremony* and Toni Morrison's *Sula* who join the armed forces not only out of economic necessity but also from the desire to seek honor and citizenship in a world where there is little tangible evidence of either. Moreover the Lakota phrase "Today is a good day to die" and the myth of slaves at Ibo Landing in South Carolina demonstrate the profound belief among Native and African American peoples that "if you surrendered to the air, you could *ride* it" (Toni Morrison, *Song of Solomon* [New York: Knopf, 1977], 337).

22. Henry Louis Gates Jr., "Niggaz with Latitude," *New Yorker*, 21 March 1994, 147 (italics mine). For related articles on *Menace* and representing blackness, see Ed Guerrero, "Framing Blackness: The African-American Image in the Cinema of the Nineties," *Cineaste* 20, no. 2 (1993): 24–31; Herman Grey, "Black Masculinity and Visual Culture," *Callaloo* 18, no. 2 (1995): 401–405; and Grant Farred, "*Menace II Society*: No Way Out for the Boys in the Hood," *Michigan Quarterly Review* 35, no. 3 (1996): 475–492.

23. Paul Rabinow, ed., *The Foucault Reader* (New York: Pantheon, 1984), 260.

24. Michel Foucault, *The Birth of the Clinic: An Archaeology of Medical Perception*, trans. A. M. Sheridan Smith (New York: Vintage, 1973), 146.

25. Simon During, *Foucault and Literature: Towards a Genealogy of Writing* (New York: Routledge, 1992), 49.

26. In an essay, "Right of Death and Power over Life," Foucault writes: "That death is so carefully evaded is linked less to a new anxiety which makes death unbearable for our societies than to the fact that the procedures of power have not ceased to turn away from death" (Rabinow, *Foucault Reader*, 261).

27. Caroline Ramazanoglu, ed., *Up against Foucault: Explorations of Some Tensions between Foucault and Feminism* (New York: Routledge, 1993), 108.

28. See Sander Gilman's discussion of Saartjie Baartman (known as the Venus Hottentot), "Black Bodies, White Bodies: Toward an Iconography of Female Sexuality in Late Nineteenth-Century Art, Medicine, and Literature," in *"Race," Writing, and Difference*, ed. Henry Louis Gates Jr. (Chicago: University of Chicago Press, 1985), 223–261.

29. Philippe Ariès, *Western Attitudes toward DEATH: From the Middle Ages to the Present*, trans. Patricia M. Ranum (Baltimore: Johns Hopkins University Press, 1974), 13.

30. Foucault, *Birth of the Clinic*, 109.

31. Michael Perry, "The *Ars Moriendi* and Breaking the Conspiracy of Silence," in *Perspectives on Death and Dying: Cross-Cultural and Multi-Disciplinary Views*, ed. Arthur Berger et al. (Philadelphia: Charles Press, 1989), 225.

32. For an excellent elaboration on the evolution of this complicated debate, see James Grantham Turner, ONE FLESH: *Paradisal Marriage and Sexual Relations in the Age of Milton* (Oxford: Clarendon, 1987). See also Steven Marcus, *The Other Victo-*

rians: A Study of Sexuality and Pornography in Mid-Nineteenth-Century England (New York: Norton, 1964).

33. Michel Foucault, *The History of Sexuality. Volume 1: An Introduction*, trans. Robert Hurley (New York: Vintage, 1980), 156.

34. This is a perspective that I will return to in chapters 3 and 4 during my discussion of Silko's *Almanac of the Dead* and Randall Kenan's *A Visitation of Spirits*, respectively. Both Silko and Kenan tend to reaffirm this brief liaison between death and sex and create a landscape where sexual practice and freedom mingle with death and ghostly presence. Foucault even articulates such a tacit connection: "Broadly speaking, at the juncture of the 'body' and the 'population,' sex became a crucial target of a power organized around the management of life rather than the menace of death" (Rabinow, *Foucault Reader*, 268).

35. Loring M. Danforth, *The Death Rituals of Rural Greece* (Princeton: Princeton University Press, 1982), 31.

36. Sogyal Rinpoche, *The Tibetan Book of Living and Dying* (San Francisco: Harper and Row, 1993), 11.

37. See Karla F. C. Holloway, *The Character of the Word: The Texts of Zora Neale Hurston* (New York: Greenwood Press, 1987), for a discussion of the importance of "nommo" as a West African retention in the literary endeavors of African Americans.

38. In 1997 the remains of the "unknown soldier" buried at Arlington National Cemetery were determined by DNA tests to be those of Air Force 1st Lt. Michael Blassie, whose plane went down in South Vietnam in 1972. He is now buried at Jefferson Barracks National Cemetery.

39. In Zora Neale Hurston's *Their Eyes Were Watching God*, black workers are told to separate black and white bodies for burial after the hurricane on the muck. But the visage of death prevents the working men from being able to distinguish white from black. See also my piece, "Who's God am 'I, god'?: A Reading of Zora Neale Hurston's *Their Eyes Were Watching God*," in *All About Zora: Proceedings of the Academic Conference of the First Annual Zora Neale Hurston Festival of the Arts* (Winter Park, Fla.: Four-G Publishers, 1991), 3–15.

40. This observation finds particular support in Harriet Beecher Stowe's *Uncle Tom's Cabin* and Harriet Wilson's *Our Nig: Or, Sketches from the Life of a Free Black*. Both authors present white characters who are confronted with a mirror of themselves in their mulatto counterparts. For more detailed critiques of African American women's writing in the nineteenth century, see Claudia Tate, *Domestic Allegories of Political Desire: The Black Heroine's Text at the Turn of the Century* (New York: Oxford University Press, 1992); and for treatment across periods, see Ann duCille, *The Coupling Convention: Sex, Text, and Tradition in Black Women's Fiction* (New York: Oxford University Press, 1993).

41. Peter Singer, *Rethinking Life and Death: The Collapse of Our Traditional Ethics* (New York: St. Martin's, 1994), 51.

42. The Harvard Committee published its report in the *Journal of the American Medical Association* in August of 1968, stating as their mission "to define irrevers-

ible comas as a new criterion for death" (Singer, *Life and Death* 25). Singer's book provides a detailed discussion of the impact of the committee's findings on modern medical practice.

43. Even in 1997, in a *New York Times* article about dying, doctors debated about societal and medical notions of "what constitutes a good death and how it can be achieved" (Sheryl Gay Stolberg, "The Good Death: Embracing a Right to Die Well," *New York Times*, 29 June 1997, sec. 4, p. 2). The pages of the *Times* were covered with stories about death because of the impending Supreme Court decision in mid-June of 1997 about physician-assisted suicide and the Constitutional right to die. As usual, the Court decided *not* to decide by rejecting claims that physician-assisted suicide is a crime while simultaneously rejecting the belief that the Constitution protects an "abstract right to die" (See Jeffrey Rose, "Nine Votes for Judicial Restraint," *New York Times*, Op-ed, 29 June 1997; and Gina Kolata, "Beyond Science: When Death Begins," *New York Times*, 20 April 1997, sec. 4, p. 1.

2 Bakulu Discourse:
Bodies Made "Flesh" in Toni Morrison's *Beloved*

1. See Houston Baker, *Modernism and the Harlem Renaissance* (Chicago: University of Chicago Press, 1987); Cheryl A. Wall, *Women of the Harlem Renaissance* (Bloomington: Indiana University Press, 1995); and Deborah G. Plant, *Every Tub Must Sit on Its Own Bottom: The Philosophy and Politics of Zora Neale Hurston* (Urbana: University of Illinois Press, 1995).

2. See Gloria T. Hull, Patricia Bell Scott, and Barbara Smith, eds., *All the Women Are White, All the Blacks Are Men, but Some of Us Are Brave: Black Women's Studies* (Old Westbury, N.Y.: Feminist Press, 1982); Barbara Smith, ed., *Home Girls: A Black Feminist Anthology* (New York: Kitchen Table Press, 1983); Audre Lorde, *Sister Outsider: Essays and Speeches* (Trumansburg, N.Y.: Crossing Press, 1984); Barbara Christian, *Black Feminist Criticism: Perspectives on Black Women Writers* (New York: Pergamon Press, 1985); Marjorie Pryse and Hortense J. Spillers, eds., *Conjuring: Black Women, Fiction, and Literary Tradition* (Bloomington: Indiana University Press, 1985); Joanne M. Braxton and Andrée Nicola McLaughlin, eds., *Wild Women in the Whirlwind: Afro-American Culture and the Contemporary Literary Renaissance* (New Brunswick: Rutgers University Press, 1990); and Beverly Guy-Sheftall, ed., *Words of Fire: An Anthology of African-American Feminist Thought* (New York: New Press, 1995). For specific emphasis on the academy, see Patricia Hill Collins, "Learning from the Outsider Within: The Sociological Significance of Black Feminist Thought," and Joyce A. Joyce, "Black Woman Scholar, Critic, and Teacher: The Inextricable Relationship among Race, Sex, and Class," in *(En)-Gendering Knowledge: Feminists in Academe*, ed. Joan E. Hartman and Ellen Messer-Davidow (Knoxville: University of Tennessee Press, 1991), 40–65, 159–178;

Daphne Patai, "U.S. Academics and Third-World Women: Is Ethical Research Possible?" in *Feminist Nightmares: Women at Odds*, ed. Susan Ostrov Weisser and Jennifer Fleischner (New York: New York University Press, 1994), 21–43.

3. Ann duCille, "The Occult of True Black Womanhood: Critical Demeanor and Black Feminist Studies," *Signs* 19, no. 3 (spring 1994): 623. For a similar reading of black women in a literary context, see Barbara Christian, "Being the Subject and the Object: Reading African-American Women's Novels," in *Changing Subjects: The Making of Feminist Literary Criticism*, ed. Gayle Greene and Coppélia Kahn (London: Routledge, 1993).

4. Hortense J. Spillers, "Interstices: A Small Drama of Words," in *Pleasure and Danger: Exploring Female Sexuality*, ed. Carole S. Vance (Boston: Routledge and Kegan Paul, 1984), 76 (italics mine).

5. Houston A. Baker Jr., *Workings of the Spirit: The Poetics of Afro-American Women's Writing* (Chicago: University of Chicago Press, 1991), 38.

6. Here blackness writes itself over and against whiteness. But Baker forgets about the presence of indigenous peoples, a presence that surely transforms this "blank"/white space into a much more complex terrain.

7. See the debates in Vance's *Pleasure and Danger*, in particular Gayle Rubin's article, "Thinking Sex: Notes for a Radical Theory of the Politics of Sexuality" (267–319).

8. The exchange between Nancy K. Miller and Peggy Kamuf in the pages of *Diacritics* is an example of this dramatic shift in feminist criticism. Nancy K. Miller, "The Text's Heroine: A Feminist Critic and Her Fictions," and Peggy Kamuf "Replacing Feminist Criticism," *Diacritics* 12, no. 2 (summer 1982): 48–53, 42–47. See also Linda Alcoff, "Cultural Feminism Versus Post-Structuralism: The Identity Crisis in Feminist Theory," *Signs* 13, no. 3 (spring 1988): 405–436. The debates about the direction of feminist scholarship raged into the 1990s: see Alice Parker and Elizabeth Meese, "Critical Negotiations: Calling Feminism Out of Its Name," in *Feminist Critical Negotiations*, ed. Alice A. Parker and Elizabeth A. Meese (Amsterdam/Philadelphia: John Benjamins, 1992).

9. Spillers, "Mama's Baby, Papa's Maybe," 67. Angela Davis also calls for a more accurate evaluation of "the historical matrix of [the black woman's] oppression" (140); "Reflections on the Black Woman's Role in the Community of Slaves" in *Contemporary Black Thought: The Best from* The Black Scholar, ed. Robert Chrisman and Nathan Hare (Indianapolis: Bobbs-Merrill, 1973).

10. See Gilman's "Black Bodies/White Bodies" for an in-depth discussion of the Venus Hottentot and the atomization of black female bodies and their "use" in determining standards of female sexuality.

11. In her examination of *Beloved*, Lorraine Liscio observes that "In *Beloved*, the agent unseating the father's law, white language, is above all the black mother-infant daughter bond, a doubly invisible participant in white patriarchal history" ("*Beloved*'s Narrative: Writing Mother's Milk," *Tulsa Studies in Women's Literature* 11, no. 1 [spring 1992]: 39).

12. See Emily Burdick's discussion of desire and Paul D, "Absence, Loss, and the Space of History in Toni Morrison's *Beloved*," *Arizona Quarterly* 48, no. 2 (summer 1992): 117–138.

13. This ghosting of Patterson is present in Spillers's explication of Harriet Jacobs's *Incidents in the Life of a Slave Girl*. Using the scene between Mrs. Flint and "Linda" as "a classic instance of sexual 'jealousy' and appropriation," Spillers surmises that "we cannot unravel one female's narrative from the other, cannot decipher one without tripping over the other. In that sense, these 'threads cablestrong' of an incestuous, interracial genealogy uncover slavery in the United States as one of the richest displays of the psychoanalytic dimensions of culture before the science of European psychoanalysis takes hold" ("Mama's Baby, Papa's Maybe," 77). Patterson's theory of genealogical isolation meshes with Spillers's conceptualization of imbricated genealogies and the cultural imaginary.

14. Toni Morrison, *Beloved* (New York: Knopf, 1987), 273.

15. Morrison, "Unspeakable Things Unspoken," 32.

16. Deborah Horvitz, "Nameless Ghosts: Possession and Dispossession in *Beloved*," *Studies in American Fiction* 17, no. 2 (fall 1989): 157.

17. See William Wordsworth, "Lucy Gray," *William Wordsworth*, The Oxford Authors, ed. Stephen Gill (Oxford: Oxford University Press, 1984), 149–150.

18. Marsha Jean Darling, "Ties That Bind," *Vital Signs* [Newsletter of the National Black Women's Health Project] (1988), 13.

19. In "Feminist Fiction and the Uses of Memory," Gayle Greene writes: "Morrison shows that even a past as horrific as this is not fixed but is open to revision by 'rememory'" (315). *Signs* 16, no. 2 (winter 1991): 290–321.

20. Karla F. C. Holloway, "*Beloved*: A Spiritual," *Callaloo* 13, no. 3 (summer 1990): 517.

21. Barbara Christian asserts that "central to African ritual is the concept that the body and spirit are one. Thus sensuality is essential to the process of healing and rebirth of the spirit" (*Black Feminist Criticism*, 156).

22. John Michael Vlach, *The Afro-American Tradition in Decorative Arts* (Cleveland: Cleveland Museum of Art, 1978), 143.

23. Migene González-Wippler, *Santería: The Religion* (New York: Harmony, 1989), 59–60.

24. Diedre L. Bádéjò, "The Goddess Ósun as a Paradigm for African Feminist Criticism," *Sage* 6, no. 1 (summer 1989): 27. Spelling variations for the names of the orishas are quite common.

25. Luisah Teish, *Jambalaya: The Natural Woman's Book of Personal Charms and Practical Rituals* (San Francisco: Harper and Row, 1985), 121. Oshun is also called "Erzulie," as in Ishmael Reed's *Mumbo Jumbo*. However, Reed's depiction of the orisha is more stereotypical. He envisions an Erzulie who is chiefly a prostitute, without paying much attention to her other attributes.

26. Terry Otten, *The Crime of Innocence in the Fiction of Toni Morrison* (Columbia: University of Missouri Press, 1989), 89.

27. For a detailed account of the Margaret Garner story, see Cynthia G. Wolff, "'Margaret Garner': A Cincinnati Story," in *Discovering Difference: Contemporary Essays in American Culture*, ed. Christoph K. Lohmann (Bloomington: Indiana University Press, 1993): 105–122; see also Gloria Naylor, "A Conversation: Gloria Naylor and Toni Morrison," *Southern Review* 21, no. 3 (summer 1985): 567–593.

28. Wilfred D. Samuels and Clenora Hudson-Weems, *Toni Morrison* (Boston: Twayne, 1990), 117.

29. Unlike many enslaved subjects writing themselves, Beloved chooses to say "I am," rather than "I was born." Her statement belies her divine nature, and the "nonissue" of her "being" (human) that Holloway articulates could stem from her connection to a pantheon of orishas rather than to a legion of human beings.

30. Holloway, "*Beloved*," 520. See also Mae G. Henderson, "Toni Morrison's *Beloved*: Re-membering the Body as Historical Text," in *Comparative American Identities: Race, Sex, and Nationality in the Modern Text*, ed. Hortense J. Spillers (New York: Routledge, 1991), 62–86.

31. Harriet Ngubane, *Body and Mind in Zulu Medicine: An Ethnography of Health and Disease in Nyuswa-Zulu Thought and Practice* (London: Academic Press, 1977): 77.

32. Morrison's character Ella is particularly outraged by the events at 124: "Ella didn't like the idea of past errors taking possession of the present. . . . As long as the ghost showed out from its ghostly place—shaking stuff, crying, smashing and such—Ella respected it. But if it took flesh and came into her world, well, the shoe was on the other foot. She didn't mind a little communication between the two worlds, but this was an invasion" (256–257).

33. Morrison, "Unspeakable Things Unspoken," 33 (italics mine).

34. Robert Ferris Thompson, *Flash of the Spirit* (New York: Vintage, 1983), 142.

35. See also Sandra Drake's wonderful study of Jean Rhys's *Wide Sargasso Sea*. Drake writes, "The African attitude, characteristically, is that the living and the dead may almost be said to form one community. The spirit-world of the ancestors continues to function as part of the living community" (106–107). "All that foolishness/That All Foolishness: Race and Caribbean Culture as Thematics of Liberation in Jean Rhys's *Wide Sargasso Sea*," *Critica* 2, no. 2 (fall 1990): 97–112.

3 Telling the Story of Genocide
in Leslie Marmon Silko's *Almanac of the Dead*

1. See the following reviews: John Skow, review of *Almanac of the Dead*, by Leslie Marmon Silko, *Time*, 9 December 1991, 86; Malcolm Jones Jr., "Reports from the Heartland," review of *Almanac of the Dead*, by Leslie Marmon Silko, *Newsweek*, 18 November 1991, 84; Sven Birkerts, review of *Almanac of the Dead*, by Leslie Marmon Silko, *New Republic*, 4 November 1991, 39–41; Review of *Almanac of the Dead*,

by Leslie Marmon Silko, *Publisher's Weekly,* 6 September 1991, 94; and Review of *Almanac of the Dead,* by Leslie Marmon Silko, *Kirkus Reviews,* 15 August 1991.

2. David Roediger, *Towards the Abolition of Whiteness* (New York: Verso, 1994), 12.

3. See note 9, chapter 1.

4. Michael Taussig, *Shamanism, Colonialism, and the Wild Man: A Study in Terror and Healing,* 5.

5. Bernard McElroy, *Fiction of the Modern Grotesque* (London: Macmillan, 1989), 1.

6. See Janet St. Clair, "Death of Love/Love of Death: Leslie Marmon Silko's *Almanac of the Dead,*" *Melus* 21, no. 2 (summer 1996): 141–156. St. Clair's argument rests on the theory that Silko's project in *Almanac* mirrors that of *Ceremony,* where white egoism and individualism are exposed as corrupt and inherently misogynistic.

7. Critiquing Native American trickster figures, Kenneth Lincoln proposes, "To progress simultaneously on different planes of thought is to do two things at once, bridging incongruities, combining opposites. This doubling perspective runs basic to comic paradigms the world over, and Tricksters from Africa to the arctic act out the primordial tenets of comedy: the ritual scapegoating and slaying of reality's fool, his springing back from death, his integrating liminally into the tribe as sacred buffoon" (*Native American Renaissance,* 129).

8. Lincoln, *Native American Renaissance,* 24–25.

9. Hertha D. Wong, *Sending My Heart Back across the Years: Tradition and Innovation in Native American Autobiography* (New York: Oxford University Press, 1992), 19; see also Gloria Bird, "Towards a Decolonization of the Mind and Text 1: Leslie Marmon Silko's *Ceremony,*" *Wicazo Sa Review* 9, no. 2 (fall 1993): 1–8.

10. Herbert Hirsch, *Genocide and the Politics of Memory: Studying Death to Preserve Life* (Chapel Hill: University of North Carolina Press, 1995), 32. Hirsch focuses his account on European events rather than events in the Americas. In his work memory seems able to speak in only a foreign tongue; therefore, little attention is paid to genocide at home.

11. Leslie Marmon Silko, *Storyteller* (New York: Little, Brown and Company 1981), 227.

12. Leslie Marmon Silko, *Almanac of the Dead* (New York: Simon and Schuster, 1991), 574.

13. Leslie Marmon Silko, interview by Kim Barnes, *Journal of Ethnic Studies* 13, no. 4 (winter 1986): 104. See also Joy Harjo, review of *Almanac of the Dead,* by Leslie Marmon Silko, *Blue Mesa Review,* no. 4 (spring 1992): 207–210. Harjo writes: "One could calculate history by observing the shift and return of days as they shuffled through an eternal circle. It's as if the days were ancestors of themselves, much as humans. They are born and return in circular time. Each day embodies a story. In this manner her new novel is an almanac. This is a groundbreaking concept for the American novel but when one considers the novel as an American form, it makes all the sense in the world" (209).

14. Paula Gunn Allen, "Special Problems in Teaching Leslie Marmon Silko's *Ceremony,*" *American Indian Quarterly* 14, no. 4 (1990): 384.

15. My colleague Robert Allen Warrior has also suggested to me that this lack of "milk" might be Silko's humorous attempt at demonstrating the people's severe lactose intolerance.

16. I was introduced to Taussig's work by a graduate student, Victoria Bomberry, in a paper she submitted to my graduate seminar at Stanford University on "Death and the Grotesque in Native and African American Literature." Bomberry's work on Silko is part of a larger dissertation project.

17. Lincoln, *Native American Renaissance*, 203.

18. Richard Luxton with Pablo Balam, *Mayan Dream Walk: Literate Shamanism in the Yucatan* (London: Rider, 1981), 226.

19. Munro S. Edmonson, trans., *The Ancient Future of the Itza: The Book of Chilam Balam of Tiziman* (Austin: University of Texas Press, 1982), 26 n.

20. Paula Gunn Allen, *The Sacred Hoop: Recovering the Feminine in American Indian Traditions* (Boston: Beacon, 1986), 20.

21. Ralph L. Roys, *The Book of Chilam Balam of Chumayel* (Norman, Okla.: University of Oklahoma Press, 1967), 83.

22. Larry Evers and Felipe S. Molina, eds. *Yaqui Deer Songs/Maso Bwikam: A Native American Poetry* (Tucson: University of Arizona Press, 1987). It is possible that this text influenced some of Silko's understandings of the Yaqui, as she was on the editorial committee for the Sun Tracks's American Indian Series.

23. Evers and Molina, *Deer Songs*, 8. See also Evelyn Hu-DeHart, *Missionaries, Miners, and Indians: Spanish Contact with the Yaqui Nation of Northwestern New Spain, 1533–1820* (Tucson: University of Arizona Press, 1981); and Edward H. Spicer, *The Yaquis: A Cultural History* (Tucson: University of Arizona Press, 1980).

24. Here Silko also takes part in reformulating the myth of Malenche, who produced the mestizo and doomed her race to constant occupation.

25. Richard Luxton describes the Mayan shaman as someone who "is able to retrieve lost souls, and read peoples' thoughts. He/she has the powers of clairvoyance and telepathy; he/she can see the future, as well, they can enter through the paradoxical gateway to the spirit world where past and future are one and the same" (31).

26. Allen, *Sacred Hoop*, 57.

27. In *Storyteller* Silko repeats a Laguna narrative about how witchery brought about the coming of the "alien invaders" (130, 132–137).

28. Luxton, *Dream Walk*, 137.

29. For further elucidation of the homosocial paradigm, see Eve Sedgwick, *Between Men: English Literature and Male Homosocial Desire* (New York: Columbia University Press, 1985).

30. Mikhail Bakhtin, *Rabelais and His World*, trans. Helen Iswolsky (Bloomington: Indiana University Press, 1984), 317.

31. Lincoln, *Native American Renaissance*, 123.

32. Janet St. Clair, "Death of Love / Love of Death: Leslie Marmon Silko's *Almanac of the Dead*," *MELUS* 21, no. 2 (summer 1996): 214.

33. Bakhtin, *Rabelais*, 336.

34. Paco Ignacio Taibo, "¡Zapatista! The Phoeniz Rises," *Nation*, 28 March 1994, 410.

4 (Pro)Creating Imaginative Spaces and Other Queer Acts: Randall Kenan's *A Visitation of Spirits* and Its Revival of James Baldwin's Absent Black Gay Man in *Giovanni's Room*

1. See Michael S. Sherry, "The Language of War in AIDS Discourse," in *Writing AIDS: Gay Literature, Language, and Analysis*, ed. Timothy F. Murphy and Suzanne Poirier (New York: Columbia University Press, 1993), 39–53.

2. Robert Bone, *The Negro Novel in America* (New Haven: Yale University Press, 1965), 226 (italics mine). I want to give thanks and credit to my colleague and friend Ann duCille, who brought *Giovanni's Room* to my attention and who opened her classroom to me so that I could participate in a discussion about this wonderful book. Many of the ideas here were inspired by that discussion.

3. James Oliver Horton, "In Search of Identity: James Baldwin and the Black American Intellectual Tradition," in *James Baldwin: His Place in American Literary History and His Reception in Europe*, ed. Jakob Köllhofer (Frankfurt am Main, Germany: Peter Lang, 1991), 98 (italics mine).

4. Houston A. Baker Jr., *Long Black Song: Essays in Black American Literature and Culture* (Charlottesville: University Press of Virginia, 1972), 108.

5. For a broader theoretical discussion of value, see Lindon Barrett's *Blackness and Value: Seeing Double* (New York: Cambridge University Press, 1999).

6. David Bergman, "The African and the Pagan in Gay Black Literature," in *Sexual Sameness: Textual Differences in Lesbian and Gay Writing*," ed. Joseph Bristow (New York: Routledge, 1992), 159.

7. Cheryl Clarke, "Living the Texts Out: Lesbians and the Uses of Black Women's Traditions," in *Theorizing Black Feminisms: The Visionary Pragmatism of Black Women*, ed. Stanlie M. James and Abena P. A. Busia (New York: Routledge, 1993), 216.

8. Horace Porter, *Stealing the Fire: The Art and Protest of James Baldwin* (Middletown, Conn.: Wesleyan University Press, 1990), 133.

9. Ron Simmons, "Some Thoughts on the Challenges Facing Black Gay Intellectuals," in *Brother to Brother: New Writings by Black Gay Men*, ed. Essex Hemphill (Boston: Alyson, 1991), 222. For an excellent analysis of biblical references that explicitly prohibit same-sex relations, see Gary David Comstock, *Violence against Lesbians and Gay Men* (New York: Columbia University Press, 1991), 120–140.

10. Arthur Flannigan Saint-Aubin's "TESTERIA: The Dis-ease of Black Men in White Supremacist, Patriarchal Culture" gives a psychoanalytic reading of black

masculinity in American culture. His work provides an interesting (heterosexual) parallel to this argument. See *Callaloo* 17, no. 4 (fall 1994): 1054–1073.

11. Nero, "Toward a Black Gay Aesthetic: Signifying in Contemporary Black Gay Literature," in *Brother to Brother*, 235.

12. Nikki Giovanni, *Gemini: An Extended Autobiographical Statement on My First Twenty-Five Years of Being a Black Poet* (Indianapolis: Bobbs-Merrill, 1971), 41 (italics mine).

13. Simmons, in *Brother to Brother*, 211.

14. As quoted in Essex Hemphill, *Ceremonies: Prose and Poetry* (New York: Plume, 1992), 54.

15. For a discussion of exorcism and its relationship to the Black Pentecostal Church, see Nero in *Brother to Brother*, 238–243.

16. I am referring particularly to the distribution of the video "The Gay Agenda" (1992), produced by the Antelope Valley Springs of Life Ministries and distributed to black churches in an effort to spearhead an attack on gay and lesbian peoples from within the black community. For an examination of the video in the context of the military ban against gay men and lesbians, see Alycee J. Lane, "Black Bodies / Gay Bodies: The Politics of Race in the Gay / Military Battle," *Callaloo* 17, no. 4 (fall 1994): 1074–1088. The group also produced another video released in 1996, entitled "The Ultimate Target of the Gay Agenda: Same Sex Marriages."

17. Wole Soyinka, "Foreword: James Baldwin at the Welcome Table," in *James Baldwin: The Legacy*, ed. Quincy Troupe (New York: Simon and Schuster, 1989), 11–12.

18. In a 1984 interview with Richard Goldstein, Baldwin comments that "*Giovanni's Room* is not really about homosexuality. It's the vehicle through which the book moves. *Go Tell It on the Mountain*, for example, is not about a church and *Giovanni* is not really about homosexuality. It's about what happens to you if you're afraid to love anybody. Which is much more interesting than the question of homosexuality" ("'Go the Way Your Blood Beats': An Interview with James Baldwin," in *James Baldwin: The Legacy*, 176).

19. Robert McRuer, "A Visitation of Difference: Randall Kenan and Black Queer Theory," *Journal of Homosexuality* 26, nos. 2 and 3 (1993): 227–228.

20. James Baldwin, *Giovanni's Room* (New York: Dell, 1964), 9–10.

21. I do not mean to imply that Joey's brown body is the only one that racializes Baldwin's text. I am simply using this early encounter to illustrate the fear of blackness that pervades Baldwin's text.

22. Audre Lorde, *Sister Outsider* (Trumansburg, N.Y.: Crossing Press, 1984), 110–113.

23. During his youth Baldwin became a youth minister in the local Pentecostal Church.

24. Bergman, in *Sexual Sameness*, 158.

25. Simmons, in *Brother to Brother*, 224.

26. Judith Butler, "Against Proper Objects," *differences* 6, nos. 2 and 3 (summer–fall 1994): 8. See also the special issue, *Queer Theory,* in *differences* 3, no. 2 (summer 1991).

27. This is not the first time that Butler has sequestered her comments about the place of race or the work of women of color. In "Against Proper Objects" these theorists are constantly listed but never engaged. As well, in *Bodies That Matter: On the Discursive Limits of "Sex"* (New York: Routledge, 1993), Butler's discussion of Nella Larson's *Passing* includes the work of Deborah McDowell and others as a segue into her own discussion.

28. I am thinking here about the 1975 film *Mandingo*, which chronicled an aspect of slavery that all of us would rather forget. Nonetheless, the sexual life of white men and women in the film, fictional though it might be, still awaits appropriate attention from the critical community. Lodged in the psyche of all Americans is that memory of the "first" revolution. Butler's use of the tension between Foucault and psychoanalysis, and the role of kinship and sexuality, is ripe terrain for an examination of kinship systems under slavery—a move that Spillers makes in "Mama's Baby, Papa's Maybe." It is ironic that Butler refers to Hortense Spillers in passing, but when she interrogates systems of kinship and their relationship to sexuality, she finds no room to engage with Spillers's findings on the subject. This omission represents one of the most troubling missed opportunities in Butler's article.

29. In her examination of the Africanist presence in American literature, Morrison writes: "Looking at the scope of American literature, I can't help thinking that the question should never have been 'Why am I, an Afro-American, absent from it?' It is not a particularly interesting query anyway. The spectacularly interesting question is 'What intellectual feats had to be performed by the author or his critic to erase me from a society seething with my presence, and what effect has that performance had on the work?'" ("Unspeakable Things Unspoken," 11–12).

30. Spillers, "Mama's Baby, Papa's Maybe," 67.

31. McRuer, "A Visitation of Difference," 221–232.

5 "From This Moment Forth, We Are Black Lesbians":
Querying Feminism and Killing the Self in Consolidated's
Business of Punishment

1. In particular I am thinking about "oi" music, which extols the virtues of white nationalism and supremacy, as well as some forms of "gangsta rap," which has made such terms as *bitch, ho,* and *niggah* current among America's youth.

2. In this chapter I am concerned more with the politics of Consolidated's music than with the music itself. It can be said, however, that the band's musical form, which is itself a pastiche (industrial and '70s R&B), articulates the clash

and confluence of identities, cultures, and communities. I am grateful to my friend Carrie Perdue for introducing me to some of industrial music's alternative politics.

3. In a 1991 press release I. R. S. Records notes that Consolidated's "unconditional support for women's equality . . . set it far apart from those in all music genres who have long upheld an overwhelmingly sexist tradition in entertainment" (from *Consolidated 1991 Biography*).

4. Regenia Gagnier, *Subjectivities* (New York: Oxford University Press, 1988), 10.

5. Gagnier refers to subjects as social creatures who read themselves through identification or nonidentification with different structures. Her use of *embeddedness* refers not to a model of autonomous subjectivity but to a subjectivity negotiating various terrains, seeking to arrive at some agency in the midst of institutions and ideas.

6. I am also reminded here of Marjorie Garber's findings in "Spare Parts: The Surgical Construction of Gender." She notes that surgeons who perform transsexual operations share with their patients "the conviction that masculine identity, male subjectivity is determined and signified by the penis" (*differences* 1, no. 3 [fall 1989]: 142). No other figure in popular culture is proof of the static nature of "blackness" than Michael Jackson and his several attempts at "unracing" himself. For an excellent evaluation of critical approaches to Jackson's racial dilemma, see Michael Awkward, *Negotiating Difference: Race, Gender, and the Politics of Positionality* (Chicago: University of Chicago Press, 1995), 175–192.

7. Evelynn Hammonds, "Black (W)holes and the Geometry of Black Female Sexuality," *differences* 6, nos. 2 and 3 (summer–fall 1994): 131.

8. See Dick Hebdige, *Subculture: The Meaning of Style* (London: Routledge, 1988); and George Lipsitz, "Land of a Thousand Dances: Youth, Minorities, and the Rise of Rock and Roll," in *Recasting America: Culture and Politics in the Age of Cold War*, ed. Larry May (Chicago: University of Chicago Press, 1989).

9. I am thinking here of Toni Morrison's groundbreaking, *Playing in the Dark: Whiteness and the Literary Imagination* (Cambridge: Harvard University Press, 1992) and of David Roediger's *Towards the Abolition of Whiteness*.

10. George P. Cunningham, "Body Politics: Race, Gender, and the Captive Body," in *Representing Black Men*, ed. Marcellus Blount and George P. Cunningham (New York: Routledge, 1996), 135–136.

11. I drop the word *lesbian* momentarily because it is obvious from the popularity of works by lesbian feminists that lesbians are no longer the stepchildren of feminism but rather its most recent inheritors.

12. For readings on the Second Wave of feminism see Anne Koedt, Ellen Levine, and Anita Rapone, *Radical Feminism* (New York: Quadrangle Books, 1973); Judith Hole and Ellen Levine, *Rebirth of Feminism* (New York: Quadrangle, 1971); Redstockings, *Feminist Revolution* (New York: Random House, 1978); Leslie B. Tanner, *Voices from Women's Liberation* (New York: New American Library, 1971);

(Jo Freeman), *The Voice of the Women's Liberation Movement*, newsletter, March 1968–69; *Notes from the Second Year*, 1968; *Notes from the Third Year*, 1970; *Notes on Women's Liberation* (Detroit: News and Letters, 1970); Ti-Grace Atkinson, *Amazon Odyssey: The First Collection of Writings by the Political Pioneer of the Women's Movement* (New York: Links Books, 1974); Shulamith Firestone, *The Dialectic of Sex: The Case for Feminist Revolution* (New York: Morrow, 1970); and Kate Millett, *Sexual Politics* (New York: Simon and Schuster, 1969).

13. Lila Karp was an original member of The Feminists in New York. She is also the author of *The Queen Is in the Garbage* (New York: Vanguard Press, 1969). She was director of the Princeton University Women's Center when I was an undergraduate there, 1982–1987.

14. See Cellestine Ware, *Woman Power: The Movement for Women's Liberation* (New York: Tower, 1970); Florence Kennedy, *Born in Flames*, video recording, 1983; and Patricia Robinson, "A Historical and Critical Essay for Black Women of the Cities," *No More Fun and Games*, no. 3 (November 1969).

15. The publications of the Second Wave are legion. Many were either published in pamphlet form or by individuals and groups. Here are a few: *Free Space: A Perspective on the Small Group in Women's Liberation*, Pam Allen (January 1970); *The Hidden History of the Female: The Early Feminist Movement in the United States*, Martha Atkins; *Tooth and Nail*, Bay Area Women's Liberation, vol. 1, no. 4 (January 1970); *The Political Economy of Women's Liberation*, Margaret Benston (September 1969); *Amazon Expedition: A Lesbianfeminist Anthology*, Phyllis Birkby, Bertha Harris, Jill Johnston, Esther Newton, and Jane O'Wyatt (1973); *The Demands of Women's Liberation*, Boston Women United (9 October 1970); *No More Fun and Games*, Cell 16, vols. 1–4 (October 1968; November 1969; April 1970); *The Fight for Women's Freedom*, Clara Colon (March 1969); *Rape, Racism, and the White Women's Movement: An Answer to Susan Brownmiller*, Alison Edwards; *Socialism, Anarchism, and Feminism*, Carol Ehrlich (January 1977); *The Tyranny of Structurelessness*, Jo Freeman (1970) reprinted—British; *Which Way for the Women's Movement?* Cindy Jaquith and Willie Mae Reid (April 1977); *The Lesbian Tide*, Tide Collective, vol. 1, no. 9 (April 1972); *Liberation of Women: Sexual Repression and the Family*, Laurel Limpus; *Working Women and Their Organizations: 150 Years of Struggle*, Joyce Maupin (1974); *Women: The Longest Revolution*, Juliet Mitchell (reprinted from *New Left Review*, November–December 1966); *How Harvard Rules Women*, New University Conference (1970); *Notes from the Third Year: Women's Liberation* (June 1970); *Abortion and the Catholic Church: Two Feminists Defend Women's Rights*, Evelyn Reed and Claire Moriarty (March 1973); *Women's Liberation and the New Politics*, Sheila Rowbotham, Women's, no. 17 (October 1971—British); *Sex and the State; or, Let's Kill Ozzie and Harriet: A Lesbian Perspective*, Shim and Cedar (paper delivered April 1976); *Sisterhood Is Powerful*, Betsey Stone (March 1972); *Woman and Her Mind: The Story of Daily Life*, Meredith Tax (Bread and Roses 1970); *The Politics of Women's Liberation Today*, Mary-Alice Waters (June 1970); The Woman's Center Northampton, Massachusetts, *Woman's Journal*, vol. 1, no. 3 (December 1971); and *Dick and*

Jane as Victims: Sex Stereotyping in Children's Readers, Women on Words and Images (1975, expanded edition). All of the above pamphlets are from my private collection.

16. For a critique of Second Wave feminism, see Alice Echols, *Daring to Be Bad: Radical Feminism in America 1967–1975* (Minnesota: University of Minnesota Press, 1989).

17. For a discussion of women in the midst of the new left movement see Jane Alpert, *Growing Up Underground* (New York: Morrow, 1981); Paul Jacobs and Saul Landau, *The New Radicals: A Report with Documents* (New York: Random House, 1966); and Sara Evans, *Personal Politics: The Roots of Women's Liberation in the Civil Rights Movement and the New Left* (New York: Knopf, 1979).

18. Jane Alpert, "Mother Right: A New Feminist Theory," *Ms.*, August 1973, 91.

19. Barbara Burris, "The Fourth World Manifesto," *Notes from the Third Year: Women's Liberation*, June 1970, 118.

20. Jill Johnston, *Lesbian Nation: The Feminist Solution* (New York: Simon and Schuster, 1973), 174.

21. Gina Covina and Laurel Galana, *The Lesbian Reader: An Amazon Quarterly Anthology* (Oakland, Calif.: Amazon Press, 1975), 105.

22. Andrew Ross, "New Age Technoculture," in *Cultural Studies*, ed. Lawrence Grossberg, Cary Nelson, and Paula Treichler (New York: Routledge, 1992), 545.

23. Judith Grant, *Fundamental Feminism: Contesting the Core Concepts of Feminist Theory* (New York: Routledge, 1993). There have been extremely cogent critiques of Echols's *Daring*, two of which are found in *Radically Speaking: Feminism Reclaimed*, ed. Diane Bell and Renate Klein (Melbourne: Spinifex Press, 1996). Diane Richardson, "Misguided, Dangerous, and Wrong: On the Maligning of Radical Feminism," and Tania Lienert, "Who Is Calling Radical Feminists 'Cultural Feminists' and Other Historical Sleights of Hand," both take Echols to task for taking the position that radical feminism gave way to cultural feminism. I think the difference among scholars here is one of place, not purpose; I believe that radical feminism is alive and well *outside* the academy but that its relationship to a broader intellectual project has been sorely marginalized by the popularity of cultural feminist concerns. I am grateful to my London-based colleague Clare Hemmings for her critique of this portion of the book and for her suggestion of the Spinifex volume.

24. Consolidated, *Business of Punishment* (London Records USA, 1994), track 10.

25. Judith Butler, *Gender Trouble: Feminism and the Subversion of Identity* (New York: Routledge, 1990), 5.

26. It is not the purpose of this chapter to illuminate the myriad problems with Butler's theory. Scholars such as Linda Alcoff, Paula Moya, and Seyla Benhabib have already launched a concerted effort to dismantle Butler's basis of inquiry.

27. Kobena Mercer, *Welcome to the Jungle: New Positions in Black Cultural Studies* (New York: Routledge, 1994), 259.

28. Tomás Almaguer, *Racial Fault Lines: The Historical Origins of White Suprem-acy in California* (Berkeley: University of California Press, 1994), 210–211 (italics mine).

29. Proposition 184 was passed by public referendum in the autumn of 1994 and called for a "three strikes, you're out" policy toward repeat offenders. Propo-sition 187, known as the "anti-immigrant" referendum, passed in the same year and mandated the denial of health care and schooling to undocumented people. In the autumn of 1996, Proposition 209, erroneously named the "California Civil Rights Initiative," demanded the immediate suspension of existing affirmative action policies and programs in the public sphere.

30. Peter Schrag, "Son of 187: Anti-Affirmative Action Propositions," *New Re-public*, 30 January 1995, 16–18.

31. I would argue that there are three movements in this country that demon-strate both legitimate and illegitimate forms of white male anger: early HIV/AIDS activism, Christian coalition politics, and paramilitary militia activity. These groups are similar because they demonstrate cognate beginnings—that the initial call to political action rested on the sense that white men were not getting all that they were entitled to receive at the hands of government.

32. See the early work of Denesh D'Souza, and Jesse Helms's early campaign against the NEA (National Endowment for the Arts) and, subsequently, NPR (Na-tional Public Radio).

33. Several collections of essays place early struggles against HIV/AIDS in prac-tical and theoretical perspective: Douglas Crimp, ed., *AIDS: Cultural Analysis and Cultural Activism* (Cambridge: MIT Press, 1988); Judith Pastore, ed., *Confronting AIDS through Literature: The Responsibilities of Representation* (Urbana: University of Illinois Press, 1993); Timothy F. Murphy and Suzanne Poirier, eds. *Writing AIDS: Gay Literature, Language, and Analysis* (New York: Columbia University Press, 1993); and Simon Watney, *Practices of Freedom: Selected Writings on HIV/ AIDS* (Durham: Duke University Press, 1994).

34. Leo Bersani, "Is the Rectum a Grave?" *AIDS: Cultural Analysis and Cultural Activism*, ed. Douglas Crimp (Cambridge: MIT Press, 1988), 206.

35. For a discussion of white male rage, see Ann Hulbert, "Angels in the Out-field," *New Republic*, 18 November 1996, 46; Schrag, "Son of 187," 16–18; and Mary B. Harris, "Sex and Ethnic Differences in Past Aggressive Behaviors," *Jour-nal of Family Violence* 7, no. 2 (1992): 85–103.

36. For an understanding of the outgrowth of various Christian coalition poli-tics, see Joe Conason, Alfred Ross, and Lee Cokorinos, "The Promise Keepers Are Coming: The Third Wave of the Religious Right," *Nation*, 7 October 1996, 11–19.

37. I am referring to the FBI siege of the compound in Waco, Texas, and the Oklahoma City bombing and the subsequent FBI crackdown on paramilitary groups in the nation. Many of the nation's extremist paramilitary groups have as their ideological foundation some of the tenets expressed in Andrew Macdon-ald's novel, *The Turner Diaries* (Hillsboro, W.Va.: National Vanguard Books, 1995).

38. For example, in the acknowledgments to their 1992 release, *Play More Music*, band members rail against vestiges of white supremacy with "No thanks and a big FUCK YOU to the NRA, Ted Nugent, Operation Rescue, Patriarchy, Procter and Gamble, The Sky God, and all the slamdancers."

39. See Eric Lott, *Love and Theft: Blackface Minstrelsy and the American Working Class* (New York: Oxford University Press, 1993).

40. Ann Powers, "The Left Stuff: Consolidated Mix Politics with Humor," *Rolling Stone*, 13 December 1994, 33.

41. Sabina Sawhney, "The Joke and the Hoax: (Not) Speaking as the Other," in *Who Can Speak? Authority and Critical Identity*, ed. Judith Roof and Robyn Wiegman (Urbana: University of Illinois Press, 1995), 216. I am grateful to Jennifer DeVere Brody for calling my attention to Sawhney's work.

42. *The Black Scholar* devoted an entire issue to the Thomas confirmation, giving leading black intellectuals and community members a chance to voice their opinions about the issue (vol. 22 [winter 1991–spring 1992]).

43. Karla F. C. Holloway, *Codes of Conduct: Race, Ethics, and the Color of Our Character* (New Brunswick: Rutgers University Press, 1995), 15.

44. Ann duCille has remarked, "The most important questions, I have begun to suspect, may not be about the essentialism and territoriality, the biology, sociology or even the ideology about which we hear so much but, rather, about professionalism and disciplinarity; about cultural literacy and intellectual competence; about taking ourselves seriously and insisting that we be taken seriously not as objectified subjects in someone else's histories—as native informants—but as critics and as scholars reading and writing our own literature and history" ("The Occult of True Black Womanhood," 603).

45. Morrison, *Playing in the Dark*, 85.

46. After the publication of Gilman's piece in *"Race," Writing, and Difference* (1985), critics took issue with Gilman's decision to reprint the pictures of Sarah Bartmann's genitalia, crafted by George Cuvier. See also Anne Fausto-Sterling, "Gender, Race, and Nation: The Comparative Anatomy of 'Hottentot' Women in Europe, 1815–1817," in *Deviant Bodies: Critical Perspectives on Difference in Science and Popular Culture*, ed. Jennifer Terry and Jacqueline Urla (Bloomington: Indiana University Press, 1995), 19–48.

47. The exception would be Lynda Hart's *Fatal Women: Lesbian Sexuality and the Mark of Aggression* (Princeton: Princeton University Press, 1994).

48. Anita Cornwell, *The Black Lesbian in White America* (Tallahassee, Fla.: Naiad Press, 1983), and Audre Lorde, *Zami: A New Spelling of My Name* (Freedom, Calif.: Crossing Press, 1982), are probably the only in-depth studies of their kind. See also Barbara Smith, *Home Girls: A Black Feminist Anthology* (New York: Kitchen Table Press, 1983).

49. Judith Roof, *A Lure of Knowledge: Lesbian Sexuality and Theory* (New York: Columbia University Press, 1991), 217.

50. I have commented more extensively on the subject of black bodies and

queer studies in my essay "(White) Lesbian Studies," in *New Lesbian Studies: Into the Twenty-First Century*, ed. Bonnie Zimmerman and Toni A. H. McNaron (New York: Feminist Press, 1996), 247–255.

51. Although the term *heteronormativity* would seem more appropriate here, I stick with *patriarchy* because although it lacks cultural currency in queer studies, it still tells us a lot about the historiography of feminist critiques of systems of power and the role that men play in them. My choice of *patriarchy* over *heteronormative* implies that although we have done the work of interrogating systems of power based on proliferating sexualities and sex roles, we have yet to formulate a politics of this moment that changes the bodies at and on the top. To do this work, we need to recirculate a notion that patriarchy *still* exists, even if the representative patriarchal body has managed to mask itself.

52. Evelynn Hammonds, "Black (W)holes," 141.

53. Andrew Parker and Eve Kosofsky Sedgwick, eds., *Performativity and Performance* (New York: Routledge, 1995), 16 (italics mine).

6 Critical Conversations at the Boundary
between Life and Death

1. For a discussion of de Man's life and work, see David Lehman, *Signs of the Times: Deconstruction and the Fall of Paul de Man* (New York: Poseidon Press, 1992).

2. Elizabeth A. Meese, *(Ex)Tensions: Re-Figuring Feminist Criticism* (Urbana: University of Illinois Press, 1990), 2.

3. For more information about the socioeconomic status of women in the United States, see Ruth Sidel, *Women and Children Last: The Plight of Poor Women in Affluent America* (New York: Penguin, 1986).

4. Arnold Krupat, *For Those Who Came After: A Study of Native American Autobiography* (Berkeley: University of California Press, 1985), 11.

5. Arnold Krupat, *The Voice in the Margin: Native American Literature and the Canon* (Berkeley: University of California Press, 1989), 37. For a similar, but brief, study of African American literature, see Henry Louis Gates Jr., "Authority, (White) Power, and the (Black) Critic: It's All Greek to Me," *Cultural Critique* 6 and 7 (spring–fall 1987): 19–46.

6. Leslie Marmon Silko, "An Old-Time Indian Attack Conducted in Two Parts," *Shantih* 4, no. 2 (1979): 4.

7. I am thinking of Audre Lorde's articulation of the difference between the two terms in the poem "Power": "The difference between poetry and rhetoric / is being ready to kill / yourself / instead of your children" (*The Black Unicorn* [New York: Norton, 1978], 108).

8. Gates briefly observes that West African characters like Esu-Elegbara, "the Yoruban sacred trickster who is truly Pan-African," provide a template for discussions of African American literature. *Figures in Black: Words, Signs, and the "Ra-*

cial" *Self* (New York: Oxford University Press, 1987), 48. In *The Signifying Monkey: A Theory of Afro-American Literary Criticism* (New York: Oxford University Press, 1988), Gates uses his earlier remarks as a framework for the book. Earlier critiques of the place of West African beliefs in African American folk culture can be found in Lawrence W. Levine, *Black Culture and Black Consciousness: Afro-American Folk Thought from Slavery to Freedom* (New York: Oxford University Press, 1977), and Zora Neale Hurston, *Mules and Men* (1935; reprint, Bloomington: Indiana University Press, 1978).

9. Audre Lorde, *Sister Outsider*, 122.

10. bell hooks, "marginality as site of resistance," in *Out There: Marginalization and Contemporary Cultures*, ed. Russell Ferguson, Martha Gever, Trinh T. Minh-ha, and Cornel West (New York: New Museum of Contemporary Art, 1990), 341.

11. Leslie Marmon Silko, "Language and Literature from a Pueblo Indian Perspective," in *English Literature: Opening Up the Canon*, ed. Leslie A. Fiedler and Houston A. Baker Jr. (Baltimore: Johns Hopkins University Press, 1981), 54.

12. Allen, "Special Problems," 382.

13. Leslie Marmon Silko, interview by Kim Barnes, *Journal of Ethnic Studies*, 89.

14. Allen, "Special Problems," 379.

15. Allen's unspecified use of the word *white* to constitute any subject outside of an essentialized "Indian" experience continually frustrates any attempt to read the book without utilizing such dichotomies.

16. Morrison, "Unspeakable Things Unspoken," 20.

17. See Kimberle Crenshaw's reading of Gates's defense in "Beyond Racism and Misogyny: Black Feminism and 2 Live Crew," *Boston Review*, 6 December 1991, 30–33.

18. Houston A. Baker Jr., "There Is No More Beautiful Way: Theory and the Poetics of Afro-American Women's Writing," in *Afro-American Literary Study in the 1990s*, ed. Houston A. Baker Jr. and Patricia Redmond (Chicago: University of Chicago Press, 1989), 135.

19. Henderson, "Re-membering," 159 (italics mine). What Henderson is referring to here is Baker's *Workings of the Spirit*, the work that grew from this earlier essay. The book includes a photo essay, dispersed throughout the text, that is meant to augment or depict what the "spirit workings" of language cannot. The photos are without captions and present quite a problem for the text and the "autobiographical situationality" of its male author in relationship to these unnamed black women.

20. I am alluding particularly to Spillers's theory of body and flesh in "Mama's Baby, Papa's Maybe." Spillers maintains that "those undecipherable markings on the captive body render a kind of hieroglyphics of the flesh whose severe disjunctures come to be hidden to the cultural seeing by skin color" (67). As well, she later argues that the "flesh is the concentration of 'ethnicity' that contemporary critical discourses neither acknowledge nor discourse away" (67). Spillers provides a more complex and nuanced approach to the reading of black female presence historically, and her work is further explored in the next chapter.

21. Allen, *Sacred Hoop*, 208.

22. Carol Shepherd McClain, ed., *Women as Healers: Cross-Cultural Perspectives* (New Brunswick: Rutgers University Press, 1989).

23. Harriet Ngubane, *Body and Mind in Zulu Medicine: An Ethnography of Health and Disease in Nyuswa-Zulu Thought and Practice* (London: Academic Press, 1977), 77.

24. Much of the belief that indigenous North American societies feared menstruating women stems from erroneous reports from anthropologists who assumed that native cultural practices were much like their own. Paula Allen observes that "the Crow and many other American Indians do not perceive signs of womanness as contamination; rather, they view them as so powerful that other 'medicines' may be canceled by the very presence of that power" (*Sacred Hoop*, 253).

25. Trudier Harris, "Reconnecting Fragments: Afro-American Folk Tradition in *The Bluest Eye*," in *Critical Essays on Toni Morrison*, ed. Nellie McKay (Boston: G. K. Hall, 1988), 69.

26. For more on this subject see Michael Grosso, "A Postmodern Mythology of Death," in *Perspectives on Death and Dying: Cross-Cultural and Multi-Disciplinary Views*, ed. Arthur Berger et al. (Philadelphia: Charles Press, 1989), 232–243. See also Vincent B. Leitch, "Writing Cultural History: The Case of Post-Modernism," in *Feminism and Institutions: Dialogues on Feminist Theory*, ed. Linda Kauffman (Cambridge, Mass.: Basil Blackwell, 1989), 166–173.

27. Michael Grosso, "Postmodern Mythology," 232.

28. Environmental activist Cynthia Hamilton offers the following statistics on the impact of hazardous wastes on communities of color: "Three out of every five Black and Hispanic Americans live in communities with uncontrolled toxic sites; 75 percent of the residents in rural areas in the Southwest, mainly Hispanics, are drinking pesticide-contaminated water; more than 2 million tons of uranium tailings are dumped on Native-American reservations each year, resulting in Navajo teenagers having seventeen times the national average of organ cancers; more than 700,000 inner city children, 50 percent of them black, are said to be suffering from lead poisoning, resulting in learning disorders" ("Women, Home, and Community: the Struggle in an Urban Environment," in *Reweaving the World: The Emergence of Ecofeminism*, ed. Irene Diamond and Gloria Feman Orenstein [San Francisco: Sierra Club, 1990], 216).

29. Winona LaDuke, "They Always Come Back," in *A Gathering of Spirit: Writing and Art by North American Indian Women*, ed. Beth Brant (Rockland, Maine: Sinister Wisdom Books, 1984), 66–67 (italics mine).

30. Luisah Teish, *Jambalaya: The Natural Woman's Book of Personal Charms and Practical Rituals* (San Francisco: Harper and Row, 1985), 69.

31. Abdul JanMohamed and David Lloyd, introduction to a special issue of *Cultural Critique: The Nature of Minority Discourse* 6 and 7 (spring–fall 1987): 6 (italics mine).

32. As historian Jack D. Forbes notes, "The spirit powers of the Black Africans

are said to have established a close cooperative relationship with the spirit-powers of the Americans. This same cooperation and reciprocal relationship can also be seen in Brazil, where Tupinamba and Guarani *candombles* exist side by side with those of Congo-Angola and Nago orientation and where Native American and African spiritual powers are called upon for assistance in various contexts" (*Africans and Native Americans*, 6).

33. Paula Gunn Allen, *Spider Woman's Granddaughters: Traditional Tales and Contemporary Writing by Native American Women* (New York: Fawcett Columbine, 1989), 3.

34. Marsha Jean Darling, "In the Realm of Responsibility: A Conversation with Toni Morrison," *Vital Signs*, 8.

Epilogue: "I'm in the Zone": Bill T. Jones, Tupac Shakur, and the (Queer) Art of Death

1. Playing the dead is not the only relationship between the two. There is some psychic connection in their comments about black fathers. In an interview with *Vibe* writer Kevin Powell, Shakur reflected on his adolescence: "I believe a mother can't give a son ways on how to be a man. Especially not a black man. It made me bitter seeing all those other niggas with fathers getting answers to questions that I have. Even now, I still don't get them" (February 1994, 37). Compare Shakur's psychic wound to Jones's comments on being an absentee father in an interview with Henry Louis Gates Jr. for the *New Yorker*: "Being a gay son, I've felt somehow morally above my brothers. My brothers were gangsters in terms of women's lives. I was superior to that, or so I thought. So how do I feel? I feel irresponsible. Too bad there's another black child in the world without a father" (28 November 1994, 117). These comments indicate the complex role that ideas of masculinity and black (male) performance of it play in the lives of two contemporary performers. What Jones once said about himself—"My eroticism, my sensuality on-stage is always coupled with a wild anger and belligerence. I know that I can be food for fantasy" (*New Yorker* 121)—is mirrored in the media's depiction of Shakur's (healthy) body's currency: "Shakur was a self-proclaimed thug. A macho tantrum thrower embarrassed by the limp of his thoughtfulness" (Danyel Smith, "Home At Last," in *Tupac Shakur*, ed. Alan Light [New York: Three Rivers Press, 1998], 129).

2. *New Yorker*, 28 November 1994, 112.

3. Arlene Croce, "Discussing the Undiscussable," *New Yorker* (26 December 1994–2 January 1995), 55.

4. Marcia B. Siegel, "Virtual Criticism and the Dance of Death," *TDR: The Drama Review* 40, no. 2 (summer 1996): 61.

5. David L. Eng, "Out Here and Over There: Queerness and Diaspora in Asian American Studies," *Social Text* 52/53 15, nos. 3 and 4 (fall–winter 1997): 40.

6. As I have already discussed in chapter 4, Judith Butler addresses similar con-

cerns in "Against Proper Objects" (1994), where she tackles the question of the appropriateness of bodies and therefore discourses to fields of inquiry. Her primary concern is with the gender/sexuality split between feminism and queer studies, respectively, and whether disciplines should create territories out of categories that aren't so mutually exclusive.

7. Lauren Berlant and Elizabeth Freeman, "Queer Nationality," *boundary 2* 19, no. 1 (spring 1992): 151.

8. José Esteban Muñoz, "'The White to Be Angry': Vaginal Davis's Terrorist Drag," *Social Text* 52/53 15, nos. 3 and 4 (fall/winter 1997): 85.

9. *Special Tribute to Tupac Shakur* (Paramus, N.J.: Starline Publications, 1996), 12.

Selected Bibliography

Abelove, Henry, Michèle Aina Barale, and David M. Halperin. *The Lesbian and Gay Studies Reader.* New York: Routledge, 1993.

Adams, Stephen. *The Homosexual as Hero in Contemporary Fiction.* London: Vision, 1980.

Alcoff, Linda. "Cultural Feminism Versus Post-Structuralism: The Identity Crisis in Feminist Theory." *Signs* 13, no. 3 (1988): 405–436.

Allen, Paula Gunn. *The Sacred Hoop.* Boston: Beacon, 1986.

———. "Special Problems in Teaching Leslie Marmon Silko's *Ceremony.*" *American Indian Quarterly* 14, no. 4 (1990): 379–386.

———, ed. *Spider Woman's Granddaughters: Traditional Tales and Contemporary Writing by Native American Women.* New York: Fawcett Columbine, 1989.

Almaguer, Tomás. *Racial Fault Lines: The Historical Origins of White Supremacy in California.* Berkeley: University of California Press, 1994.

Alpert, Jane. *Growing Up Underground.* New York: Morrow, 1981.

———. "Mother Right: A New Feminist Theory." *Ms.,* August 1973, 52–55, 88–94.

Anderson, Benedict. *Imagined Communities: Reflections on the Origin and Spread of Nationalism.* Rev. ed. London: Verso, 1991.

Anzaldua, Gloria. *Borderlands/La Frontera: The New Mestiza.* San Francisco: Spinsters/Aunt Lute Books, 1987.

Ariès, Philippe. *The Hour of Our Death.* Translated by Helen Weaver. New York: Vintage Books, 1982.

———. *Western Attitudes toward DEATH: From the Middle Ages to the Present.* Translated by Patricia M. Ranum. Baltimore: Johns Hopkins University Press, 1974.

Astrov, Margot. *The Winged Serpent: An Anthology of American Indian Prose and Poetry.* 1946. New York: John Day, 1972.

Atkinson, Ti-Grace. *Amazon Odyssey: The First Collection of Writings by the Political Pioneer of the Women's Movement.* New York: Links Books, 1974.

Atlas, Marilyn Judith. "Toni Morrison's Beloved and the Reviewers." *Midwestern Miscellany* 18 (1990): 45–57.

Awkward, Michael. *Negotiating Difference: Race, Gender, and the Politics of Positionality.* Chicago: University of Chicago Press, 1995.

————. *New Essays on* Their Eyes Were Watching God. New York: Cambridge University Press, 1990.

Bádéjò, Diedre L. "The Goddess Ósun as a Paradigm for African Feminist Criticism." *Sage* 6, no. 1 (1989): 27–31.

Badham, Paul, and Linda Badham, eds. *Death and Immortality in the Religions of the World*. New York: Paragon Press, 1987.

Baker, Houston A., Jr. *Long Black Song: Essays in Black American Literature and Culture*. Charlottesville: University Press of Virginia, 1972.

————. *Workings of the Spirit: The Poetics of Afro-American Women's Writing*. Chicago: University of Chicago Press, 1991.

Baker, Houston A., Jr., and Patricia Redmond, eds. *Afro-American Literary Study in the 1990s*. Chicago: University of Chicago Press, 1989.

Bakhtin, Mikhail. *Rabelais and His World*. Translated by Helen Iswolsky. Bloomington: Indiana University Press, 1984.

Baldwin, James. *Giovanni's Room*. New York: Dell, 1964.

Bambara, Toni Cade. *The Salt Eaters*. New York: Vintage, 1980.

Bamunoba, Y. K. *La Mort dans la vie africaine*. Paris: Presence africaine, 1979.

Barrett, Lindon. *Value and Blackness: Seeing Double*. New York: Cambridge University Press, 1999.

Becker, Ernest. *The Denial of Death*. New York: Free Press, 1973.

Bell, Bernard. "*Beloved*: A Womanist Neo-Slave Narrative; or Multivocal Remembrances of Things Past." *African American Review* 26, no. 1 (1992): 7–15.

Belton, Don. *Speak My Name: Black Men on Masculinity and the American Dream*. Boston: Beacon, 1995.

Berger, Arthur, et al. *Perspectives on Death and Dying: Cross-Cultural and Multi-Disciplinary Views*. Philadelphia: Charles Press, 1989.

Berlant, Lauren, and Elizabeth Freeman. "Queer Nationality." *boundary 2* 19, no. 2 (spring 1992): 149–189.

Bernal, Martin. *Black Athena: The Afroasiatic Roots of Classical Civilization*. New Jersey: Rutgers University Press, 1987.

Berry, Mary Frances, and John W. Blassingame. *Long Memory: The Black Experience in America*. New York: Oxford University Press, 1982.

Bierhorst, John, ed. and trans. *Four Masterworks of American Indian Literature*. New York: Farrar, Straus, and Giroux, 1974.

Bird, Gloria. "Towards a Decolonization of the Mind and Text 1: Leslie Marmon Silko's *Ceremony*." *Wicazo Sa Review* 9, no. 2 (1993): 1–8.

Blackshire-Belay, Carol Aisha, ed. *Language and Literature in the African American Imagination*. Westport, Conn.: Greenwood Press, 1992.

Blount, Marcellus, and George P. Cunningham, eds. *Representing Black Men*. New York: Routledge, 1996.

Bone, Robert. *The Negro Novel in America*. New Haven: Yale University Press, 1965.

Brant, Beth, ed. *A Gathering of Spirit: Writing and Art by North American Indian Women*. Rockland, Maine: Sinister Wisdom Books, 1984.

Braxton, Joanne M., and Andrée Nicola McLaughlin, eds. *Wild Women in the Whirlwind: Afra-American Culture and the Contemporary Literary Renaissance.* New Brunswick: Rutgers University Press, 1990.

Bristow, Joseph. *Sexual Sameness: Textual Differences in Lesbian and Gay Writing.* New York: Routledge, 1992.

Budick, Emily Miller. "Absence, Loss, and the Space of History in Toni Morrison's *Beloved.*" *Arizona Quarterly* 48, no. 2 (1992): 117–138.

Burns, Allan F., trans. *An Epoch of Miracles: Oral Literature of the Yucatec Maya.* Austin: University of Texas Press, 1983.

Burris, Barbara. "The Fourth World Manifesto." *Notes from the Third Year: Women's Liberation,* June 1970, 102–119.

Butler, Judith. "Against Proper Objects." *differences* 6, nos. 2 and 3 (summer–fall 1994): 1–26.

———. *Bodies That Matter: On the Discursive Limits of "Sex."* New York: Routledge, 1993.

———. *Gender Trouble: Feminism and the Subversion of Identity.* New York: Routledge, 1990.

Butler, Judith, and Joan W. Scott. *Feminists Theorize the Political.* New York: Routledge, 1992.

Butler-Evans, Elliott. *Race, Gender, and Desire: Narrative Strategies in the Fiction of Toni Cade Bambara, Toni Morrison, and Alice Walker.* Philadelphia: Temple University Press, 1989.

Calloway, Colin G. *New Directions in American Indian History.* Norman: University of Oklahoma Press, 1988.

Carby, Hazel. *Reconstructing Womanhood.* New York: Oxford University Press, 1987.

Case, Sue-Ellen, Philip Bret, and Susan Leigh Foster, eds. *Cruising the Performative: Interventions into the Representation of Ethnicity, Nationality, and Sexuality.* Bloomington: Indiana University Press, 1995.

Chametzky, Jules, ed. *Black Writers Redefine the Struggle: A Tribute to James Baldwin.* Amherst, Mass.: University of Massachusetts Press, 1989.

Chrisman, Robert, and Nathan Hare. *Contemporary Black Thought: The Best from The Black Scholar.* Indianapolis: Bobbs-Merrill, 1973.

Christian, Barbara. "Being the Subject and the Object: Reading African-American Women's Novels." In *Changing Subjects: The Making of Feminist Literary Criticism,* edited by Gayle Greene and Coppélia Kahn, 195–200. London: Routledge, 1993.

———. *Black Feminist Criticism: Perspectives on Black Women Writers.* New York: Pergamon Press, 1985.

Clarke, Cheryl. "Living the Texts Out: Lesbians and the Uses of Black Women's Traditions." In *Theorizing Black Feminisms: The Visionary Pragmatism of Black Women,* edited by Stanlie M. James and Abena P. A. Busia, 214–227. New York: Routledge, 1993.

Clinton, Catherine. *The Plantation Mistress: Woman's World in the Old South.* New York: Pantheon, 1982.

Cole, Susan Letzler. *The Absent One: Mourning Ritual, Tragedy, and the Performance of Ambivalence*. University Park: Pennsylvania State University Press, 1985.

Collier, George, with Elizabeth Lowery Quaratiello. *Basta!: Land and the Zapatista Rebellion in Chiapas*. Oakland, Calif.: Institute for Food and Development Policy, 1994.

Comstock, Gary David. *Violence against Lesbians and Gay Men*. New York: Columbia University Press, 1991.

Conason, Joe, Alfred Ross, and Lee Cokorinos. "The Promise Keepers are Coming: The Third Wave of the Religious Right." *Nation*, 7 October 1996, 11–19.

Cornwell, Anita. *Black Lesbian in White America*. Tallahassee, Fla.: Naiad Press, 1983.

Covina, Gina, and Laurel Galana. *The Lesbian Reader: An Amazon Quarterly Anthology*. Oakland, Calif.: Amazon Press, 1975.

Crimp, Douglas, ed. *AIDS: Cultural Analysis and Cultural Activism*. Cambridge: MIT Press, 1988.

Crosby, Alfred W., Jr. *The Columbian Exchange: Biological and Cultural Consequences of 1492*. Westport, Conn.: Greenwood Press, 1972.

Crowley, Daniel J. *African Folklore in the New World*. Austin: University of Texas Press, 1977.

Danforth, Loring M. *The Death Rituals of Rural Greece*. Princeton: Princeton University Press, 1982.

Davis, F. James. *Who Is Black? One Nation's Definition*. University Park: Pennsylvania State University Press, 1991.

de Beauvoir, Simone. *The Second Sex*. Translated by H. M. Parshley. New York: Vintage, 1952.

Debo, Angie. *And Still the Waters Run: The Betrayal of the Five Civilized Tribes*. 1940. Reprint, Princeton: Princeton University Press, 1968.

de Lauretis, Teresa, ed. *Feminist Studies, Critical Studies*. Bloomington: Indiana University Press, 1986.

Demetrakopoulos, Stephanie A. "Maternal Bonds as Devourers of Women's Individuation in Toni Morrison's *Beloved*." *African American Review* 26, no. 1 (1992): 51–59.

de Weever, Jacqueline. *Mythmaking and Metaphor in Black Women's Fiction*. New York: St. Martin's, 1991.

Diamond, Irene, and Gloria Feman, eds. *Reweaving the World: The Emergence of Ecofeminism*. San Francisco: Sierra Club, 1990.

Donnelly, John, ed. *Language, Metaphysics, and Death*. New York: Fordham University Press, 1978.

Douglass, Carol Anne. *Love and Politics: Radical Feminist and Lesbian Theories*. San Francisco: ISM Press, 1990.

Drake, Sandra. "All that foolishness / That All Foolishness: Race and Caribbean Culture as Thematics of Liberation in Jean Rhys's *Wide Sargasso Sea*." *Critica* 2, no. 2 (1990): 97–112.

duCille, Ann. *The Coupling Convention: Sex, Text, and Tradition in Black Women's Fiction*. New York: Oxford University Press, 1993.

———. "The Occult of True Black Womanhood: Critical Demeanor and Black Feminist Studies." *Signs* 19, no. 3 (1994): 591–629.

Dunne, John S. *The City of the Gods: A Study in Myth and Mortality*. New York: Macmillan, 1965.

During, Simon. *Foucault and Literature: Towards a Genealogy of Writing*. New York: Routledge, 1992.

Echols, Alice. *Daring to Be Bad: Radical Feminism in America 1967–1975*. Minneapolis: University of Minnesota Press, 1989.

Edmonson, Munro S., trans. *The Ancient Future of the Itza: The Book of Chilam Balam of Tiziman*. Austin: University of Texas Press, 1982.

Eisenstein, Hester, and Alice Jardine, eds. *The Future of Difference*. New Brunswick: Rutgers University Press, 1985.

Eng, David. "Out Here and Over There: Queerness and Diaspora in Asian American Studies." *Social Text 52/53* 15, nos. 3 and 4 (fall–winter 1997): 31–52.

Evans, Charlene Taylor. "Mother-Daughter Relationships as Epistemological Structures: Leslie Marmon Silko's *Almanac of the Dead* and *Storyteller*." In *Women of Color: Mother-Daughter Relationships in Twentieth-Century Literature*, edited by Elizabeth Brown-Guillory, 172–187. Austin: University of Texas Press, 1996.

Evans, Sara. *Personal Politics: The Roots of Women's Liberation in the Civil Rights Movement and the New Left*. New York: Knopf, 1979.

Evers, Larry, and Felipe S. Molina. *Yaqui Deer Songs/Maso Bwikam: A Native American Poetry*. Tucson: University of Arizona Press, 1987.

Fausto-Sterling, Anne. "Gender, Race, and Nation: The Comparative Anatomy of 'Hottentot' Women in Europe, 1815–1817." In *Deviant Bodies: Critical Perspectives on Difference in Science and Popular Culture*, edited by Jennifer Terry and Jacqueline Urla 19–48. Bloomington: Indiana University Press, 1995.

Feral, Josette. "The Powers of Difference." In *The Future of Difference*, edited by Hester Eisenstein and Alice Jardine, 88–94. New Brunswick: Rutgers University Press, 1985.

Fiedler, Leslie. *Love and Death in the American Novel*. New York: Anchor, 1992.

Firestone, Shulamith. *The Dialectic of Sex: The Case for Feminist Revolution*. New York: Morrow, 1970.

Forbes, Jack D. *Africans and Native Americans: The Language of Race and the Evolution of Red-Black Peoples*. 2d ed. Urbana: University of Illinois Press, 1993.

Foucault, Michel. *The Birth of the Clinic: An Archaeology of Medical Perception*. Translated by A. M. Sheridan Smith. New York: Vintage, 1973.

———. *The History of Sexuality*. Vol. 1, *An Introduction*. Translated by Robert Hurley. New York: Vintage, 1980.

Fox-Genovese, Elizabeth. *Within the Plantation Household: Black and White Women of the Old South*. Chapel Hill: University of North Carolina Press, 1988.

Frazier, E. Franklin. *The Negro Family in the United States*. Rev. ed. 1939. Reprint, Chicago: University of Chicago Press, 1966.

Frith, Simon. *Performing Rites: On the Value of Popular Music*. Cambridge: Harvard University Press, 1996.

Fuss, Diana. *Essentially Speaking: Feminism, Nature, and Difference*. New York: Routledge, 1989.

Fuss, Diana, ed. *Inside/Out: Lesbian Theories, Gay Theories*. New York: Routledge, 1991.

Gagnier, Regenia. *Subjectivities*. New York: Oxford University Press, 1988.

Gallenkamp, Charles, and Regina Elise Johnson, gen. eds. *Maya: Treasures of an Ancient Civilization*. New York: H. N. Abrams, in association with the Albuquerque Museum, 1985.

Garber, Marjorie. "Spare Parts: The Surgical Construction of Gender." *differences* 1, no. 3 (1989): 137–159.

Gates, Henry Louis, Jr. *Figures in Black: Words, Signs, and the "Racial" Self*. New York: Oxford University Press, 1987.

———. *The Signifying Monkey: A Theory of Afro-American Literary Criticism*. New York: Oxford University Press, 1988.

———, ed. *Black Literature and Literary Theory*. New York: Methuen, 1984.

Geertz, Clifford. *Local Knowledge: Further Essays in Interpretive Anthropology*. New York: Basic Books, 1983.

Gervais, Karen Grandstand. *Redefining Death*. New Haven: Yale University Press, 1986.

Gilman, Sander. "Black Bodies / White Bodies: Toward an Iconography of Female Sexuality in Late Nineteenth-Century Art, Medicine, and Literature." In *"Race," Writing, and Difference*, edited by Henry Louis Gates Jr., 223–261. Chicago: University of Chicago Press, 1985.

———. *Picturing Health and Illness: Images of Identity and Difference*. Baltimore: Johns Hopkins University Press, 1995.

Gilroy, Paul. *The Black Atlantic: Modernity and Double Consciousness*. Cambridge: Harvard University Press, 1993.

Giovanni, Nikki. *Gemini: An Extended Autobiographical Statement on My First Twenty-Five Years of Being a Black Poet*. Indianapolis: Bobbs-Merrill, 1971.

Gleason, Judith. *Oya: In Praise of the Goddess*. New York: Shambhala Press, 1987.

Goodwin, Sarah Webster, and Elisabeth Bronfen, eds. *Death and Representation*. Baltimore: Johns Hopkins University Press, 1993.

González-Wippler, Migene. *Santeria: The Religion*. New York: Harmony Books, 1989.

Goss, Linda, and Marian E. Barnes. *Talk That Talk: An Anthology of African-American Storytelling*. New York: Simon and Schuster, 1989.

Grahn, Judy. *Another Mother Tongue: Gay Words, Gay Worlds*. Boston: Beacon, 1984.

Grant, Judith. *Fundamental Feminism: Contesting the Core Concepts of Feminist Theory*. New York: Routledge, 1993.

Gray, Herman. *Watching Race: Television and the Struggle for "Blackness."* Minneapolis: University of Minnesota Press, 1995.

Greene, Gayle. "Feminist Fiction and the Uses of Memory." *Signs* 16, no. 2 (1991): 290–321.

Gualtieri, Antonio R. *The Vulture and the Bull: Religious Responses to Death*. Lanham, Md.: University Press of America, 1984.

Guy-Sheftall, Beverly, ed. *Words of Fire: An Anthology of African-American Feminist Thought*. New York: New Press, 1995.

Haggerty, George E., and Bonnie Zimmerman, eds. *Professions of Desire: Lesbian and Gay Studies in Literature*. New York: Modern Language Association Publications, 1995.

Hamilton, Cynthia. "Women, Home, and Community: The Struggle in an Urban Environment." In *Reweaving the World: The Emergence of Ecofeminism*, edited by Irene Diamond and Gloria Feman Orenstein, 215–22. San Francisco: Sierra Club, 1990.

Hammonds, Evelynn. "Black (W)holes and the Geometry of Black Female Sexuality." *differences* 6, nos. 2 and 3 (summer–fall 1994): 126–145.

Harris, Mary B. "Sex and Ethnic Differences in Past Aggressive Behaviors." *Journal of Family Violence* 7, no. 2 (1992): 85–103.

Harris, Trudier. "Reconnecting Fragments: Afro-American Folk Tradition in *The Bluest Eye*." In *Critical Essays on Toni Morrison*, edited by Nellie McKay, 68–76. Boston: G. K. Hall, 1988.

Hart, Lynda. *Fatal Women: Lesbian Sexuality and the Mark of Aggression*. Princeton: Princeton University Press, 1994.

Hartman, Joan E., and Ellen Messer-Davidow, eds. *(En)Gendering Knowledge: Feminists in Academe*. Knoxville: University of Tennessee Press, 1991.

Hebdige, Dick. *Subculture: The Meaning of Style*. London: Routledge, 1988.

Herrmann, Anne C., and Abigail J. Stewart, eds. *Theorizing Feminism: Parallel Trends in the Humanities and Social Sciences*. Boulder, Colo.: Westview Press, 1994.

Hemphill, Essex. *Ceremonies: Prose and Poetry*. New York: Plume, 1992.

———, ed. *Brother to Brother: New Writings by Black Gay Men*. Boston: Alyson, 1991.

Henderson, Mae G. "Toni Morrison's *Beloved*: Re-membering the Body as Historical Text." In *Comparative American Identities: Race, Sex, and Nationality in the Modern Text*, edited by Hortense J. Spillers, 62–86. New York: Routledge, 1991.

Herskovitz, Melville J. *Dahomey: An Ancient West African Kingdom*. 2 vols. Evanston: Northwestern University Press, 1967.

Hertz, Robert. *Death and the Right Hand*. Translated by Rodney and Claudia Needham. Glencoe, Ill.: Free Press, 1960.

Himelblau, Jack J. *Quiche Worlds in Creation: The Popol Vuh as a Narrative Work of Art*. Culver City, Calif.: Labyrinthos, 1989.

Hirsch, Herbert. *Genocide and the Politics of Memory: Studying Death to Preserve Life.* Chapel Hill: University of North Carolina Press, 1995.

Holbrook, David. *Images of Women in Literature.* New York: New York University Press, 1989.

Hole, Judith, and Ellen Levin. *Rebirth of Feminism.* New York: Quadrangle, 1971.

Holland, Sharon. "'If You Know I Have a History, You Will Respect Me': A Perspective on Afro–Native American Literature." *Callaloo* 17, no. 1 (1994): 334–350.

———. "(White) Lesbian Studies." In *The New Lesbian Studies: Into the Twenty-First Century,* edited by Bonnie Zimmerman and Toni A. H. McNaron, 247–61. New York: Feminist Press, 1996.

Holloway, Karla F. C. "*Beloved*: A Spiritual." *Callaloo* 13, no. 3 (1990): 516–525.

———. *The Character of the Word: The Texts of Zora Neale Hurston.* New York: Greenwood Press, 1987.

———. *Codes of Conduct: Race, Ethics, and the Color of Our Character.* New Brunswick: Rutgers University Press, 1995.

Holloway, Karla F. C., and Stephanie A. Demetrakopoulos. *New Dimensions of Spirituality: A Biracial and Bicultural Reading of the Novels of Toni Morrison.* New York: Greenwood Press, 1987.

hooks, bell. *Black Looks: Race and Representation.* Boston: South End Press, 1992.

———. "Marginality as site of resistance." In *Out There: Marginalization and Contemporary Cultures,* edited by Russell Ferguson, Martha Gever, Trinh T. Minh-ha, and Cornel West, 337–40. New York and Cambridge, Mass.: New Museum of Contemporary Art and MIT Press, 1990.

Horvitz, Deborah. "Nameless Ghosts: Possession and Dispossession in *Beloved*." *Studies in American Fiction* 17, no. 2 (1989): 157–167.

Houlbrooke, Ralph, ed. *Death, Ritual, and Bereavement.* London: Routledge, 1989.

Hu-DeHart, Evelyn. *Missionaries, Miners, and Indians: Spanish Contact with the Yaqui Nation of Northwestern New Spain, 1533–1820.* Tucson: University of Arizona Press, 1981.

Hull, Gloria T., Patricia Bell Scott, and Barbara Smith, eds. *All the Women Are White, All the Blacks Are Men, but Some of Us Are Brave: Black Women's Studies.* Old Westbury, N.Y.: Feminist Press, 1982.

Hurston, Zora Neale. *Mules and Men.* 1935. Reprint, Bloomington: Indiana University Press, 1978.

———. *Tell My Horse: Voodoo and Life in Haiti and Jamaica.* 1938. Reprint, New York: Harper, 1990.

———. *Their Eyes Were Watching God.* 1937. Reprint, Urbana: University of Illinois Press, 1978.

Jacobs, Paul, and Saul Landau. *The New Radicals: A Report with Documents.* New York: Random House, 1966.

James, Stanlie, and Abena P. A. Busia, eds. *Theorizing Black Feminisms: The Visionary Pragmatism of Black Women.* New York: Routledge, 1993.

JanMohamed, Abdul R. *Manichean Aesthetics: The Politics of Literature in Colonial Africa.* Amherst: University of Massachusetts Press, 1983.

Johnson, Barbara. *A World of Difference.* Baltimore: Johns Hopkins University Press, 1987.

Johnston, Jill. *Lesbian Nation: The Feminist Solution.* New York: Simon and Schuster, 1973.

Kamuf, Peggy. "Replacing Feminist Criticism." *Diacritics* 12, no. 2 (1982): 42–47.

Karp, Lila. *The Queen Is in the Garbage.* New York: Vanguard Press, 1969.

Katz, William Loren. *Black Indians: A Hidden Heritage.* New York: Atheneum, 1986.

Kauffman, Linda, ed. *Feminism and Institutions: Dialogues on Feminist Theory.* New York: Basil Blackwell, 1989.

Keenan, Sally. "Four Hundred Years of Silence": Myth, History, and Motherhood in Toni Morrison's *Beloved.* In *Recasting the World: Writing after Colonialism,* edited by Jonathan White, 45–81. Baltimore: Johns Hopkins University Press, 1993.

Kenan, Randall. *A Visitation of Spirits.* New York: Anchor Books, 1989.

Kennedy, J. Gerald. *Poe, Death, and the Life of Writing.* New Haven: Yale University Press, 1987.

Koedt, Anne, Ellen Levine, and Anita Rapone. *Radical Feminism.* New York: Quadrangle Books, 1973.

Köllhofer, Jakob, ed. *James Baldwin: His Place in American Literary History and His Reception in Europe.* Frankfurt am Main: Peter Lang, 1991.

Kramer, Kenneth Paul. *The Sacred Art of Dying: How World Religions Understand Death.* New York: Paulist, 1988.

Krumholz, Linda. "The Ghosts of Slavery: Historical Recovery in Toni Morrison's *Beloved.*" *African American Review* 26, no. 3 (1992): 395–408.

Krupat, Arnold. *Ethnocriticism: Ethnography, History, Literature.* Berkeley: University of California Press, 1992.

———. *For Those Who Came After: A Study of Native American Autobiography.* Berkeley: University of California Press, 1985.

———. *The Voice in the Margin: Native American Literature and the Canon.* Berkeley: University of California Press, 1989.

Kubler-Ross, Elisabeth. *On Death and Dying.* New York: Collier Books, 1969.

———. *Working It Through.* New York: Macmillan, 1982.

Laderman, Gary. *The Sacred Remains: American Attitudes toward Death, 1799–1883.* New Haven: Yale University Press, 1996.

Lane, Alycee J. "Black Bodies / Gay Bodies: The Politics of Race in the Gay / Military Battle." *Callaloo* 17, no. 4 (1994): 1074–1088.

Langer, Lawrence L. *The Age of Atrocity: Death in Modern Literature.* Boston: Beacon, 1978.

Larson, Charles R. *American Indian Fiction.* Albuquerque: University of New Mexico Press, 1978.

Lawrence, David. "Fleshly Ghosts and Ghostly Flesh: The Word and the Body in *Beloved*." *Studies in American Fiction* 19, no. 2 (1991): 189–201.

Lehman, David. *Signs of the Times: Deconstruction and the Fall of Paul de Man*. New York: Poseidon Press, 1992.

Levine, Lawrence W. *Black Culture and Black Consciousness: Afro-American Folk Thought from Slavery to Freedom*. New York: Oxford University Press, 1977.

Levy, Andrew. "Telling *Beloved*." *Texas Studies in Literature and Language* 33, no. 1 (1991): 114–123.

Lincoln, Kenneth. *Native American Renaissance*. Berkeley: University of California Press, 1983.

Lipsitz, George. "Land of a Thousand Dances: Youth, Minorities, and the Rise of Rock and Roll." In *Recasting America: Culture and Politics in the Age of Cold War*, edited by Larry May, 267–84. Chicago: University of Chicago Press, 1989.

———. "The Possessive Investment in Whiteness: Racialized Social Democracy and the 'White' Problem in American Studies." *American Quarterly* 47, no. 3 (1995): 369–387.

Liscio, Lorraine. "*Beloved*'s Narrative: Writing Mother's Milk." *Tulsa Studies in Women's Literature* 11, no. 1 (1992): 31–46.

Lorde, Audre. *The Black Unicorn*. New York: Norton, 1978.

———. *Sister Outsider*. New York: Crossing Press, 1985.

———. *Zami: A New Spelling of My Name*. Trumansburg, N.Y.: Crossing Press, 1982.

Lott, Eric. *Love and Theft: Blackface Minstrelsy and the American Working Class*. New York: Oxford University Press, 1993.

Lummis, Charles F. *Mesa, Canyon, and Pueblo*. New York: Century, 1925.

Luxton, Richard, with Pablo Balam. *Mayan Dream Walk: Literate Shamanism in the Yucatan*. London: Rider, 1981.

Macey, David. *The Lives of Michel Foucault: A Biography*. New York: Pantheon, 1993.

Mack, Arien, ed. *Death in American Experience*. New York: Schocken Books, 1973.

Makemson, Maud Worchester, comp. *The Book of the Jaguar Priest: A Translation of the Book of Chilam Balam of Tizimin*. New York: Schuman, 1971.

Marcus, Steven. *The Other Victorians: A Study of Sexuality and Pornography in Mid-Nineteenth-Century England*. New York: Bantam, 1967.

Margolies, Edward. *Native Sons: A Critical Study of Twentieth-Century Negro American Authors*. Philadelphia: Lippincott, 1968.

Mbiti, John S. *African Religions and Philosophy*. New York: Doubleday, 1970.

———. *Introduction to African Religion*. 2d rev. ed. Portsmouth, N. H.: Heinemann Educational, 1991.

McAdoo, Harriette Pipes, ed. *Black Families*. Beverly Hills, Calif.: Sage, 1981.

McClain, Carol Shepherd, ed. *Women as Healers: Cross-Cultural Perspectives*. New Brunswick: Rutgers University Press, 1989.

McDowell, Deborah E. *"The Changing Same": Black Women's Literature, Criticism, and Theory*. Bloomington: Indiana University Press, 1995.

McElroy, Bernard. *Fiction of the Modern Grotesque*. London: MacMillan, 1989.

McKay, Nellie Y. *Critical Essays on Toni Morrison*. Boston: G. K. Hall, 1988.

McRuer, Robert. "A Visitation of Difference: Randall Kenan and Black Queer Theory." *Journal of Homosexuality* 26, nos. 2 and 3 (1993): 221–232.

Medina, Angel. *Reflection, Time, and the Novel: Toward a Communicative Theory of Literature*. London: Routledge and Kegan Paul, 1979.

Meese, Elizabeth A. *(Ex)Tensions: Re-Figuring Feminist Criticism*. Urbana: University of Illinois Press, 1990.

Mellon, James, ed. *Bullwhip Days: The Slaves Remember*. New York: Avon, 1988.

Mercer, Kobena. *Welcome to the Jungle: New Positions in Black Cultural Studies*. New York: Routledge, 1994.

Miller, Nancy K. "The Text's Heroine: A Feminist Critic and Her Fictions." *Diacritics* 12, no. 2 (1982): 48–53.

Millett, Kate. *Sexual Politics*. New York: Simon and Schuster, 1969.

Mohanty, Satya. "The Epistemic Status of Cultural Identity: On *Beloved* and the Postcolonial Condition." *Cultural Critique* (spring 1993): 41–80.

Moody, Raymond A., Jr. *Life after Death: The Investigation of a Phenomenon — Survival of Bodily Death*. Harrisburg, Pa.: Stackpole Books, 1976.

Morrison, Toni. *Beloved*. New York: Knopf, 1987.

———. *The Bluest Eye*. New York: Washington Square Press, 1970.

———. *Playing in the Dark: Whiteness and the Literary Imagination*. Cambridge, Mass.: Harvard University Press, 1992.

———. *Race-ing Justice, En-gendering Power: Essays on Anita Hill, Clarence Thomas, and the Construction of Social Reality*. New York: Pantheon, 1992.

———. *Sula*. New York: Knopf, 1973.

———. "Unspeakable Things Unspoken: The Afro-American Presence in American Literature." *Michigan Quarterly Review* 28, no. 1 (1989): 1–34.

Mumford, Kevin J. 1996. "Homosex Changes: Race, Cultural Geography, and the Emergence of the Gay. *American Quarterly* 48, no. 3 (1996): 395–414.

Muñoz, José Esteban. " 'The White to Be Angry': Vaginal Davis's Terrorist Drag." *Social Text* 52/53 15, nos. 3 and 4 (fall–winter 1997): 80–103.

Murphy, Joseph M. *Santeria: An African Religion in America*. Boston: Beacon, 1988.

Murphy, Timothy F., and Suzanne Poirier, eds. *Writing AIDS: Gay Literature, Language, and Analysis*. New York: Columbia University Press, 1993.

Ngubane, Harriet. *Body and Mind in Zulu Medicine: An Ethnography of Health and Disease in Nyuswa-Zulu Thought and Practice*. London: Academic Press, 1977.

Nuland, Sherwin B. *How We Die: Reflections on Life's Final Chapter*. New York: Knopf, 1994.

O'Daniel, Therman. *James Baldwin: A Critical Evaluation*. Washington, D.C.: Howard University Press, 1977.

Ortiz, Alfonso. *The Tewa World: Space, Time, Being, and Becoming in a Pueblo Society*. Chicago: University of Chicago Press, 1969.

———, *New Perspectives on the Pueblos*. Albuquerque: University of New Mexico Press, 1972.

Ortiz, Alfonso, and Richard Erodoes, eds. *American Indian Myths and Legends*. New York: Pantheon, 1984.

Otten, Terry. *The Crime of Innocence in the Fiction of Toni Morrison*. Columbia: University of Missouri Press, 1989.

Owens, Louis. *Other Destinies: Understanding the American Indian Novel*. Norman: University of Oklahoma Press, 1992.

Page, Philip. "Circularity in Toni Morrison's *Beloved.*" *African American Review* 26, no. 1 (1992): 31–39.

Parker, Alice A., and Elizabeth A. Meese, eds. *Feminist Critical Negotiations*. Amsterdam/Philadelphia: John Benjamins, 1992.

Parker, Andrew, and Eve Kosofsky Sedgwick. *Performativity and Performance*. New York: Routledge, 1995.

Pastore, Judith, ed. *Confronting AIDS through Literature: The Responsibilities of Representation*. Urbana: University of Illinois Press, 1993.

Patai, Daphne. "U.S. Academics and Third-World Women: Is Ethical Research Possible?" In *Feminist Nightmares: Women at Odds*, edited by Susan Ostrov Weisser and Jennifer Fleischner, 21–43. New York: New York University Press, 1994.

Patterson, Orlando. *Slavery and Social Death: A Comparative Study*. Cambridge: Harvard University Press, 1982.

Porter, Horace A. *Stealing the Fire: The Art and Protest of James Baldwin*. Middletown, Conn.: Wesleyan University Press, 1989.

Pryse, Marjorie, and Hortense Spillers. *Conjuring: Black Women, Fiction, and Literary Tradition*. Bloomington: Indiana University Press, 1985.

Rabinow, Paul, ed. *The Foucault Reader*. New York: Pantheon, 1984.

Ramazanoglu, Caroline, ed. *Up against Foucault: Explorations of Some Tensions between Foucault and Feminism*. New York: Routledge, 1993.

Redstockings. *Feminist Revolution*. New York: Random House, 1978.

Rigney, Barbara Hill. "'A Story to Pass On': Ghosts and the Significance of History in Toni Morrison's *Beloved.*" In *Haunting the House of Fiction: Feminist Perspectives on Ghost Stories by American Women*, edited by Lynette Carpenter and Wendy K. Kolmar, 229–235. Knoxville: University of Tennessee Press, 1991.

Rinpoche, Sogyal. *The Tibetan Book of Living and Dying*. San Francisco: Harper and Row, 1993.

Roach, Joseph. *Cities of the Dead: Circum-Atlantic Performance*. New York: Columbia University Press, 1996.

Roediger, David. "Guineas, Wiggers, and the Dramas of the Racialized Culture." *American Literary History* 7, no. 4 (1995): 654–68.

———. *Towards the Abolition of Whiteness: Essays on Race, Politics, and Working Class History*. London: Verso, 1994.

Roof, Judith. *A Lure of Knowledge: Lesbian Sexuality and Theory*. New York: Columbia University Press, 1991.

Rosaldo, Renato. *Culture and Truth: The Remaking of Social Analysis*. Boston: Beacon, 1989.

Rosen, Kenneth, ed. *Voices of the Rainbow: Contemporary Poetry by American Indians.* New York: Viking, 1975.

Ross, Andrew. "New Age Technoculture." In *Cultural Studies,* edited by Lawrence Grossberg, Cary Nelson, and Paula Treichler, 531–555. New York: Routledge, 1992.

Rowe, Dorothy. *The Construction of Life and Death.* Chichester, England: John Wiley, 1982.

Roys, Ralph L., trans. *The Book of Chilam Balam of Chumayel.* Norman: University of Oklahoma Press, 1967.

Rushdy, Ashraf H. A. "Daughters Signifyin(g) History: The Example of Toni Morrison's *Beloved." American Literature* 64, no. 3 (1992): 567–597.

Saint-Aubin, Arthur Flannigan. "TESTERIA: The Dis-ease of Black Men in White Supremacist, Patriarchal Culture." *Callaloo* 17, no. 4 (1994): 1054–1073.

Saldívar, José David. *The Dialectics of Our America: Genealogy, Cultural Critique, and Literary History.* Durham: Duke University Press, 1991.

Sale, Maggie. "Call and Response as Critical Method: African-American Oral Traditions and *Beloved." African American Review* 26, no. 1 (1992): 41–50.

Samuels, Wilfred D., and Clenora Hudson-Weems. *Toni Morrison.* Boston: Twayne, 1990.

Sartre, Jean-Paul. *Being and Nothingness: A Phenomenological Essay on Ontology.* Translated by Hazel E. Barnes. New York: Washington Square Press, 1956.

Schmudde, Carol E. "The Haunting of 124." *African American Review* 26, no. 3 (1992): 409–416.

Scholes, Robert. *Semiotics and Interpretation.* New Haven: Yale University Press, 1982.

Schrag, Peter. "Son of 187: Anti-Affirmative Action Propositions." *New Republic,* 30 January 1995, 16–18.

Sedgwick, Eve Kosofsky. *Between Men: English Literature and Male Homosocial Desire.* New York: Columbia University Press, 1985.

Sheffey, Ruthe T. *Trajectory: Fueling the Future and Preserving the African-American Past.* Baltimore: Morgan State University Press, 1989.

Shibles, Warren. *Death: An Interdisciplinary Analysis.* Whitewater, Wis.: Language Press, 1974.

Sidel, Ruth. *Women and Children Last: The Plight of Poor Women in Affluent America.* New York: Penguin, 1986.

Siegel, Marcia. "Virtual Criticism and the Dance of Death." *TDR: The Drama Review* 40, no. 2 (summer 1996): 60–70.

Silko, Leslie Marmon. *Almanac of the Dead.* New York: Simon and Schuster, 1991.

———. "Language and Literature from a Pueblo Indian Perspective." In *English Literature: Opening Up the Canon,* edited by Leslie A. Fiedler and Houston A. Baker Jr., 54–72. Baltimore: Johns Hopkins University Press, 1981.

———. "An Old-Time Indian Attack Conducted in Two Parts." *Shantih* 4, no. 2 (1979): 3–5.

———. *Storyteller*. New York: Little, Brown and Company, 1981; distributed by Grove Press.

———. *Yellow Woman and a Beauty of the Spirit: Essays on Native American Life Today*. New York: Simon and Schuster, 1996.

Simmons, Marc. *Witchcraft in the Southwest: Spanish and Indian Supernaturalism on the Rio Grande*. Lincoln: University of Nebraska Press, 1974.

Singer, Peter. *Rethinking Life and Death: The Collapse of Our Traditional Ethics*. New York: St. Martin's, 1994.

Sitter, Deborah Ayer. "The Making of a Man: Dialogic Meaning in *Beloved*." *African American Review* 26, no. 1 (1992): 17–29.

Smith, Barbara. *Home Girls: A Black Feminist Anthology*. New York: Kitchen Table Press, 1983.

———. *On the Margins of Discourse: The Relation of Literature to Language*. Chicago: University of Chicago Press, 1978.

Smith, Sidonie. *A Poetics of Women's Autobiography: Marginality and the Fictions of Self-Representation*. Bloomington: Indiana University Press, 1987.

Smith, Valerie. " 'Loopholes of Retreat': Architecture and Ideology in Harriet Jacobs's *Incidents in the Life of a Slave Girl*." In *Reading Black, Reading Feminist: A Critical Anthology*, edited by Henry Louis Gates Jr., 212–26. New York: Meridian, 1990.

———. *Self-Discovery and Authority in Afro-American Narrative*. Cambridge, Mass.: Harvard University Press, 1987.

Spense, Lewis. *Popol Vuh: The Mythic and Heroic Sagas of the Kiches of Central America*. 1908. Reprint, New York: AMS, 1972.

Spicer, Edward H. *The Yaquis: A Cultural History*. Tucson: University of Arizona Press, 1980.

Spillers, Hortense J. " 'All the Things You Could Be by Now, If Sigmund Freud's Wife Was Your Mother': Psychoanalysis and Race." *boundary 2* 23, no. 3 (1996): 75–141.

———. "Interstices: A Small Drama of Words." In *Pleasure and Danger: Exploring Female Sexuality*, edited by Carole S. Vance, 73–100. Boston: Routledge and Kegan Paul, 1984.

———. "Mama's Baby, Papa's Maybe: An American Grammar Book." *Diacritics* 17, no. 2 (1987): 64–81.

———, ed. *Comparative American Identities: Race, Sex, and Nationality in the Modern Text*. New York: Routledge, 1991.

Spretnak, Charlene. *The Politics of Women's Spirituality: Essays on the Rise of Spiritual Power within the Feminist Movement*. Garden City, N.Y.: Anchor, 1982.

Stallybrass, Peter, and Allon White. *The Politics and Poetics of Transgression*. Ithaca: Cornell University Press, 1986.

Stampp, Kenneth. *The Peculiar Institution: Slavery in the Ante-Bellum South*. New York: Vintage, 1956.

St. Clair, Janet. "Death of Love / Love of Death: Leslie Marmon Silko's *Almanac of the Dead*. *MELUS* 21, no. 2 (1996): 141–156.

Stuart, David E. *Glimpses of the Ancient Southwest*. 1st ed. Santa Fe, N.Mex.: Ancient City Press, 1985.

Swann, Brian, and Arnold Krupat, eds. *I Tell You Now: Autobiographical Essays by Native American Writers*. Lincoln: University of Nebraska Press, 1987.

————. *Recovering the Word: Essays on Native American Literature*. Berkeley: University of California Press, 1987.

Taibo, Paco Ignacio. "Zapatista! The Phoenix Rises." *The Nation*, 28 March 1994, 406–410.

Takaki, Ronald T. *Violence in the Black Imagination: Essays and Documents*. New York: Oxford University Press, 1993.

Tanner, Leslie B. *Voices from Women's Liberation*. New York: New American Library, 1971.

Tate, Claudia. *Black Women Writers at Work*. New York: Continuum, 1989.

————. *Domestic Allegories of Political Desire: The Black Heroine's Text at the Turn of the Century*. New York: Oxford University Press, 1982.

Taussig, Michael T. *The Nervous System*. New York: Routledge, 1992.

————. *Shamanism, Colonialism, and the Wild Man: A Study in Terror and Healing*. Chicago: University of Chicago Press, 1987.

Taylor-Guthrie, Danille, ed. *Conversations with Toni Morrison*. Jackson: University of Mississippi Press, 1994.

Teish, Luisah. *Jambalaya: The Natural Woman's Book of Personal Charms and Practical Rituals*. San Francisco: Harper and Row, 1985.

Terry, Jennifer, and Jacqueline Urla, eds. *Deviant Bodies*. Bloomington: Indiana University Press, 1995.

Thompkins, Jane P. "Sentimental Power: Uncle Tom's Cabin and the Politics of Literary History." In *The New Feminist Criticism: Essays on Women, Literature, and Theory*, edited by Elaine Showalter, 81–104. New York: Pantheon, 1985.

Thompson, Edward Herbert. *The People of the Serpent: Life and Adventure among the Mayas*. Boston: Houghton Mifflin, 1932.

Thompson, Robert Ferris. *Flash of the Spirit*. New York: Vintage, 1983.

Trace, Jacqueline. "Dark Goddesses: Black Feminist Theology in Morrison's *Beloved*." *Obsidian II: Black Literature in Review* 6, no. 3 (1991): 14–30.

Travis, Molly Abel. "*Beloved* and *Middle Passage*: Race, Narrative and the Critic's Essentialism." *Narrative* 2, no. 3 (1994): 179–200.

Troupe, Quincy, ed. *James Baldwin: The Legacy*. New York: Simon and Schuster, 1989.

Turner, James Grantham. *ONE FLESH: Paradisal Marriage and Sexual Relations in the Age of Milton*. Oxford [Oxfordshire]: Clarendon Press, 1987.

Turner, Victor. *The Ritual Process: Structure and Anti-Structure*. Ithaca: Cornell University Press, 1969.

Tyler, Hamilton A. *Pueblo Gods and Myths*. Norman: University of Oklahoma Press, 1964.

Underhill, Ruth M. *First Penthouse Dwellers of America*. New York: J. J. Augustin, 1938.

Vance, Carole S., ed. *Pleasure and Danger: Exploring Female Sexuality*. Boston: Routledge and Kegan Paul, 1984.

Van Sertima, Ivan. *They Came before Columbus: The African Presence in Ancient America*. New Brunswick: Transaction, 1983.

Velie, Alan R. *Four American Indian Literary Masters*. Norman: University of Oklahoma Press, 1982.

———, ed. *American Indian Literature: An Anthology*. Norman: University of Oklahoma Press, 1979.

———. ed. *The Lightening Within: An Anthology of Contemporary American Indian Fiction*. Lincoln: University of Nebraska Press, 1991.

———. *Native American Perspectives on Literature and History*. Norman: University of Oklahoma Press, 1994.

Vizenor, Gerald. *Crossbloods: Bone Courts, Bingo, and Other Reports*. 1976. Reprint, Minneapolis: University of Minnesota Press, 1990.

———. *Earthdivers: Tribal Narratives on Mixed Descent*. Minneapolis: University of Minnesota Press, 1981.

———. *Interior Landscapes: Autobiographical Myths and Metaphors*. Minneapolis: University of Minnesota Press, 1990.

Vlach, John Michael. *The Afro-American Tradition in Decorative Arts*. Cleveland: Cleveland Museum of Art, 1978.

Walker, Alice. *Meridian*. New York: Pocket Books, 1976.

Walker, Melissa. *Down from the Mountaintop: Black Women's Novels in the Wake of the Civil Rights Movement, 1966–1989*. New Haven: Yale University Press, 1991.

Walters, Anna Lee. *Ghost Singer*. Flagstaff, Ariz.: Northland Publishing, 1988.

———. *The Sun Is Not Merciful*. Ithaca: Firebrand Books, 1985.

Ware, Cellestine. *Woman Power: The Movement for Women's Liberation*. New York: Tower, 1970.

Warrior, Robert. *Tribal Secrets: Recovering American Indian Intellectual Traditions*. Minneapolis: University of Minnesota Press, 1995.

Waters, Lindsay. "Dreaming with Tears in My Eyes." *Transition* 7, no. 2 (1999): 78–102.

Watney, Simon. *Practices of Freedom: Selected Writings on HIV/AIDS*. Durham: Duke University Press, 1994.

Weatherby, W. J. *James Baldwin: Artist on Fire*. New York: Donald Fine, 1989.

Weir, Robert F. *Death in Literature*. New York: Columbia University Press, 1980.

West, Cornel. *Race Matters*. Boston: Beacon, 1993.

White, Armond. *Rebel for the Hell of It: The Life of Tupac Shakur*. New York: Thunder's Mouth Press, 1997.

White, Deborah Gray. *Ar'n't I a Woman? Female Slaves in the Plantation South*. New York: Norton, 1985.

Williams, Walter L. *The Spirit and the Flesh: Sexual Diversity in American Indian Culture*. Boston: Beacon, 1986.

Williamson, Joel. *The Crucible of Race: Black/White Relations in the American South since Emancipation*. New York: Oxford University Press, 1984.

————. *William Faulkner and Southern History.* New York: Oxford University Press, 1993.

Wilson, Robin. "Among White Males, Jokes and Anecdotes." *Chronicle of Higher Education,* 28 April 1995, A20.

Winik, Marion. *First Comes Love.* New York: Pantheon, 1996.

Wolff, Cynthia G. "'Margaret Garner': A Cincinnati Story." In *Discovering Difference: Contemporary Essays in American Culture,* edited by Christoph K. Lohmann, 105–22. Bloomington: Indiana University Press, 1993.

Wong, Hertha Dawn. *Sending My Heart Back across the Years: Tradition and Innovation in Native American Autobiography.* New York: Oxford University Press, 1992.

Zahan, Dominique. *The Religion, Spirituality, and Thought of Traditional Africa.* Translated by Kate Ezra Martin and Lawrence M. Martin. Chicago: University of Chicago Press, 1979.

Zitkala-Sa. *Old Indian Legends.* 1901. Reprint, Lincoln: University of Nebraska Press, 1985.

Index

ACT UP, 103–4, 139
Affirmative action, 139
African Americans. *See* Blacks
African American studies, 3, 119–22
African spirituality, 54–56, 192 n.21, 192 n.24, 206–7 n.32
AIDS, 104
Ali, Shahrazad, 109–10
Allen, Paula Gunn: on Aztec deities, 80; on complexity of existence, 164; on dogmatism of Western literary criticism, 170; on Laguna Pueblo culture, 171; on male/female equilibrium in Laguna culture, 166; on Native American views of womanness, 206 n.24; on secretiveness, 160; on self-esteem in Native American culture, 88; on white vs. Indian experience, 205 n.15
Almaguer, Tomás, 139
Almanac of the Dead (Silko), 68–99; Beaufrey character, 94–95; Beaufrey's hatred of mother/self, 95; beginning of, 76–77; borders in/organization of, 75–76; and *Ceremony*, 77, 92, 194 n.6; the children flee north, 88–89; critical response to, 68, 69; death's dual role in, 7; death/sex in, 36, 96, 189 n.34; differences in, 75, 76; drug use in, 77–78, 81; Ferro character, 77; frontispiece to, 14; the general's erection, 91–92; generational stories in, 85; genocide theme in, 71, 74, 78–79, 83–84, 96, 97, 98; geographic settings of, 75; the grotesque in, 71–72, 85, 90, 94, 95, 97–98; Guzman character, 83, 84; Guzman's trees, 84; Leah Blue's exploitation of the land, 96–97; Lecha character, 75, 77, 80; Lecha's dream-visions, 85–88; Lecha's note-

book, 88; Lecha's pain/addiction, 87; male body in, 94; Malenche myth in, 195 n.24; masculinism/misogyny in, 97; memory/imagination in, 73–74, 81–82; Menardo character, 89; Menardo's business dealings, 90, 91; Menardo's dream-vision, 93; Menardo's house, 90; Menardo's Indian ancestry, 89–90; milk's absence in, 78, 79, 195 n.15; Monte's kidnapping, 81; narrative structure of, 75; Native American influences on, 75, 79–80, 195 n.22; ordering of events in, 75–76; postmodernism of, 7; realism of, 98; rebirth theme in, 85; sacred/profane in, 80; Seese's dream-visions, 81–82; serial killer in, 86, 87; Serlo's alternative earth project, 95–96; sexual/physical violence in, 70, 76, 91–92, 93–94; simultaneity in, 75; spirits in, 72, 87, 90–91; and *Storyteller*, 92; trickster character in, 72; Trigg bleeds hitchhikers, 96; vignettes in, sources for, 69; vision of the future in, 98; whiteness in, negative characterization of, 68–69, 84–85; witchery in, 89, 92; Yoeme sees lynchings, 84; Yoeme's stories, 83; Zeta character, 75, 77, 80; Zeta's dye, 77, 79–80
Alpert, Jane, 131, 132, 133–34
American Indian culture. *See* Native American culture
American Indian literature. *See* Native American literature
American literature/culture, 154. *See also* Literature
American poets, 155–56
"American," status of, 16
Anderson, Benedict, 6; on the dead/nation/language, 13, 16, 22–28, 36,

n.8. *See also* Black women, literature of

Blackness: critical theory's disinheriting of, 135–36; fear of, 177–78; and whiteness, 6, 127, 128, 199 n.6. *See also* Black gay/lesbian subjectivity; Black subjectivity

Black Panthers, 130

Black power movement, 132

Blacks: naming/unnaming of, 47; oppression of, and Eurocentrism, 108

Black subjectivity, 6; and ancestors/heritage, 15; as invisible, 31, 38; as nonhuman vs. nonentity, 15; and self–U.S. relationship, 16. *See also* Black gay/lesbian subjectivity; Blackness; Slaves

Black women: anger of, 143–44; feminist scholarship on, 42; as instigators of black men's demise, 41; liminality of, 42–43; motherhood of, 49–50; as passage between humanity and nonhumanity, 42–43; and reproduction/eugenics, 145; as serving community/academy, 42, 43–44; status of, 6–7, 145, 201 n.44; strength/perseverance of, 49. See also *Beloved*

Black women, literature of: criticism of, 44–45, 190 n.6; detemporalized universe in, 53; and gaze, 162–63; inversion in, 66–67; as site of discursive power, 163; tangible/intangible in, 160–61

"Black Women in Defense of Ourselves" campaign, 143–44

Blassie, Michael, 189 n.38

The Bluest Eye (Morrison), 160–61

Body/bodies: black vs. white bodies, in medical research, 38–39; and eugenics, 145, 201 n.46; in life/death, 175; mutilated female bodies, 46, 66; and performance, 176; and pollution, 165–66, 204 n.24; and power, 31–32; racialization of, 32; Spillers on, 58, 66, 120, 162, 205 n.19

Bone, Robert, 105

Book of Chilam Balam, 75

"Born of a Woman" (Consolidated), 129

Brown, Elsa Barkley, 143

Brown, Rosellen, 1, 183 n.1, 184 n.4

Buckley, William F., 143

Burris, Barbara, 131

Business of Punishment (Consolidated), 125, 141–42

Butler, Judith, 149; on feminism and lesbian/gay studies, 118–19, 134, 207–8 n.6; on gender/sexuality, 118–19, 134; on identity, 136, 142; on kinship/sexuality, 198 n.28; on Martin, 119; on race, 119, 120, 198 n.27; on radical politics, 136; on the social/symbolic, 121; on women as subject of feminism, 137

"Butyric Acid" (Consolidated), 129

California Civil Rights Initiative, 202 n.29

Canon debates/formation, 2–3, 153–54, 160–61, 184–85 n.7

Carpentier, Alejo, 1

Cell 16 (feminist group), 130–31

Centeredness, 150, 152, 153, 158, 159, 169–70, 171. *See also* Marginality

Ceremony (Silko), 77, 92, 157–59, 169, 186 n.21, 192 n.6

Ceremony and writing, 158

Chiapas rebellion (Mexico, 1994), 98

Christian, Barbara, 61, 192 n.21

Christian coalition politics, 140, 202 n.31

Christian culture/tradition, 88, 108

Civil rights movement, 139

Clarke, Cheryl, 107

Colonial life, 70

Commodities, fetishism of, 187 n.18

Consciousness raising, 132

Conservative Right, 110, 197 n.16

Consolidated: "Born of a Woman," 129; *Business of Punishment*, 125, 141–42; "Butyric Acid," 129; "Consolidated Buries the Mammoth," 143, 144; fans of, 127–28; feminism of, 125, 129, 134–36, 137, 199 n.3; identities assumed by, 127, 138, 141–42; killing of self by, 8, 126–27; members of, 124; musical form of, 198–99 n.2; *The Myth of the Rock*, 124–25; "No Answer for a Dancer," 129; *Play More Music*, 125, 202–3 n.38; pleasure/desire in listening to, 128; politics of, 124–26, 127, 138–39, 141, 143, 202–203 n.38; self-representation resisted by, 143; Thomas ritually

killed by, 143, 144, 145, 146; and
transcendence of whiteness, 128;
"Woman Shoots John," 125, 135
"Consolidated Buries the Mammoth"
(Consolidated), 143, 144
Critical theory, 135–36
Croce, Arlene, 176–77
Cross-disciplinary study, 120–22, 149,
170
Cunningham, George, 128–29
Cuvier, George, 201 n.46

Danforth, Loring, 37
Darling, Marsha, 52
Davis, Vaginal, 179
Death: as absolute difference, 123; and
abstract existence/life-in-death, 17–
18; anonymity of, 38, 47, 189 n.39;
brain death, 39–40, 189–90 n.42;
commodification of, 187–88 n.20;
fear of, 23, 38–39, 149, 176–77, 179–
80; and fetishism, 187 n.18; good
death, 190 n.43; and grieving, 37;
knowledge/discussion of, 15; and
life, 6, 32–33, 164–65, 166, 175; and
living/dead as one community, 193
n.35; and meaning of life, 38; medicalization of, 29–31, 33–34, 35, 37;
physician-assisted suicide, 190 n.43;
as private, 29; and queer subjects,
179; and right to die, 190 n.43; scientific vs. spiritual views of, 167–68;
and sexuality, 35–36, 189 n.34;
silence as equal to, 103–4, 152;
silencing about, 36–37; social, in
slavery, 13–14; space of, 4–5, 122,
179; subjectivity of, 4–5; as a victory,
186 n.7
de Man, Paul, 149
Demetrakopoulos, Stephanie, 164
Dichotomous societies, 88
Difference, 16–17, 46, 123, 158
Disidentification, 179
Drake, Sandra, 191 n.35
Du Bois, William, 110
duCille, Ann, 42, 43–44, 45, 201 n.44
During, Simon, 29–30, 31, 149

Echols, Alice, 134, 201 n.23
Edmonson, Munro S., 80
Edwards, Thomas, 183 n.1
Eng, David, 178

Erasure, 161–62
Erzulie. See Oshun/Osun
Esu-Elegbara, 107
Ethnic studies, 170
Eugenics movement, 145
Eurocentrism, 108

Family, 33–35, 48–49. See also Kinship
Family values, 140
Fanon, Franz, 2, 133
FBI, 202 n.37
Female/matriarchal culture, 132
Feminism: and biology as source of
revolution, 131, 132, 134; and the
black lesbian, 127, 141–47, 199 n.11;
on the black mother, 50; and canonicity, 154, 160–61; on capital, 130; cultural, 130, 131–34, 201 n.23; and
difference, 158; and ghosting of
whiteness, 135; and identities, 136–
38, 142; and lesbian/gay studies,
118–19, 134, 145–46, 207–8 n.6; and
lesbian separatism, 132–34; liberal,
130; marginality of, 150–51; on
marriage, 130; and materiality of
women's lives, 152; multivocality
of, 151; New Age, 134, 135; and patriarchy, 146–47, 204 n.51; and race,
119, 120, 121, 129; on racism, 130;
radical, 130–31, 132–33, 201 n.23;
and reconciliation between men and
women, 134; Second Wave, 130–35,
200 n.15; separatism within, 132; on
sexuality/gender, 45, 118–19, 120,
121–22; women's centrality to, 45,
50, 137
Feminists, The (New York), 130–31,
200 n.13
Feral, Josette, 16–17, 159
Firestone, Shulamith, 131
Forbes, Jack D., 206–7 n.32
Foucault, Michel: on bodies/power,
31, 32; on dead/nations, 29, 30, 188
n.26; on death, medical view of, 35;
on death-in-life, 30–31; on family,
medical view of, 34; influence of,
149; on knowledge, 160; on sex, 36,
189 n.34
Fox, Reuben, 102
Freedom, 3
Freeman, Elizabeth, 178–79
Fugitive Slave Law, 59

Gagnier, Regenia, 126, 199 n.5
Gangsta rap, 198 n.1
Gangster movie, genre of, 24, 27
Garber, Marjorie, 199 n.6
Garner, Margaret, 57
Gates, Henry Louis, Jr.: defense of Two
  Live Crew, 161; on Esu-Elegbara,
  107, 204 n.8; on *Menace II Society*, 27;
  West African contexts used by, 157,
  204–5 n.8
"Gay Agenda, The," 197 n.16
Gay subjectivity. *See* Black gay/lesbian
  subjectivity
Gender, 5–6, 45, 118–19, 120, 121–22
Genesis, 64–65
Genocide, 78–79. See also under *Alma-
  nac of the Dead*
Ghetto, and the American id, 27
Gilman, Sander L., 32, 145, 203 n.46
Giovanni, Nikki, 108–9
Giovanni's Room (Baldwin), 104–15;
  critical response to, 104–5, 106, 107;
  David's affair with Giovanni and
  Helen, 111; David's American,
  white identity, 112–13; David's fear
  about affair with Joey, 111–12;
  David's flight to Europe, 113;
  David's nightmarish image, 117–18;
  David's paranoia, 7; David's self-
  hatred, 117; fear of blackness in, 112,
  197 n.21; the grotesque in, 117;
  homosexuality in, 104–5, 107, 111–
  12, 197 n.18; love/human condition
  in, 110, 197 n.18; queerness/black-
  ness in, 7–8, 113; tradition in, 104–5,
  107
González-Wippler, Migene, 55
Good, Karen R., 179–80
Goodfellas (Scorsese), 24
Go Tell It on the Mountain (Baldwin),
  197 n.18
Grant, Judith, 134
Gray, Paul, 183 n.1
Greene, Gayle, 192 n.19
Grieving, 37
Grosso, Michael, 167–68
Grotesque, theories of, 70–74, 88, 94, 97
Gúzman, Diego de, 83

Hammonds, Evelynn, 127, 147
Harjo, Joy, 76, 194 n.13
Harris, Trudier, 166

Harvard Brain Death Committee, 39,
  189–90 n.42
Hawthorne, Nathaniel, 1–2
Hemingway, Ernest: *To Have and Have
  Not*, 144–45
Hemphill, Essex, 103
Henderson, Mae, 61, 162–63, 164, 205
  n.19
Heteronormativity, 204 n.51
Heterosexism, 47, 48, 106–7
Hill, Anita, 143, 144
Hip hop culture, 27
Hiroshima, 76
Hirsch, Herbert, 73, 194 n.10
History, remaking of, 73
HIV/AIDS activism, 139–40, 202 n.31
Holloway, Karla F. C., 53, 55, 61, 66,
  144, 164, 193 n.29
Homophobia, 106, 108, 109
Homosexuality, 48, 108. *See also* Black
  gay/lesbian subjectivity
hooks, bell, 15, 159
Horton, James Oliver, 106
Horvitz, Deborah, 51–52, 54
Hudson-Weems, Clenora, 58, 63
Hughes, Allen and Albert: *Menace II
  Society*, 6, 19–22, 23–28, 122–23
Hurston, Zora Neale: *Their Eyes Were
  Watching God*, 189 n.39

Ibo Landing (South Carolina), 188 n.21
Identity: Butler on, 136, 142; and femi-
  nism, 136–38, 142; and performance,
  147–48; as subjectivity, 126–27
Incidents in the Life of a Slave Girl
  (Jacobs), 192 n.13
Indian culture. *See* Native American
  culture
Indian literature. *See* Native American
  literature
Industrial music, 124, 198–99 n.2
Inversion, 66–67
Invisibility, 16
Iron John movement, 134
Islam, 108

Jackson, Michael, 199 n.6
Jacobs, Harriet, 185 n.3; *Incidents in the
  Life of a Slave Girl*, 192 n.13
Jaguar priest, 80
JanMohamed, Abdul, 169–70
Jefferson, Margo, 130

Johnston, Jill, 133
Jones, Bill T., 175, 178, 179, 180, 207 n.1;
 "Still/Here," 176–77
Jones, Malcolm, Jr., 68, 69
Judeo-Christian tradition, 108

Karenga, Ron, 130
Karp, Lila, 130, 200 n.13
Kenan, Randall. See *A Visitation of
 Spirits*
Kennedy, Florence, 130
Keres culture, 166
Kevorkian, Jack, 37–38
Kinship, 47–49, 198 n.28. *See also*
 Family
Knowledge, desire for, 159–61
Krupat, Arnold, 153–57

LaDuke, Winona, 168
Laguna Pueblo people, 76, 160, 166
Lakota people, 188 n.21
Language: and fatality, 22–23, 26; and
 historical truth, 46–47; and importance of the word, 160; and inversion, 66–67; and life, 152; patriotic,
 26–27; and power, 72–73, 152; and
 writing-ceremony relationship, 158
Lee, Ang: *The Wedding Banquet*, 178
Leonard, John, 184–85 n.7
Lesbian/gay studies: and feminism,
 118–19, 134, 145–46, 207–8 n.6; and
 race, 120, 121; sexuality as a subject
 of, 118–19
Lesbian subjectivity. *See* Black gay/les-
 bian subjectivity
Lienert, Tania, 201 n.23
Life: and death, 6, 32–33, 164–65, 166,
 175; and language, 152; life-in-
 death, 17–18; meaning of, 38
Limbaugh, Rush, 143
Liminality, 8, 40, 42–44
Lincoln, Kenneth, 79–80, 94, 194 n.7
Lipsitz, George, 186 n.6
Liscio, Lorraine, 191 n.11
Literary criticism, 163, 164–65
Literary theory, 98, 157
Literature: canonical, 2–3, 153–54, 160–
 61, 184–85 n.7; vs. discourse, 157;
 mixing levels of diction in, 170–71;
 Native American, 153–54, 155, 156–
 57. *See also* Black literature; Black
 women, literature of
Little House on the Prairie, 116

Lloyd, David, 169–70
Lorde, Audre, 158; "Power," 204 n.7
Los Angeles riots (1992), 27
Lott, Eric, 141
"Lucy Gray" (Wordsworth), 52
Luxton, Richard, 91, 195 n.25

Macdonald, Andrew: *The Turner Diaries*, 202 n.37
Magical realism, 1
Male political groups, 134
Male subjectivity, 128, 199 n.6
Mandingo, 198 n.28
Mapplethorpe, Robert, 177
Marginality: and bringing others back
 from the dead, 158; vs. center, 150,
 152, 158, 159, 169–70, 171; within cul-
 ture, 5; definitions of, 165; and differ-
 ence, 16–17; and discourse, 152;
 discourse on, 5, 8, 16–17; of empow-
 ered subjects, 159; of feminism, 150–
 51; and literary theory, 98; and post-
 modernism, 166–67; and power, 5,
 16–17
Martin, Biddy, 119
Marxist/socialist discourse, 138
Mayan culture, 75, 91, 195 n.25
McClain, Carol, 165
McElroy, Bernard, 70–71, 94
McKay, Claude, 110
McRuer, Robert, 110–11, 122
Meaning, production of, 159–60
Meaning of life, 38
Media, 141
Medicine: and black vs. white bodies
 used in research, 38–39; and death,
 29–31, 33–34, 35, 37; empirical
 knowledge, 35; and family, 33–35
Meese, Elizabeth, 18, 150, 151–53, 154;
 on *Ceremony*, 157–59, 169
Melville, Herman, 3
Memory, 73–74
Menace II Society (Hughes brothers), 6,
 19–22, 23–28, 122–23
Mercer, Kobena, 136–38
Michelet, Jules, 27
Militia groups, 140, 202 n.31, 202 n.37
Million Man March, 134
Momaday, Scott, 74
Moody, Raymond, 37–38
Morrison, Toni: on Afro-American
 presence and canon debates, 2–3,
 185 n.9, 198 n.29; on being black in

the U.S., 16; on being "outdoors," 17–18; *The Bluest Eye*, 160–61; on dichotomies, 171; folk beliefs in works of, 166; *Playing in the Dark*, 185 n.9; *Sula*, 60, 186 n.21; on *To Have and Have Not*, 145; "Unspeakable Things Unspoken," 2, 3–4. See also *Beloved*

Multicultural discourse / experience, 169–71, 206–7 n.32

Mumbo Jumbo (Reed), 192 n.25

Muñoz, José, 179

Music, 124, 198–99 n.2, 198 n.1. *See also* Consolidated

Myth of the Rock , The (Consolidated), 124–25

Nagasaki, 76

National Endowment for the Humanities (NEH), 169–70

Nation of Islam, 108

Nations and the dead, 18–28; Anderson on, 13, 16, 22–28, 36, 144, 187–88 n.20, 187 n.18; and brain death, 39–40; and embodiment, 23; and family, 34–35; Foucault on, 29, 30, 188 n.26; and language, 22–23, 26–27; and medicalization of death, 29–31, 33–34, 35, 37; *Menace II Society* as commentary on, 19–22, 23–28; and national imaginings, attachment to, 26; and religion, 22; and Rwandan ethnic conflict, 19

Native American culture: authority in, 153; dynamic self-esteem in, 88; fear of menstruating women in, 206 n.24; secretness / sacredness in, 160; trickster figures in, 72, 194 n.7; women and life / death in, 166. *See also specific peoples*

Native American literature: language / being in, 72–73; marginality of, 153–54, 155, 156–57

Navajo people, 206 n.28

Necromancy vs. sorcery, 115

Negrophobia, 2

NEH (National Endowment for the Humanities), 169–70

Nero, Charles, I., 106, 108, 110

Newsweek, 19

New York Radical Feminists (NYRF), 130–31

Ngubane, Harriet, 62, 165–66

Nine Lords, 91

"No Answer for a Dancer" (Consolidated), 129

Nugent, Ted, 143

NYRF (New York Radical Feminists), 130–31

Nyuswa-Zulu culture, 165–66

Obscenity, 35

Oi music, 198 n.1

Oklahoma City bombing, 202 n.37

Orishas (African deities), 55–56, 192 n.24

Oshun / Osun (a Yoruban divinity), 55–56, 192 nn.24–25

Otherness, 154

Otten, Terry, 56

Our Nig: Or, Sketches from the Life of a Free Black (Wilson), 189 n.40

Oya (Yoruban deity), 166

Parker, Andrew, 147–48

Parliament Funkadelic, 41

Past / present, 6

Patriarchy, 146–47, 165–66, 204 n.51

Patterson, Orlando, 13, 14, 48, 192 n.13

Pentecostal Black Church, 107–8, 110, 115, 197 n.16

People of color: hazardous wastes' impact on, 206 n.28; memory for, 73; status as "living," 15–16. *See also entries beginning with "Black" and "Native American"*

Perdue, Carrie, 199 n.2

Performativity / performance, 147–48, 179

Perry, Michael, 35

Personal as political, 8

Physician-assisted suicide, 190 n.43

Picasso, Pablo, 177

Pietri, Arturo Uslar, 1

Pistel, Mark, 124. *See also* Consolidated

Playing in the Dark (Morrison), 185 n.9

Play More Music (Consolidated), 125, 202–3 n.38

Poe, Edgar Allan, 1–2

Poetics, 161

Poetry, 155–56, 204 n.7

Political movements, of white males, 139–41, 202 n.31

Pollution, 8, 165–66, 206 n.24

Poor people, 151

Porter, Horace, 107

Postmodernism, 146, 166–67, 168
Poststructuralism, 146
Power: and the body, 31–32; discursive, of black women's literature, 163; and language, 72–73, 152; and marginality, 5, 16–17
"Power" (Lorde), 204 n.7
President's Commission for the Study of Ethical Problems in Medicine, 39
Promise Keepers, 134
Propositions 184, 187, and 209 (California), 139, 202 n.29
Prostitution, 145
Pueblo people, 76, 160, 166

Queer acts, and bringing back the dead, 103–4, 121
Queer studies, 178–79, 180
Queer subjectivity. *See* Black gay / lesbian subjectivity
Quetzalcoatl, 80

Race: and the body, 32; Butler on, 119, 120, 198 n.27; and feminism, 119, 120, 121, 129; and lesbian / gay studies, 120, 121
Racism, 130, 145, 186 n.6
Rap music, 124, 198 n.1
Reed, Ishmael: *Mumbo Jumbo*, 192 n.25
Religion, 22. *See also* Pentecostal Black Church
Rhetoric, 156, 204 n.7
Richardson, Diane, 201 n.23
Right to die, 190 n.43
Rinpoche, Sogyal, 38
Roach, Joseph, 9, 186 n.11
Robinson, Patricia, 130
Roediger, David, 69
Rogin, Michael, 3
Roof, Judith, 146
Ross, Andrew, 133–34
Ross, Elisabeth Kübler, 37–38
Rushdie, Salman: *Satanic Verses*, 80
Rwanda, ethnic conflict in, 19, *19*

Samuels, Wilfred, 58, 63
Sanchez, Sonya, 175
Sartre, Jean-Paul, 187 n.17
Satanic Verses (Rushdie), 80
Sawhney, Sabina, 142
Schrag, Peter, 139
Schreiber, Flora Rheta, 12

Scientific materialism, 167, 168
Scorsese, Martin: *Goodfellas,* 24
Secretness / sacredness, 160–61
Sedgwick, Eve Kosofsky, 147–48
Sexuality: and death, 35–36, 189 n.34; deviant, and racism, 145; and feminism, 45, 118–19, 120, 121–22; as a lesbian / gay studies subject, 118–19; silences about, 104
Shakur, Tupac, 175, 176, 179, 180, 207 n.1
Shamanism, 86, 195 n.25
Sherburne, Adam, 124, 125, 141–42. *See also* Consolidated
Siegel, Marcia, 177
"Silence = death," 103–4, 152
Silko, Leslie Marmon: *Ceremony,* 77, 92, 157–59, 169, 188 n.21, 194 n.6; on Louis Simpson, 155–56; *Storyteller,* 73, 77, 92, 195 n.27. See also *Almanac of the Dead*
Simmons, Ron, 108, 109
Simpson, Louis, 155–56, 160
Simpson, O. J., 146
Singer, Peter, 38, 39–40
Skow, John, 68
Slaves, 3; anonymity / naming of, 47; as enslaved / freed subjects, 14–15; and gender difference, 46; at Ibo Landing, 188 n.21; kinship of, 47–49, 198 n.28; and master / slave dynamic as male, 48; and mutilated female bodies, 46; and sexual revolution for white subjects, 120, 198 n.28; social death of, 13–14; and whites as mirrored in mulattos, 14, 39, 189 n.40
Sly and the Family Stone, 125
Snyder, Gary, 156
Sorcery vs. necromancy, 115
Soyinka, Wole, 110
Space of death, 4–5, 122, 179
Spillers, Hortense J., 6, 55; on body / flesh / slavery, 50, 53, 58, 120, 162, 205 n.19; on gender / slavery, 45–46, 49–50, 121; on genealogies, 192 n.13; on *Incidents in the Life of a Slave Girl,* 192 n.13; on kinship, 47–49, 198 n.28; on liminality of black women, 42–44; on mutilated female bodies, 41, 46, 66; on naming of Africans, 47
Spirit / spirituality: African, 54–56, 192 n.21, 192 n.24, 206–7 n.32; definition

Sharon Patricia Holland is Assistant Professor of
English at Stanford University.

Library of Congress Cataloging-in-Publication Data

Holland, Sharon Patricia.
Raising the dead: readings of death and (black) subjectivity /
Sharon Patricia Holland.
p. cm.—(New Americanists)
Includes bibliographical references (p.) and index.
ISBN 0-8223-2475-x (cloth : alk. paper)—ISBN 0-8223-2499-7
(paper : alk. paper)
1. American fiction—20th century—History and criticism.   2. Death in literature.   3. Death—Social aspects—United States—History—20th century.
4. American literature—Afro-American authors—History and criticism.   5. Homosexuality and literature—United States—History—20th century.   6. Feminism and literature—United States—History—20th century.   7. Performing arts—United States—History—20th century.   8. Marginality, Social, in
literature.   9. Afro-Americans in literature.   10. Subjectivity in literature.
I. Title.   II. Series.
PS374.D34 H65 2000
-dc21   99-046234